"In his lucid book on grace and human action, Aiken offers a much-needed contemporary contribution from the field of moral theology/Christian ethics to this too-often-neglected topic. He establishes the need in contemporary theology for the sophistication and precision of St. Thomas Aquinas' thought on grace, and also draws on contemporary thinkers (Stanley Hauerwas and Reinhard Hütter) to extend the communal emphasis of the Angelic Doctor's work. Aiken's book is one of the first in an impending deluge of studies augmenting recent work on virtue with more detailed attention to the relationship between God's grace and human action."

—WILLIAM C. MATTISON III

Associate Professor of Moral Theology, Catholic University of America
Author of *Introducing Moral Theology: True Happiness and the Virtues* (2008)

"Aikin's accomplishment is most impressive. Conversant with certain influential contemporary discussions of Christian moral agency, Aikin also knows his Aquinas very well, making intelligent use of Aquinas on grace and the Holy Spirit to depict more fully the working of God in the Christian moral life, both individually and communally. God's acting is not at the expense of human agency; God's intimate involvement in human acting, depicted in its ecclesial setting, is genuinely empowering. Aikin's project is ecumenical and charitable in the best sense, and his careful, thoughtful, uplifting analyses show convincingly how Aquinas and Hauerwas and Huetter, can be mutually enriching."

—JOSEPH WAWRYKOW

Associate Professor of Theology, University of Notre Dame
Author of *The Westminster Handbook to Thomas Aquinas* (2005)

Moved by God to Act

Moved by God to Act
An Ecumenical Ethic of Grace in Community

WM. CARTER AIKIN

CASCADE *Books* • Eugene, Oregon

MOVED BY GOD TO ACT
An Ecumenical Ethic of Grace in Community

Copyright © 2014 Wm. Carter Aikin. All rights reserved. Except for brief quotations in critical publications or reviews, no part of this book may be reproduced in any manner without prior written permission from the publisher. Write: Permissions, Wipf & Stock, 199 W. 8th Ave., Eugene, OR 97401.

Cascade Books
An Imprint of Wipf and Stock Publishers
199 W. 8th Ave., Suite 3
Eugene, OR 97401
www.wipfandstock.com

ISBN 13: 978-1-61097-520-9

Cataloging-in-Publication data:

Aikin, Wm. Carter.

   Moved by God to act : an ecumenical ethic of grace in community / Wm. Carter Aikin.

   xii + 252 p. ; cm. Includes bibliographical references and index.

   ISBN 13: 978-1-61097-520-9

   1. Christian ethics. 2. Thomas, Aquinas, Saint, 1225?–1274—Ethics. 3. Hauerwas, Stanley, 1940–. 4. Hütter, Reinhard, 1958–I. Title.

BJ1251 .A34 2014

Manufactured in the U.S.A.

New Revised Standard Version Bible, copyright © 1989, Division of Christian Education of the National Council of Churches of Christ in the United States of America. Used by permission. All rights reserved.

For Diane

with gratitude and love

Contents

Acknowledgments xi

Introduction: Christian Moral Action 1

1. Stanley Hauerwas 31
2. Reinhard Hütter 67
3. Common Threads 115
4. Thomas Aquinas 150
5. Toward an Ecumenical Ethic of Grace 184

Conclusion: A Community-Centered Ecumenical Ethic of Grace 220

Bibliography 241

Index 245

Acknowledgments

THE CORE CHAPTERS OF this book began as my 2006 University of Notre Dame doctoral dissertation, and much of its technical merit I owe to the instruction, encouragement, and wisdom of my dissertation advisor, Professor Jean Porter. Among my other readers of this project in its early stages, particular thanks are due to Joseph Wawrykow, whose theology continues to inform and inspire, and to Gerald McKenny, for encouragement and help. Thanks also to James Helmer, whose prayers and friendship weave in and out of the pages of this book. Especially in the case of *Evangelische Ethik als kirchliches Zeugnis*, my translations from the German would not have been possible without the generous help of my friend Sieglinde Pölzler-Kamatali and the support of John Cavadini. Sieglinde's efforts and John's support have prevented many potential errors. As to any translation errors that remain, I take full responsibility. Thanks to Aaron Canty for his help with Thomas's biblical commentaries. The community of learning at the University of Notre Dame provided a supportive and helpful environment for this project in its origins. My particular thanks go to Jennifer Herdt, Brian Daley, John Cavadini, and Maura Ryan, as well as Paul Martens, Matthew Loverin, John Perry, Elizabeth Agnew-Cochran, Deonna Neal, and Mary Hirschfeld for their friendship, their patience, and their invaluable input.

I am grateful to Reinhard Hütter and Paul Wadell, who became real friends to me as this book grew and matured. Few people have the stomach to aid in evaluating the limitations and promise of their own work, but this Reinhard has done, while at the same time kindly encouraging me through this process. Thank you also to Paul for his invaluable friendship, support, and guidance. His example of gentle leadership, of pedagogy in humility, and of holy kindness inspires me deeply.

I would like to acknowledge and thank the Hastings College community and the hard-working staff of Perkins Library at Hastings College. Most especially I need to thank Sheri Schneider who found for me, with remarkable speed, even the most obscure of resources for my research, and Clark Hendley who offered very tangible administrative support for this research.

Finally, many thanks to Jack, Niki, Ed, Sharon, and to my Stoneybrook family. Their daily living of an ecumenical community of grace teaches me a theological depth to which I hope to have done some small justice in the final chapter of this book. The debt of gratitude flows from charity, which the more it is paid the more it is due" (*ST* II-II 106.6.RO2).

Introduction

Christian Moral Action

> The Spirit is given to each one who receives Him as if He were the possession of that person alone, yet He sends forth sufficient grace to fill all the universe. . . . Through Him hearts are lifted up, the infirm are held by the hand, and those who progress are brought to perfection. He shines upon those who are cleansed from every spot, and makes them spiritual men through fellowship with Himself. When a sunbeam falls on a transparent substance, the substance itself becomes brilliant, and radiates light from itself. So too Spirit-bearing souls, illumined by Him, finally become spiritual themselves, and their grace is sent forth to others.[1]

ST. BASIL, THE FOURTH-CENTURY bishop of Caesarea, writes that upon each person cleansed by the grace of God in Jesus Christ shines the gift of the Holy Spirit. This gift is so intimate that, in Basil's description, its reception might be to that person alone. Yet this gift is so abundant that, through it, God's grace is sufficient to fill all that is. To the light of the Holy Spirit, as Basil describes it, the Christian is not merely receptive, but transparent. For this reason, the received gift of the Holy Spirit (perhaps the most paradoxical of human possessions) shines forth from the Christian with a light not belonging to her, illuminating her and others. She is no less herself for being illumined, yet this light shining from her is by no means hers. As St. Basil describes it, this gift of the Holy Spirit does not compete with the humanity of the Christian in the world—quite the opposite, in fact. Neither does the gift of the Holy Spirit perfecting the individual compete with that individual's social, ecclesial,

---

1. St. Basil the Great, *On the Holy Spirit*, 43–44.

and community context. The efficacy of God's grace competes neither with human agency nor with human fellowship. The shining forth of the light of the Holy Spirit through that individual renders her no less human and makes the shining no less hers, while at the same time shining as light that can only be called God's.

Two Defining Elements

In this book, I present a conversation that articulates the ecumenical foundation of Christian ethics in that noncompetitive cooperation between God's agency and human agency in the Christian moral act. The notion of the Christian moral act rarely receives attention in and of itself in contemporary theology. In this treatment, however, I examine a number of Christian theologians to see how they treat the Christian moral act and all that goes into its formation. Christian moral action, as it will be treated here, stands out as the most unique and yet least obviously identifiable kind of human action. Basil's description of a person in "possession" of the light of the Holy Spirit that shines through her aids in framing this idea. Christian moral action does not receive its definition from appearance, from the belief system of the human being involved, or from harmony with a set of moral norms. Rather Christian moral action, as treated in these pages, traces the deepest moments of relation between God and human beings—those moments in which God shines through free human agency in noncompetitive relation. God's invitation to these points of contact is by no means under human control, nor are these points of contact always visibly identifiable for what they are. Yet, the qualifier of "Christian" remains. Not for the appearance of the action, but rather for its source—God's grace in Christ through the Holy Spirit. Certainly, there are times when non-Christians act morally. Indeed, a great many times. There are also a great many times when Christians act morally in such a way that is not quintessentially Christian. One might, in both cases, wish that these times would occur more often than they do, but they are by no means a rarity. Likewise, Christians and non-Christians alike fail to do the morally good act. Christian moral acts are not simply those morally good acts done by Christians, or even those that have a particularly Christian appearance. Rather, *Christian moral action* or *Christian moral agency* refers to that peculiar kind of moral action that can be rightly said to fall under St. Basil's metaphor—those actions that are a shining forth of God's grace and still very much human action, intimately individual and inextricably communal. These pages offer an ecumenical treatment of that connection and the foundational place of that relationship in the field of Christian ethics.

Servais Pinckaers offers a wonderful definition of the discipline of Christian ethics at the beginning of his *Sources of Christian Ethics*,[2] before going on to treat the subject itself. While I will not attempt an exhaustive definition of Christian moral action (there may very well be as many different qualifiers for this definition as there are Christian moral acts themselves), I offer two elements that must be included in such a definition. First, Christian moral action is free human action. It includes the working of the unseen matrix of human intellect, reason, emotion, desire, and will. Often it includes that external orchestra of human agency—human voices, arms, legs, eyes. As human action, it is inextricably intertwined with human circumstances, human relationships, and human communities. Humans subsist almost invariably in social contexts, and human action cannot be considered without that dimension. Second, Christian moral action is God's action. That is, Christian moral action is the work of the Holy Spirit in and through the Christian. This, in fact, distinguishes Christian adherence to a moral code from Christian ethical action as a thing in and of itself. Christian moral action is that action accomplished, using St. Paul's words, "in the new life of the Spirit" (Rom 7:6), by "those who live according to the Spirit" (Rom 8:5)—the Spirit who "helps us in our weakness" (Rom 8:26), who "intercedes for us" (Rom 8:27) and "dwells in" us (Rom 8:11; 1 Cor 3:16), in whom "there is freedom" (2 Cor 3:17), by whom we live and in whom we are guided (Gal 5:25). Many other important elements must be included in defining Christian moral action—this action is beyond the capability of natural human capacity without God's help; it is hindered by sin without God's redemption; it is directed towards an end beyond natural human reach; it is guided by Scripture and nourished in the sacraments of the Church. No matter how long the list becomes, however, there may be no two elements of Christian moral action that are more difficult to conceptually hold together as the two I have named. The combination of Christian moral action as human action and as God's action forces the definition close to the cliff edges of Pelagianism and determinism. Such a definition threatens the idea of God's transcendence on the one hand,

---

2. Pinckaers, *The Sources of Christian Ethics*, 8.

while making God's immanence overbearing or immaterial or impossible on the other.

Yet, without the noncontrastive involvement of both human and divine agency, the Christian moral act ceases to be itself. As Robert Sokolowski nicely expresses it, Christian action is beyond its merely visible manifestation. Instead, Christian moral action "has a dimension that remains hidden in a way analogous to the way the divinity of Christ was hidden during his life on earth, and for the same reason: what is being done is, not merely an action within the setting of the world and its necessities, but an involvement with God who is not a part of the world."[3] Christian moral action is human action within the world and its necessities, but must, by definition, also involve God's entirely transcendent agency in the world. Precisely in this unseen matrix of human willing/desiring/purposing/reasoning and the stuff of human agency does God offer God's grace, shining forth into the world.

As beautiful as this may be, finding a way to apply this conjunction to Christian ethics is notoriously difficult. The purpose of this book is to offer an ecumenical conversation that reaches toward this conjunction and describes its setting in Christian community existence. I bring to this conversation a combination of theological sources that, in their unique way, aspire to articulate Christian ethics such that the grace of God in Jesus Christ and through the Holy Spirit constitutes the root of Christian action. At the same time, those theologians whose work I examine staunchly defend against the threat of determinism and insist upon Christian moral action as, in its essence, free human action. As human, Christian ethical action occurs inseparably from community context, and involves all of the internal and external means by which human action is formed.

Pursuing an ecumenical Christian ethic of faithful community and God's grace reaches far beyond simply pursuing a set of conceptual tools or a particularly accurate description. Both in the academy and in church pews across the world, few issues are more pivotal for narrating Christian existence than how God is or is not involved in our lives. Does my faithful action emerge from myself as an active gratitude for God's grace, or through my passivity to God's grace acting through me? When Scripture directs certain kinds of ethical action, are we moral islands in our obedience or disobedience? Does God care when good actions get

---

3. Sokolowski, *God of Faith and Reason*, 73.

done? If God does care about them, does that mean that God takes a part in getting them done? If and when God is involved in our actions, does that mean that we no longer have free will? When good actions get done, do they have anything to do with our salvation, or is that a denial of God's grace in some way? Jesus instructs the disciples to pray for God's aid. Is that possibility a part of the structure of human existence, or does God's agency come to us as a foreign thing—a miraculous happening, rather than a natural relationship? The shape of discipleship, the essence of prayer, the role of the sacraments (whatever their number), the purpose of Christian community, and a better description of Christian life as a whole are at stake here. While finding an interesting, ecumenical description of the relationship between divine grace and human action in Christian ethics might be a fascinating project on its own, the way that Christian life and Christian ethical action are described reaches to the very core of Christian identity and vocation. Recognizing the context, formation, and expression of God's involvement in human life gives us no more control over God's agency than we have over the sunlight's illumination of Basil's transparent substance. Yet our partaking in this relational conjunction, which results in Christian moral action, is better understood, pursued, nurtured, and prayed for when we know more about the nature of the connection sought.

Two Contemporary Voices Prompting Christian Ethics

Two contemporary theologians know the full impact of this issue quite well. Both Stanley Hauerwas and Reinhard Hütter have made substantial strides toward a better description of Christian ethical action and how such a description can change our notion of human freedom, human agency, and the direction, purpose, and meaning of Christian life. Even aside from the uniquely ecumenical character of their ethics, these theologians stand out in contemporary conversations as long-standing advocates of the centrality of God's agency in Christian action. They reach beyond the contemporary discourse in radical ways to articulate the dependence of Christian moral action upon God's grace, while at the same time never simply settling on a resulting human passivity in such action. Rather, they strive to express an interactive relationship between God's agency and human agency in the moral life. Writing from different backgrounds, these two voices grant much attention to Christian moral action as involving both human and divine agency, though they do so in very different ways. Each of them recognizes the difference made in theological ethics by what Robert Sokolowski calls "the disclosure of the theological"; he writes that "the disclosure of the theological is so special, and the kind of activity it opens for human beings is so different, that natural virtue does not render us capable in any way of behaving in the new context."[4] The virtue of which human beings are naturally capable is an important subject that merits close attention, but that is not the focus of this treatment. I am concerned (as are Hauerwas and Hütter, I believe) with this new "kind of activity" opened up through the grace of Jesus Christ by the Holy Spirit that renders a particular sort of human activity. Like them, too, this treatment looks to sources across the Christian historical landscape for a more complete picture of this new kind of activity and what it means for Christians to be a part of it.

These voices see this new kind of action as harmonious with the natural dynamics of human agency and human communities. Indeed, this is their great strength. They realize, with Kathryn Tanner, that "the transformative effects of God's grace are assumed to include genuine created dispositions for good works under God's direction; in this way the account of our salvation accords with the doctrine of creation in which divine agency is said to establish created beings in the created powers whereby they exercise their own operations and efficacy. Created beings by their own movements and activities attain what they are providentially ordered to attain by God."[5] Hauerwas and Hütter stand out of the contemporary discourse because they consistently exhibit an awareness of both the importance of the created attributes of human agency and the ways in which God transforms such attributes by grace. In treating the centrality of the grace of Jesus Christ in the Christian moral life, human operation, community, and the shape of human agency play a central role as those things by which God providentially orders Christian life. While it may be easy simply to assert the importance of God's grace, the acute awareness that these theological ethicists show for the threat of determinism prompts them to reach for articulating a harmonious conjunction between God's agency and human agency. As they treat the formation of Christian action by God's agency, they treat the transformation of understanding, community, judgment, and perception, and

---

4. Ibid., 100.

5. Tanner, *God and Creation in Christian Theology*, 112–13.

not just the revision of a list of moral norms. Hauerwas and Hütter struggle with the significant and long-standing ethical problem of describing God's agency as central to Christian ethics without compromising human freedom—how to express the formation and transformation of human action by God's agency without rendering human beings mere puppets of divine will.

Even more importantly, while championing the centrality of God's action in the Christian moral life, Hauerwas and Hütter explain the great value of Christian community and the integral connection of Christian language and narrative as a part of this process. The natural backdrop of Christian ethical action, for both of them, is not only the shape of human agency itself, but the shaping of that agency in community. The transformative effects of life in community play a prominent role in their ethical systems and function as means by which God transforms human beings and their being-in-act. Likewise, they utilize the formative power of the content of the Gospels as a part of God's involvement in Christian life, the dynamics of Christian community, and a facet of the means by which the Christian moral act is transformed. These theologians reach well beyond their backgrounds, and even beyond their connection with each other, in striving for a Christian ethic in which God's active, intimately involved agency is central to Christian moral action. While placing this heavy emphasis on the grace of God, they also manage to show the absolutely vital importance of Scripture, the context of the Christian worshipping community, and some kind of interactive relationship between God's grace and human moral agency. The theological ethics written by each emerge as shining attempts to show the Christian moral act as necessarily harmonizing God's action and our action in a noncompetitive way.

Perhaps because these theologians reach so far beyond their backgrounds and the context of the contemporary discourse, they also present a common problem. They stand, in many ways, as two of the best examples in contemporary theological ethics of sustained attempts to show the importance and centrality of the grace of God in the moral life. However, they also best exemplify the need for more sophisticated tools for speaking about this harmonious and noncompetitive bond between human and divine agency in Christian action. They are leaders in the trajectory of an ethic that reaches in ecumenical ways toward a noncompetitive relationship between divine and human agency in

Christian moral action. At the same time, however, they point to where the contemporary discourse in Christian ethics has encountered limits with the tools it has for dealing with this issue. These theologians consistently champion the necessity of a conjunction between God's action and human action in the Christian moral life. But as I hope to show, their efforts in conceptualizing ethics in the contemporary context in which God's action finds intimate involvement in human action can be supplemented in a beneficial way with additional tools.

Thomas Aquinas as a Resource

Hauerwas and Hütter take Christian ethics in exciting new directions, and yet the framework for ethics they offer could benefit from interaction with additional concepts. While both offer Christians good hope for the promise of an ethic founded on God's grace—in active, relational ways—and maintain that such an ethic can only exist in the context of the Christian worshipping community, they can benefit from dialogue with a very different theologian, also striving to describe the kind of connection between God's grace and free human agency that they seek.

Thomas Aquinas has much to contribute here. While he is not the complete solution to the contemporary ethical context that Hauerwas and Hütter address, he does have a number of very potent conceptual tools that can bring the contemporary discourse a great amount of help in figuring out just how to describe the connection between what God is doing and what people are doing in Christian ethical action. Like Hauerwas and Hütter, Thomas sees Christian ethical action as the work of the Holy Spirit and as human action, bound together in a noncompetitive and harmonious way. Like them, too, Thomas does not see a disjunction between the shape of human agency and God's action therein. Rather, Thomas seeks to show how human intellect, emotion, reason, desire, and will are a part of the means through which divine agency works in conjunction with free human action. Aquinas is certainly no less concerned with the threat of determinism than Hauerwas and Hütter, and perhaps even more eager to safeguard God's transcendence while insisting upon the intimacy of God's involvement in Christian ethical life. As I hope to show, some of his most valuable tools have been neglected by Christian ethics and have even been undertreated in Aquinas scholarship circles. Thomas' writing on the shape of the human condition, the connection between the work of the Holy Spirit and human free action, and how this free action is changed in and through its connection with God's grace are sadly underrecognized treasures in the contemporary discourse.

Though perhaps not immediately obvious, Thomas' dialogue with Hauerwas and Hütter is a natural one in many ways. Not only are they concerned with the same general goal of articulating a Christian ethic in which God's grace is firmly central, but they do so through remarkably similar (if not always similar-looking) ways. Thomas, Hauerwas, and Hütter all show the involvement of God's agency in the Christian moral life through following some common patterns, making them even better dialogue partners. In outlining God's involvement in the moral life, they look to (1) the indispensability of the Gospel narrative and the connection of that narrative with the effect of God's agency in the Christian moral life; (2) God's resituating of our character by gift as the starting point for the impact of God's agency in the moral life; (3) the necessity of God's agency as being intimately involved in the moral life, proceeding from a connection that is noncompetitive and cooperative between human and divine action. Thomas' voice is particularly useful, as his treatments of the potential for connection between divine and human agency developed across his writing career, right along with his treatments of Christology, anthropology, and pneumatology in ways that nicely carry these ambitions to coherent expression. Particularly in those sections of the *Summa theologiae* in which his articulation of the shape of Christian ethics and his pneumatology coincide (primarily his treatment of the New Law, the Gifts of the Holy Spirit, and his treatise on grace), Thomas provides invaluable tools for precisely that trajectory toward which Hauerwas and Hütter point contemporary Christian ethics.

Thomas' inclusion in this dialogue is not a one-way street, however. In fact, his theology can benefit from the robust emphasis on Christian community as a setting for God's grace that we find in the other two theologians. Where Hauerwas and Hütter are thin on conceptual tools for articulating a noncompetitive connection between divine and human agency in the moral life, Thomas proves very helpful. Where Thomas is thin on the ways in which the individual transformation of the Christian and her action must intertwine with the dynamics of the worshipping community, Hauerwas and Hütter prove very helpful. The sound impulses of each theologian are dramatically helped through an interaction between them.

Bringing Thomas Aquinas to the table of an ecumenical conversation in the contemporary context may not seem the most obvious of choices, and, indeed, prominent voices have expressed significant concerns about the place of Thomas' theology in contemporary Christian ethics. More specifically, a handful of Protestant theologians have articulated some anxieties about adopting or adapting Thomas' ethics (and specifically his treatise on grace) to the modern discourse. Theo Kobusch, Alister McGrath, and Eugene Rogers offer three of the most potent objections. Before making a case for the profound usefulness of Thomas Aquinas to the contemporary ethical discourse, it is first worth retracing some objections to his relevance and the applicability of his theology. As Kobusch, McGrath, and Rogers point out, the burden is on Aquinas to prove his usefulness in contemporary Christian ethics.

Three Objections to Thomas' Theology in Contemporary Ethics

Theo Kobusch, for one, objects to adopting Thomas' theology of grace, contending that the use he makes of Aristotle's outdated natural physics inadequately and inappropriately expresses God's grace and human freedom in the moral life. Another objection to the usability of Thomas' theology comes from Alister McGrath. In examining Thomas' explanation of the process of justification, he finds that Thomas has allowed Aristotle, rather than either Scripture or tradition, to dictate the terms and the process. While such a charge is limited in this case to justification, Aristotelian terms (especially those having to do with God's causation, human potentiality, and motion) are ubiquitous in Thomas' treatment of grace, and the charge could easily extend beyond his treatment of justification. Finally, an additional criticism is offered by Eugene Rogers, who poses some doubts about the category of habit, and the consequences that such a concept has on our view of human agency. Thomas' use of habit leads to a picture of human agency as either having possession of something through which human beings could do righteous works, or that we are enabled to do righteous works leading to eternal life apart from the immediate grace of God. These three objections—to the use of an outdated physics to describe dynamics of grace, to the use of Aristotelian categories generally to explain the effects of grace, and to the implications behind the language of habit—are very closely related, and each will be articulated as a prelude to my own arguments about the usefulness of Thomas' concepts regarding God's grace and human agency for prompting an ecumenical ethic of grace.

Theo Kobusch, in his chapter ("Grace") in *The Ethics of Aquinas*, argues for limits in the ways that the contemporary discourse draws from Aquinas' theology regarding grace and human freedom because of the ways in which Thomas uses an outdated natural physics to describe these relationships. This is especially troubling, hints Kobusch, since Aquinas is clearly aware of other, much better ways of conceptualizing grace and human agency. Kobusch questions the adequacy of Thomas' explanation of the relationship between divine and human agency, "in such natural categories as motion, although Thomas himself, even in the treatise on grace, employs other categories such as those of self-communication and gift (which transcend the Aristotelian imaginative world), and these seem to be more appropriate to freedom and grace."[6] Why should not Aquinas simply skip straight past the limitations of Aristotelian physics and proceed to the language of God's self-communicating gift? He says that this is especially harmful in the consideration of grace itself, which Thomas describes as a quality of the soul—an accident—that heals and perfects it, and in some way is a participation in God. Yet, argues Kobusch, Aquinas also spoke about the "being" of this accident.[7] Limited as he was (again, according to Kobusch) by the categories of Aristotelian terms which were appropriate only to natural things, Aquinas essentially contends that before we have this "thing" that has "being" we are unable to have a healed and perfected soul, and in some weak way participate in God, and after we have this "thing" that has "being" we are able to do righteous works (or at least partially so). The major problem here is not only the strong smell of Pelagianism, but also the needless mixing of metaphors between God's agency and things that have an existence in the natural world.[8] Because Thomas chose to express God's agency in human freedom using Aristotelian ideas about the motion of things in the natural world, Thomas reduced a change rightly seen as an ontological one to one that was merely the gaining of a naturally existing thing. In this way, he argues, Thomas uses language only appropriate to natural physics to describe a much deeper change, which results in an account of grace and human freedom robbed of its true impact.

6. Kobusch, "Grace (Ia IIae, qq. 109–14)," 214.
7. Ibid.
8. Ibid.

Kobusch's objection is an extremely important one, as it expresses the doubts of many: with conceptual tools like gift and self-communication at Thomas' disposal, why employ Aristotle's physics? Does his use of this physics not firmly cross Thomas off the list of those whose systems could be of use in the contemporary context? Alister McGrath's intensive examination of Thomas' treatment of the process of justification sharpens this critique even further. While McGrath contains his critique to a short and rather minimal inquiry into the effects of Aristotelian categories on Thomas' articulation of the process of justification, the implications of these questions go far beyond that context. McGrath argues that, following closely the Aristotelian scheme of generation and motion, Aquinas articulates a threefold process of justification: the infusion of grace, the movement of the free will, and the remission of sin. But, McGrath argues, the tradition from which he draws consistently (most especially Augustine) establishes a twofold motion of the free will in faith and in contrition. The result is a four-tiered system that ends up being based on the movement of the free will according to Aristotelian categories of motion. The movement of the will is preceded by a preparation for that motion which is the infusion of grace, and then the movement of the will itself which has relation (in good Aristotelian fashion) to both its terms—the term from which it leaves and the term toward which it goes. In short, a free will movement with regard to sin and a free will movement toward God. The final step in this causal progression is the remission of sin. McGrath argues that the resulting fourfold process of justification "is based, not upon tradition or Scripture, but on the Aristotelian analysis of motion."[9] Aquinas' use of these Aristotelian categories of generation imposes two consequences on the resulting picture of the process of justification: "1. the existence of motion implies premotion; therefore justification implies a disposition for justification. 2. the analysis of the inner structure of the *motus* of justification allows a causal sequence to be established between the *motus moventis*, the *motus mobilis* and the *terminus*, which St. Thomas demonstrates—again, on the basis of Aristotelian physics—to correspond with the traditional *processus iustificationis*."[10] While McGrath's language critiquing this picture is densely minimal, he helpfully points out that the imposition of the necessity of a "premotion" disposition required for justification, as

---

9. McGrath, "The Influence of Aristotelian Physics," 225.
10. Ibid., 229.

well as the movement regarding the whence and the whereto to get to the final movement of the remission of sin, does not reflect the process of justification as found in Scripture, nor in the tradition. McGrath points out that most of the changes readers see resulting in the treatment of grace found in the *Summa* seem to have followed from Aquinas' encounter with Eudemus' *Liber de bona fortuna* (thought by Aquinas to have been written by Aristotle). McGrath concludes, "Indeed, if the *Liber de bona fortuna* be allowed to be 'Aristotelian' for the purposes of our argument, it is possible to argue that St. Thomas' views on justification, as expressed in the *Summa theologiae* rests on a foundation that owes more to Aristotle than to St. Augustine."[11] The fourfold process of justification is a treatment that takes its structure from Aristotelian concepts of generation and movement. Rather than taking his cues from Scripture or from Augustine, Thomas offers a treatment in Aristotelian physics.

Again, the impact of this critique reaches beyond the confines of Thomas' explanation of the process of justification. Aristotle's ideas intimately inform the dynamics of grace in the context of human agency, the concepts of movement, causation, potentiality, and action as Thomas describes them. McGrath poses a useful question in asking whether in looking to adopt or adapt certain notions from Aquinas we should tolerate the framework expressed, at least in part, by an outdated Aristotelian physics.

Eugene Rogers offers some additional assistance in articulating some possible obstacles to the use of Aquinas in prompting an ecumenical ethic of grace. In particular, he voices some Protestant anxieties to the Aristotelian category of habit and to the elevation of human reason by means of grace. He argues that Aquinas' description of the interaction between the Holy Spirit and human moral agency puts too much emphasis on the abilities of our continuity in righteousness and our minds. "As the giver not of legalisms but of newness of life, [according to Aquinas] the Spirit appropriates two features of human nature that Protestants hate to see deified. They are reason and habit—the structure of knowing and the reliability of love."[12] He argues that Aquinas places far too much trust in human agency and human modes of knowing and doing things. After all, if the reason is elevated and we are given a gift of grace, which

11. Ibid.
12. Rodgers, "Faith and Reason Follow Glory," 450–51.

stays with us habitually, why would we need any connection with God's grace anymore? As Rogers writes, "Protestants worry that habits give too much continuity to the creature."[13] If human moral agency is set up in such a way that God's grace is no longer needed or that our sinfulness is no longer a serious obstacle, then is there really any difference from the kinds of habitual shaping that Aristotle describes in the cultivation of the virtues and the abilities of the reason, and the transformation Aquinas describes through grace? Is human sin even a factor anymore if such concepts are employed so dominantly? "Protestants may say, Wait! Reason and habit are the very places where the human rebellion against God takes place. Reason, in Luther's famous phrase, is the devil's whore. Habit is where sin persists even in the justified."[14] The usefulness of concepts like habit and the treatment of reason should be in articulating the problem rather than the solution. To use such categories as habit and reason to speak about righteous action rings very loudly of Pelagianism, and seems to imply that we either have a "thing" from God in the reason and/or the will by which we can do good works, or that we are, at minimum, suddenly enabled to do good works without an utter dependence upon the constantly intimate presence of the grace of God through the Holy Spirit.

These critiques are all closely connected. Each argues for some caution when it comes to using Thomas' treatment of grace and human action because of his heavy reliance on Aristotle, producing an account that might be not only outdated but also better suited to describe natural causality rather than divine causality. If the languages of justification and sanctification are reduced to discussions of natural motion, reason, habit, potency, generation, etc., then are we any longer speaking of a transcendent God upon whom sinful humanity is entirely dependent? Kobusch, McGrath, and Rogers offer a great service in voicing in different ways the concern of many Protestant readers of Aquinas: the discussion of grace sounds a lot like an Aristotelian description of the mere movements of natural causes.

Part of the root worry behind these objections is Aquinas' use of what he perceived to be the very best language about the movement of natural created things to describe the impact of God's redeeming grace and the gift of the indwelling Holy Spirit in terms of human agency.

13. Ibid., 452.
14. Ibid., 451.

Such objections neglect one of the most valuable perspectives Aquinas can offer: the language of the movement of natural, created things is appropriate (and in fact, very useful) because God's causation is so transcendent that connection with human agency does not constitute a threat to its freedom. For Thomas, the interaction between divine and human agency is a noncompetitive one. Human agency need not be (and indeed, in Aquinas' framework, cannot be) seen as its own entity, its own power, over and against the providential willing of God. Quite the contrary, as God is the creative and sustaining cause behind all that is, we are in fact forced to speak of human agency always and everywhere in the context of God's action. As Tanner says, "God brings forth the operations of created causes by working interiorly, in their depths. A transcendent God can be said to have such an extraordinary immanence of operation when discussion of God's agency accords with our rule for talk of God as transcendent. Following our rule for talk of God's agency as immediate, one can say that God operates within created causes, in the very place from which their operations arise."[15] The beauty of God's indwelling in us is not that our sinful causation is cast aside, but that it is redeemed. God does not compete with the foundations of our own causes, because God *is* the foundation of our own causes. Because God is transcendent cause and, therefore, God's cause is not competitive with those secondary causes that God creates and sustains, then it is most fitting that God's grace in Jesus Christ through the Holy Spirit should operate within (while, of course, entirely transcending) the framework of those secondary causes that God has put into place. It is most fitting and natural that God redeems us not despite our human agency, but through it—even, and dramatically, through sin-ridden human desires, thoughts, and actions that separate us from God in the first place. It is most fitting that God's entirely transcendent redemption should move and work according to (and not despite) the kinds of creatures God created us to be.

Thomas Aquinas applied what he knew as the best articulation of natural movement, causation, and action so that he could demonstrate in detail that God redeems and sanctifies human sinners in a way that closely involves the sinner's own agency. While we may wish to question the applicability of Aristotle, Thomas uses this newly arrived physics as a way to articulate the intimacy of God's love, God's transcendent,

15. Tanner, *God and Creation in Christian Theology*, 95.

noncompetitive bond with human nature, and the fittingness of speaking of God's operation through the matrix of human willing and acting as a part of God's saving grace and the action of the Holy Spirit. Thomas Aquinas' use of categories from natural physics is meant to show how entirely dependent we are upon God's transcendent agency, and the beauty and elegance of God's redemption of Christian lives and its incorporation of and redemption of our willing agency. For "God's creative powers must be said to extend to all created existence, including presumably any power or efficacy that created beings themselves have."[16] In whatever way we choose to describe or evaluate the unseen matrix of human willing and acting, Thomas Aquinas provides wonderfully useful conceptual tools for prompting an ecumenical ethic of grace by showing that Christian moral action can be both entirely dependent upon God's grace through Jesus Christ and the indwelling of the Holy Spirit, and still properly taking place in a nondeterminative way in the matrix of human willing and acting.

In the following section, I endeavor to let Thomas flex his conceptual muscles a bit and display just how useful and relevant his system is to the contemporary conversation. More specifically, I wish to demonstrate why he would be an invaluable conversation partner in precisely those directions toward which Hauerwas and Hütter are prompting ecumenical Christian ethics. Over and against those objections offered by Kobusch, McGrath, and Rogers about the specific tools Aquinas uses to achieve his system, I hope to show the great value of some of these specifics, if not for complete adoption, then at least for charitable adaptation. Thomas' inclusion in contemporary ethical discourse relies on his ability to offer tools that the contemporary conversation lacks, and to do so in a system that can be adapted to the terms of the contemporary discourse.

A Case for Thomas Aquinas as an Invaluable Conversation Partner

In what follows, I will briefly indicate why Thomas Aquinas might be a useful conversation partner to Hauerwas and Hütter to better articulate the connection between divine and human agency, in a general way. Here I make a broad case for Thomas' usefulness, particularly lifting up his explanations of movement and causation in human action. I pursue

16. Tanner, *God and Creation in Christian Theology*, 86.

this case through (1) a brief and introductory glance at a very concise moment—*ST* I-II 109.6—in which Aquinas demonstrated his conceptual agility regarding the connection between divine and human agency; (2) a glance at another brief instance in the *Summa*—I.22—in which Aquinas presents some foundational notions about human causation as considered in terms of divine causation; and (3) another look at the special connection Aquinas holds between divine and human agency in the moral life, as found in a very short passage in his commentary on Paul's Letter to the Romans. Through these three very compact moments, I hope to give some initial indicators as to why Aquinas might be such a useful conversation partner in considering the theological problem of how God's agency is involved in human action, generally, and Christian moral action, in particular. Through these three brief glances at compact moments in Thomas' theology, I also hope to show exactly what the conceptual tools at his disposal are able to accomplish. To name the potential of these tools initially, Thomas offers: (*a*) a picture of created, secondary, human agency that is rightly seen as being always in the context of divine agency, (*b*) a picture of genuinely free human will that is always rightly seen within the larger context of divine causation, and (*c*) a picture of Christian moral action in which the dependence of human action upon divine agency is brought to an especially close bond.

In Question 109, article 6 in the *Prima Secundae* of his masterful *Summa theologiae*, in his responses to the objections, Aquinas offers a concise moment demonstrating his conceptual agility with regard to the bond between divine and human agency. In Question 109, Thomas looks in ten specific ways at the necessity of grace. In the sixth article, he asks, "Whether a man by himself and without the external aid of grace, can prepare himself for grace?" This is an interesting problem in the overall topic of the necessity of grace because it not only asks whether grace is necessary (the affirmative answer to which would not draw very much skepticism from his reading audience then or now), but also what is necessary in preparation for grace. If God alone can prepare us to receive grace, then it would seem as if the freedom of the human will is severely compromised and we are merely God's puppets. On the other hand, if we prepare ourselves for God's grace, then this would seem to suggest that we could somehow demand it of God when we were ready, or at least that we could accomplish a crucial step in Christian conversion (turning away from sin, and turning to God) without any need for grace. In the first objection of 109.6, a possible answer to this question is offered in this way: Surely we must be capable of preparing ourselves for God's grace because preparing for God's grace is to turn to God. If this is indeed what we are called to do as Christians (the objector cites scriptural authority on this point), it cannot be impossible for us. If only God could turn us to God, then God could not ask us to do it. Therefore, we must be able to turn ourselves to God without the help of grace. To this formidable objection, Thomas' reply is short and simple: "Man's turning to God is by free-will; and thus man is bidden to turn himself to God. But free-will can only be turned to God, when God turns it."[17] On the surface, the reply seems to contain a central contradiction. Thomas agrees with the objector, it appears, on every point. Yes, God asks the Christian to turn to God by her own free will. Yes, if she could not turn to God by her own free will, God would not ask her to do it. So, yes, it must be possible for her. However, Thomas seems to have a set of concepts that the objector lacks. For, without any careful qualification or explanation, he simply asserts, "free-will can only be turned to God when God turns it." For reasons that we must explore, Thomas seems to hold that there is no inherent contradiction between a movement of the "free" human will and God's movement of that will. In seeking to articulate a connection between divine and human agency, Thomas can be quite useful. In a straightforward and almost brazen manner, Thomas speaks of a noncontradictory and noncompetitive connection between a genuinely free human action and God's action within it—a cordial relationship between divine and human agency.

A slight variation on this same idea occurs in the next reply to the next objection in the same *ST* I-II 109.6. The second objector tries an affirmative answer to the question ("Whether a man by himself and without the external aid of grace, can prepare himself for grace?") in this way: In preparing ourselves for grace and turning to God, the only things we can do are the things that we can do. The objector cites Matthew 7:11 and shows that Scripture itself says that if we ask for God's Spirit, God will give it to us. So, if we are told that we can receive God's Spirit if we just ask for it, then it must be within our capacity to actually receive that Spirit. It would be very cruel, after all, for God to tell us that we might ask for God's Spirit, if we were not in fact able to receive it. Since we can only do those things that we can do, we must be able to prepare ourselves

17. Aquinas, *Summa theologiae*, I-II.109.6.RO1.

to receive grace. Thomas replies to this objection in an equally brief way: "Man can do nothing unless moved by God, according to John 15:5: 'Without Me, you can do nothing.' Hence when a man is said to do what is in him to do, this is said to be in his power according as he is moved by God."[18] Thomas does not deny that we can receive grace if we ask for it. He does not deny that we can only do those things we can do. What he does deny is that doing those things that are in our power to do somehow belongs to us as self-caused actions. What he denies is the idea that our capacity for moral action, or any action, is a capacity isolated from God's agency. Again, it becomes clear why Thomas Aquinas might be so important to the involvement of God's grace in Christian ethics. He has at his disposal sufficient tools to be able to treat, quickly and boldly, the capacity for human action in connection with God's action in a noncompetitive way.

One more permutation of the same problem emerges from this question, further demonstrating why Aquinas might be a useful resource for treating a bond between divine and human agency in the moral life, especially with regard to the threat of determinism. In the fourth objection to the same article 6 of *ST* I-II 109, the objector gives one more attempt at an affirmative answer to the question of whether we can prepare ourselves for God's grace without any external aid of grace. The objector cites what would seem to be a smoking gun of a biblical passage from Proverbs 16, "it is the part of man to prepare the soul," and then goes on to give a slight variation on the previous objections. The objector argues that for an action to be "the part" of man, a human being actually has to be able to do it—and not only to do it, but to do it by himself. The Proverbs passage did not say that it is the part of human beings to prepare the soul as long as God first prepares the soul for this preparation. The clear point of the passage is that we can do this by ourselves, and so, the objector concludes, we can prepare ourselves for grace. Again, Thomas gives a clear and concise answer: "It is the part of man to prepare his soul, since he does this by his free-will. And yet he does not do this without the help of God moving him, and drawing him to Himself, as was said above."[19] Once more, Thomas does not deny the core of the objection. Indeed, we certainly prepare ourselves for grace, and we do that through the free will. But, boldly and simply,

---

18. Ibid., I-II.109.6.RO2.
19. Ibid., I-II.109.6.RO4.

Thomas asserts that God's help in moving us and the freedom of the will are not incompatible. Once more, Aquinas might be very useful in pursuing conceptual tools for articulating a bond between divine and human agency in the moral act. In the reply to this objection as well, he demonstrates that he has some tools at his disposal that enable him to speak of a connection between our movement, as asked of us by God and mandated by Scripture, and God's movement of us in such a way that our freedom is not compromised.

What might some of these tools be? Fortunately, Thomas offers a densely compact glance at these tools in his question "On the Providence of God" (*ST* I.22), in which readers are afforded a glimpse at his picture of the ways in which God's causal sovereignty extends to all other causes. While such a brief glance will by no means do justice to Thomas' complex treatment of human causation, it will aid in offering some indication as to how Thomas can give the kinds of answers that one sees in *ST* I-II 109.6, and shows some of the foundational notions Aquinas holds about the connection between divine and human causation. In *ST* I.22, Aquinas writes that "the causality of God, Who is the first agent, extends to all being, not only as to constituent principles of species, but also as to the individualizing principles; not only of things incorruptible, but also of things corruptible."[20] For Aquinas, the reason that we cannot firmly separate what is on the "part" of a human being to do and what is on the "part" of God to do, is that there is no such thing as something that is on our "part" to do and cut off from God's action. This connection is present not only as the ground of our being or of intact human nature, but even in sinful, individual existence and action. In short, there is no created action that falls outside of divine causality, for Aquinas. Even the freedom of our will itself is still caused by God and, thereby, exists under the broader heading of God's ordering causality (which is to say, God's providence). For, "since the very act of free will is traced to God as to a cause, it necessarily follows that everything happening from the exercise of free will must be subject to divine providence. For human providence is included under the providence of God, as a particular under a universal cause."[21] God's causation stands behind every free action of ours and so, as such, it is impossible to speak of the freedom of our will without also speaking of the causes on which it depends, most especially God's

20. Ibid., I.22.2.
21. Aquinas, *Summa theologiae*, I.22.2.RO4.

causality. Of course the obvious objection is that if God's sovereign and providential causality stands behind all things, then it seems really incorrect to speak of the human will as free at all. However, Aquinas makes clear that simply because there is a connection between divine and human causation does not mean that God imposes a necessity on our secondary, human causing. Instead, "Divine providence imposes necessity upon some things; not upon all . . . thus it has prepared for some things necessary causes, so that they happen of necessity; for others contingent causes, that they may happen by contingency, according to the nature of their proximate causes."[22] God safeguards the freedom of human will as God safeguards the kind of causality appropriate to our nature. Simply because we may speak of a constant connection between divine and human agency in human action does not mean that we are forced to conclude that God causes everything with necessity. Instead, while God's causality cannot be separated from our own secondary causality, God's causation does not impose necessity upon us. We may still act as it is proper in our nature to do—freely. But, this doesn't mean that God's power is thwarted either. "The effect of divine providence is not only that things should happen somehow; but that they should happen either by necessity or by contingency. Therefore whatsoever divine providence ordains to happen infallibly and of necessity happens infallibly and of necessity; and that happens from contingency, which the plan of divine providence conceives to happen from contingency."[23] The bond between divine and human agency in the freedom of the human act does not entail a weakness of God's sovereignty, nor does it entail the binding of the freedom of human will. Instead, Aquinas speaks of the freedom of the human will as standing in an inseparable causal relationship with God in which God's providential agency causes our actions in accord with our nature—which is to say, with regard to the freedom of the will. As Rudi te Velde writes in his *Participation and Substantiality in Thomas Aquinas*, "since natural causes suppose something prior to their (particular) effect, they must be understood, according to Aquinas, as secondary causes, which means that their operation depends on a prior and more universal cause."[24] As natural causes, human acts are operations that depend on God's causality. But God does not move any natural

22. Ibid., I.22.4.
23. Ibid., I.22.4.RO1.
24. Velde, *Participation and Substantiality in Thomas Aquinas*, 160.

causes in a way disproportionate to their natures. As God has granted us the freedom of will, the ways in which we are caused to act does not impose necessity on our actions. Or, as Joseph Wawrykow writes in his *God's Grace and Human Action*, "By divine ordination, the human person is not restricted to a single course of action . . . God respects this freedom and leaves human contingency intact. Nevertheless, while the human person retains dominion over his acts, his activity falls under the divine providence employed by God for the achievement of God's plan . . . God does not treat creatures as mere 'puppets' that contribute nothing of their own to the realization of God's plan. Rather, creatures possess their own causality as granted to them by God."[25] Aquinas forges a connection between divine and human agency in *every* human action such that we are dependent upon God's providential causation, but not "restricted" to only certain kinds of actions. God, instead, causes our secondary agency with the contingency and freedom appropriate to our nature. All kinds of agency stand in a dependent relationship to God's providential causality. But human agency and divine agency have a connection in which God infallibly causes our agency contingently. "In other words, he simply asserts that it is possible to ascribe real causing to the human will, while at the same time affirming the infallibility of divine willing. For modern readers, the simple assertion is jarring and perhaps puzzling. In all likelihood, Aquinas feels that he can make the claim without further explanation because he takes seriously divine transcendence."[26] Aquinas conceives of God's causation in a way very different from our own. Our will is not at war with God for control, resulting in an action either caused by us or caused by God. Instead, God's agency infallibly causes all other secondary causes. Our actions are only possible because of the dependence of our agency on God's. Yet, the freedom of our will is a part of God's providential causation and does not constitute a compromise of the connection between God's agency and our own. "St. Thomas affirmed the analogy of operation, namely, that the causation of the created cause is itself caused; that it is a procession which is made to proceed; that it is an operation in which another operates."[27] This is true for all created causes and, likewise, for human beings in the freedom God grants us. For Aquinas, to argue for

25. Wawrykow, *God's Grace and Human Action*, 155.
26. Wawrykow, "Grace," 202.
27. Lonergan, *Grace and Freedom*, 88.

the ability of human beings to cause their own free actions would be tantamount to equating our causation, power, and will with that of God's.

Still, one might object that no matter how transcendent God's agency may be, and no matter what the explanation of the relationship may be, if the act of the will is to be genuinely free, then God's agency can only be involved at a distance. However, as Bernard Lonergan points out, simply by affirming the freedom of our agency, we need not necessarily close the free human act to God's action. Instead, "there is no end of room for God to work on the free choice without violating it, to govern above its self-governance, to set the stage and guide reactions and give each character its personal role in the drama of life. Still, none of these created antecedents can be rigorous determinants of the free choice: God alone has the property of transcendence. It is only in the logico-metaphysical simultaneity of the atemporal present that God's knowledge is infallible, His will irresistible, His action efficacious."[28] To place divine and human will on par with one another such that either human will is free, or God determines human action, is to deny God's transcendence and to equate our capacity for action with God's.

Again, while these indications exhaust neither the scope of Thomas' metaphysics nor his picture of human and divine causation, they do highlight some of the reasons why Thomas could respond to the objections in *ST* I-II 109.6 in the ways that he did. The freedoms of human agency are not outside of God's providential agency, but are rather still a part of the connection between divine causation and created causation. For, "since God, then, provides universally for all being, it belongs to His providence to permit certain defects in particular effects, that the perfect good of the universe may not be hindered, for if all evil were prevented, much good would be absent from the universe. A lion would cease to live, if there were no slaying of animals; and there would be no patience of martyrs if there were no tyrannical persecution."[29] Even in the sinfulness of creation and of the human will particularly, we still are not forced into the language of opposition between God's sovereign will and our own fallen nature. Human and divine agency are not only compatible but in a necessarily dependent relationship. Such a relationship does not negate human freedom, but is, rather, "the condition of the possibility of

---

28. Ibid., 115–16.
29. Aquinas, *Summa theologiae*, I.22.2.RO2.

human freedom."³⁰ The fabric of causation in which there is a connection between God's infallible agency and our free agency "does not check human liberty but enlarges it."³¹ The affirmation that, even in the free acts of human will, we stand in dependence upon God's agency and under the sovereignty of God's providence is especially important for us. For Aquinas, the possibility of this cooperative connection between divine and human agency in the Christian moral act rests on the foundation of a conception of human agency in which we, even in the freedom of our action, are never separate from God's providential causation. Instead, "the providence of God produces effects through the operation of secondary causes,"³² even and especially by means of the freedom of human acts as contingent secondary causes.

When Aquinas turns to the specific question of Christian moral action, he speaks often of the Holy Spirit acting in the heart of the Christian. Without the above tools, this would seem to be an inherently problematic way of construing the moral life. After all, moral action can hardly be said to belong to us if it can also be described as God's action. Nevertheless, in Aquinas' system, "virtuous activity would emerge not first from ethical debate or community discipline but from the new life of the Spirit in us."³³ While much more attention will be given to the bond between the action of the Holy Spirit and human agency in the following chapters, here I wish to point out, in some simple ways, how the conceptual building blocks regarding divine and human causation (highlighted above) find direct relevance to a treatment of the Christian moral life.

Daniel A. Keating, in his helpful article "Justification, Sanctification and Divinization in Thomas Aquinas," points out that if one were to compare Thomas' biblical commentaries with his more strictly systematic treatises, "we see in *longhand* in the biblical commentaries what often appears in *shorthand* in the *Summa*."³⁴ While Keating is no doubt correct in many instances, in at least one of the commentaries he highlights, the opposite is the case. In the eighth chapter of Thomas' commentary on

---

30. Kobusch, "Grace (Ia IIae, qq. 109–14)," 211.
31. Kelly, "Gifts of the Spirit," 194.
32. Aquinas, *Summa theologiae*, I.23.5.
33. O'Meara, "Virtues in the Theology of Thomas Aquinas," 264.
34. Keating, "Justification, Sanctification and Divinization in Thomas Aquinas," 139.

Paul's Epistle to the Romans, there are moments that give a shorthand to the picture of the Christian moral life spelled out in much more detail in the *Summa*. In cap. 8, lect. 3 of this commentary, Thomas asserts the following: "Whoever are sons of God obtain the inheritance of the life of glory; but any who are guided by the Holy Spirit are sons: therefore any who are directed by the Holy Spirit, attain the inheritance of the life of glory."[35] This statement rightly joins a few things, namely the Christian identity as adopted sons and daughters of God and that such an identity is bound up with being guided by the Holy Spirit. He goes on to consider this statement in two ways, both of which deal with this connection.

> First, "how are some directed by the Spirit of God?" and it is thus able to be understood. *Whoever is led by the Spirit of God*, that is guided, as if by a certain teacher and director: indeed the Holy Spirit accomplishes that in us, namely insofar as he shows us from within what we ought to do. . . . But because he who is led is unable to accomplish such things in himself: yet the spiritual man, on the other hand, is not only instructed by the Holy Spirit as to what he should do, but also his heart is moved by the Holy Spirit; therefore it should be better understood in this sense when it says: *Whoever is led by the Spirit*. For they are said to be led who are moved by a higher inspiration . . . the spiritual man is inclined to do something not as if by the movement of his own will principally, but rather is inclined to some degree by the inspiration of the Holy Spirit. . . . That spiritual men may act by will and free choice should not be excluded, through this, however, because the Holy Spirit causes in them the very movement of the will and free choice.[36]

---

35. Quicumque sunt filii Dei consequuntur hereditatem gloriosae vitae; sed quicumque reguntur Spiritu sancto, sunt filii: ergo quicumque reguntur Spiritu sancto, consequuntur hereditatem gloriosae vitae.

36. Aquinas, *In Epistolam ad Romanos*, Cap. 8, Lect. 3. Circa primum duo consideranda sunt. Primo quidem quomodo aliqui aguntur a Spiritu Dei; et potest sic intelligi. *Quicumque Spiritu Dei aguntur*, id est reguntur, sicut a quodam doctore et directore: quod quidem in nobis facit Spiritus, scilicet inquantum illuminat nos interius quid facere debeamus, . . . Sed quia ille qui ducitur ex seipso non operatur: homo autem spiritualis non tantum instruitur a Spiritu sancto quid agere debeat, sed etiam cor eius a Spirit sancto movetur; ideo plus intelligendum est in hoc quod dicitur: *Quidcumque Spiritu Dei aguntur*. Illa enim agi dicuntur quae quodam superiori instinctu moventur: unde de brutis dicimus quod non agunt, sed aguntur, quia a natura moventur, et non ex proprio motu, ad suas actiones agendas. Similiter autem homo spiritualis non quasi ex motu propriae voluntatis principaliter, sed ex instinctu Spiritus sancti inclinatur ad aliquid agendum, . . . Non tamen per hoc excluditur quin viri spirituales per voluntatem

In this first consideration, Aquinas deals with the idea of being "led by the Spirit of God," and in the very last sentence, one can see how such an idea rests upon some of the conceptual groundwork regarding divine and human causation examined in the above paragraphs. The Holy Spirit causes movement of the will and in a way that is noncompetitive with the freedom of our will. So, in the moral life, the agency of the Holy Spirit in the heart of the believer relies on the backdrop of a broader picture of human and divine causation in which the action that is our "part" to accomplish is not ever rightly considered as separate from God's agency. If the above quotation is any indication, this seems especially true in the freedom of the Christian moral act. For, as the middle section of the quotation indicates, being led by the Spirit of God is not only to be taught what to do, for that would mean we were simply instructed by God to do things that were still very much within our own limited human capacity to do. But rather, the one who is led by the Spirit "is unable to accomplish such things in himself," and so that one "is not only instructed by the Holy Spirit as to what he should do, but also his heart is moved by the Holy Spirit." Those who are heirs to God's kingdom through Jesus Christ are also "led by a higher instinct/inspiration"— that of the Holy Spirit. While it is true, then, that all secondary, created causes are dependent on divine causation, and while it is true that even those actions of the human free will are rightly considered as dependent on God's agency and in a noncompetitive relationship with it, it seems that Christian moral action (action that is the product of the movement of the Holy Spirit teaching and leading in the Christian heart) is in more than just a noncompetitive relationship with divine agency.

Thomas here, in a brief way, indicates that in those moments of Christian moral action, the Holy Spirit is just as rightly considered the moving agent as is the human. The free Christian moral act, proceeding as it does from both human agency and the action of the Holy Spirit, implies a human dependence on God beyond the dependence on a secondary cause to the first cause. Instead, in the individual action, both the Spirit and the human agent are rightly said to act in what might, for now, loosely be called a *cooperative* relationship. In other words, in the kind of action of which Thomas speaks in the above passage, the connection between divine and human agency is more than cordial or

et liberum arbitrium operentur, quia ipsum motum voluntatis et liberi arbitrii Spiritus santus in eis causat.

noncompetitive. Rather, it is an involvement of God's action and human action together. While this certainly relies on the broader backdrop of Thomas' picture of secondary causation, it seems to reach beyond it to indicate the potential for a much deeper connection between divine and human agency in the Christian moral act. The sort of free willing that Thomas seems to affirm in instances like this is quite different from common modern, Western notions of freedom as isolated, uninhibited agency. Thomas offers a freedom that is only free (and indeed only existent at all) because of its causal dependence on God's agency. Freedom in a context of inescapable dependence opens quite a natural door for a variety of human actions that, for Thomas (and hopefully for the modern discourse as well), can still be called "free," but not in a way that eliminates God's causality.

Keating helpfully points out that the notion of the indwelling of the acting Holy Spirit is much more prevalent in Thomas' biblical commentaries than it is in the *Summa* where Thomas prefers the term "infusion."[37] Still, in this moment of shorthand, Thomas uses Scripture to speak about a unique and particular connection between God's action and our own in the moral life. In fact, as he continues in this commentary (in the second consideration), such a bond is part of what it means to be a Christian child of God, redeemed by Christ: "Further it is considered, how those who are moved by the Spirit of God, are sons of God. And this is obvious from the likeness of natural sons who are generated, proceeding by means of the natural seed of a father. But the spiritual seed proceeding from the Father is the Holy Spirit: and therefore through this seed some people are generated into children of God."[38] This internal bond with the Spirit, then, can rightly be said to be bound with our salvation through Christ, our turning to God, and our generation into children of God. This generation is bound closely with these moments of coaction by the freely willing Christian and the indwelling Holy Spirit. Such an interaction is a part of what it means to be an adopted child of God.[39] Another way of putting such things (as does Ulrich Kühn in his

37. Keating, "Justification, Sanctification and Divinization in Thomas Aquinas," 149.

38. Aquinas, *In Epistolam ad Romanos*, Cap.8, Lect. 3. Secundo considerandum est, quomodo illi qui Spiritu Dei aguntur, sunt filii Dei. Et hoc est manifestum ex similitudine filiorum carnalium, qui per semen carnale a patre procedentes generantur. Semen autem spirituale a Patre procedens, est Spiritus sanctus: et ideo per hoc semen aliqui homines in filios Dei generantur.

39. Keating, "Justification, Sanctification and Divinization in Thomas Aquinas," 150.

1965 book *Via Caritatis: Theologie des Gesetzes bei Thomas von Aquin*), the indwelling of the Holy Spirit in one's soul—instructing us in action and leading us to accomplish it—is bound up with the most intimate and intrinsic effect of the Holy Spirit in us, through which the love of God directs us in virtue. Such is what it means to be under the "New Law" or the "Law of the Spirit."[40]

While this brief glimpse of Thomas Aquinas' treating the connection between divine and human agency in the Christian moral life cannot present the whole scope of his thought on this subject, my present goal is much less ambitious. My hope here was to give a brief indication as to why Aquinas might be useful as a conversation partner in speaking about the connection between divine and human agency in the Christian moral act. Aquinas seems at least as concerned as contemporary theological ethics will prove to be, if not more so, with the problem of the freedom of the will and the threat of determinism. What makes his work uniquely useful are those conceptual tools at his disposal to consider a connection between created and uncreated agency in every movement and action. Beyond that, he has the tools to treat even the action of the free human agent as rightly contextualized in the overall picture of God's providential agency. His commentary on the book of Romans reveals an additional dimension to the bond between divine and human agency: the action of the indwelling Holy Spirit in the heart of the Christian, instructing us as to what we are to do and acting along with us in doing it. Indeed, for Thomas, such a relationship between divine and human agency in Christian moral action is not only possible, but is in some way the fabric of what it means to be an adopted child of God through Christ Jesus.

---

40. Kühn, *Via Caritatis*, 193. "Lex spiritus" meint nach Thomas einmal den in der Seele wohnenden Heiligen Geist selbst, der den Menschen über das rechte Handeln belehrt und zu ihm hinführt; zum anderen meint es die nächsten und eigentlichsten Wirkungen des Heiligen Geistes im Menschen: den durch die Liebe wirksamen Glauben, der selbst wieder innerlich über das zu Tuende belehrt. Und diese doppelte Auslegung des Begriffes "lex spiritus" nennt Thomas ausdrücklich auch Bestimmungen der "lex nova." Dabei bringt der zweite Aspekt dieser Auslegung einen für uns noch neuen Gedanken: Das neue Gesetz ist das Gesetz der durch den Geist gegebenen Tugenden Glaube und Liebe, die als Prinzip ethischer Erkenntnis und ethischen Handelns anzusprechen sind. Im Zentrum des neuen Gesetzes steht somit das, was auch im alten Gesetz als oberstes Prinzip deutlich wurde, dessen Erfüllung aber aus dem alten Gesetz selbst unmöglich war.

After thoroughly examining Hauerwas and Hütter in chapters 1 and 2, respectively, in chapter 4, I treat in more detail the conceptual framework utilized by Aquinas (which enables him to outline the connection between divine and human agency in the Christian moral act). Following that chapter will be a process of synthesis, asking questions of Aquinas' system (especially with regard to the rather thin role he gives to the Christian worshipping community in the dynamics of God's grace and human agency) and offering potential answers from Hauerwas and Hütter. Finally, drawing from Thomas' conceptual tools about grace and human agency, his notion of Christ as the Head of the Church, and utilizing Hauerwas and Hütter's treatment of the role of community in Christian ethics, I conclude by synthesizing an ecumenical ethical framework in which God's grace and Christian community play a prominent role.

1

Stanley Hauerwas

Stanley Hauerwas and Contemporary Theological Ethics

The Place of Stanley Hauerwas in the Present Treatment

STANLEY HAUERWAS RIGHTLY REFOCUSES the attention of theological ethics on the importance of community, the distinctiveness of Christian language, and the necessary bond between Christian convictions and their concrete performance. Additionally, his contribution has directed the discourse to look again for the work of an entirely transcendent God amongst the banality of dynamics internal to the Christian worshipping community. He places Jesus Christ at the center of Christian theological ethics and draws from Wesleyan notions of sanctification to argue for the importance of God's grace for Christian transformation. Even given the great importance he grants to the categories of narrative and tradition, Christian ethics is not merely an ethical system well informed by a storied reality, but is rather the possibility of moral action created anew by means of God's redeeming and sanctifying grace as given through Jesus Christ. For Hauerwas, Christian ethics is a linguistic retraining of vision and the ability to recognize the eschatological self in a truthful story within a community of memory. In these ways, Hauerwas' work adds much to the potential for articulating an ecumenical ethic of grace in community.

For Hauerwas, Christian ethics is a radical relationship with God's transforming grace through transformed vision, language, praxis, and community. This trajectory heralds a different consideration of ethics in the contemporary discourse. Christian ethical transformation is a connection between free, authentic human action and God's redeeming agency. In Hauerwas' efforts toward this cooperative and relational framework for ethics he places himself in a larger stream of theologians across the centuries who have strived to articulate that same framework for the Christian ethical life. In the present chapter, I hope to situate Hauerwas with regard to this project and show those places in which his theology points to the need for this connection between divine and human agency in the moral life, and articulate the means through which he sees this transformative connection occurring. At the same time, I hope to show how much he can benefit from other theologians who share this overall conviction about the nature of Christian ethics, but articulate the connection with complementary language around the shape of human agency, as such, which would take this ideal of an ethic of grace much further. I contend that the goal to which Hauerwas points the contemporary discourse could be sped along by a close conversation with the theology of Thomas Aquinas and the more complete picture of the causal dependence in human action and its connection with God's grace that Aquinas can provide.

Of course, Hauerwas' treatments of these dynamics have changed considerably in the past thirty-plus years. Toward the beginning of his writing career, Hauerwas argued for Christian character as completely self-determined and Christian agency as entirely self-caused (closing the structure of the Christian act to any and all external influences). Hauerwas' later writings, however, depict the reality that we are in fact determined by the communities in which we live and the narratives by which they subsist. Nonetheless, Hauerwas places strict limits on the ways in which the self can be determined by any external cause. The shape of Christian character, for instance, is quite permeated by the convictions and practices of the worshipping Church for the later Hauerwas. The tools Hauerwas utilizes as he moves toward this increased permeability of the self are truly striking. Formation is linguistic and conceptual. A story-formed community of practice shapes Christian agency through shaping language as the pattern of action and life together. The shaping of Christian character is formation to live Christian foundational grammar. Christian agency, for Hauerwas, is pliable through molding concept, grammar, and thus vision and the ability to live the truth. God speaks forth the church as a new grammar and Christians live as an extension of the Gospel narratives. Hauerwas pushes the discourse to account for Christian ethical transformation in terms of God's grace, Christian worship, and the Gospel narratives.

His description of ethics points to a deep connection with divine agency in the individual, and in the worshipping community as a whole. Hauerwas could much benefit, I contend, from a much thicker description of the shape of ethical agency in itself. While his ethics describe the impact of God's grace on the grammar, the vision, and the practice of a Christian, they rely largely on the transformative impact of foundational grammar and a narrative-formed community to do so. Other tools can carry his ethics beyond these limits and speak more directly to the pliability of human agency to the movements and non-competitive shaping action of God's grace.

As I will argue in this chapter, Hauerwas affords the grace of God in sanctification and the work of the Holy Spirit a central place in his theology, though he is in need of more detailed conceptual tools with regard to grace, the shape of human agency, and its potential to be drawn into cooperation with grace. The greater complexity with which his more recent writing offers to the shape of Christian moral action is a helpful indication that these detailed tools could move the ethical trajectory he offers forward. The overall hope of his place in this project is to articulate an ethic of grace like the one toward which he points, through placing him in interaction with other theologians aiming at the same grace-centered picture of Christian ethics.

The Centrality of Divine Agency

Stanley Hauerwas writes as a preacher and a teacher. Saying that his writing is occasional sells short these two important descriptors. Hauerwas writes not so much to provide a perfectly sound system as to give instruction where it is required, and to preach the centrality of Christ for the Christian life where it needs to be heard. His great gift is insisting on the applicability of Christian convictions and narratives to the ethical life. "Ethical reflection may exist in a highly abstract form, but men cannot. We must decide to stay married or celibate, to fight in war or not to fight, to teach our children this rather than that."[1] Hauerwas' moral

---

1. Hauerwas, *Vision and Virtue*, 98.

theology seeks to frame a lived existence, never stopping at idealistic frameworks.

The theological ethics of Stanley Hauerwas are, inarguably, christologically centered. Jesus Christ is not just the center of a faith upon which a distinctive community rests, but the promise that our lives rest on a new hope and are enfolded in a new reality. "The hope by which we journey is not of our own making. Far from arising from our own unworthiness, our hope comes as an open invitation to locate our lives in a new history that is made present in the life, death, and resurrection of Jesus Christ."[2] This invitation to locate ourselves in a new history gives hope in that it is not a story of our own making. The hope that we can locate our lives in Christ is not to be drawn *from* the story, but *is* the story. Or, as Hauerwas writes, "the claim that the story of Jesus is a social ethic means that there is no moral point or message that is separable from the story of Jesus . . . Jesus' identity is prior to the 'meaning' of the story. There is no meaning that is separable from the story itself."[3] Trying to find a core to Christian ethics beyond Christ fails to cling to the hope that moral action emerges from becoming a part of God's story. The grace of God in Jesus Christ is much more than a mere facet of theological ethics.[4] Rather, "Christians betray themselves [when] we say and act as if the cross of Christ is incidental to God's being. In fact, the God we worship and the world God created cannot be truthfully known without the cross."[5] This story in which we are enfolded is the story of God's saving action through Christ. Christian virtue is inseparable from God's redeeming and sanctifying work. Moral action emerges, then, not from reflection upon Christ, but is rather "a response to a love relation with God in Christ. That is why it makes sense for the Christian Aquinas to say that true or complete virtue is fundamentally not our own achievement but is rather infused in us by God's grace, which saves us and enables us."[6] The ethic of Stanley Hauerwas consistently indicates Christ as its center and the dynamics of Christian community as its setting. This indication is not just in the centrality of the story of Jesus, but rather

---

2. Hauerwas, *Christians Among the Virtues*, 118.
3. Hauerwas, *Community of Character*, 42–43.
4. Ibid., 37.
5. Hauerwas, *With the Grain of the Universe*, 17.
6. Hauerwas, *Christians Among the Virtues*, 68.

strives to be an ethic in which the "love relation with God in Christ" and the grace of God are the conditions *sine qua non*.

As Jeffery Stout has rightly noted, "one constant in [Hauerwas'] thinking from the beginning has been his own tradition's emphasis on the power of the Holy Spirit to transform the life of the believer."[7] The grace of God "saving and enabling us" finds voice in a variety of ways in Hauerwas' ethics, but most primarily in the Christian knowing the truth about herself through Christian narrative. For the Christian to know herself and her moral acts according to something other than the "love relation with God in Christ," is to miss this truth. "By making the story of such a Lord central to their lives, Christians are enabled to see the world accurately and without illusion . . . by being trained through Jesus' story we have the means to name and prevent these powers from claiming our lives as their own."[8] Hauerwas consistently points theological ethics to the cross as the lens through which we might see ourselves and our actions truthfully. This direction provides vital correctives to those who would pursue theological ethics in such a way as to separate the intimacy of this "love relation" from Christian action. For, in much of contemporary ethics, "God has been driven into the universe of the 'wholly other' . . . even if he is present or is the God of history, he does little more than confirm the irrepressible march of human creativity. On such a view, any life-directing attraction toward God's creative and redemptive being becomes unintelligible."[9] Hauerwas argues that merely placing God as central in theological ethics does not go far enough. In fact, it is the intimacy of God through God's "creative and redemptive being" that rightly directs ethical action. Without such an emphasis (as Hauerwas continues), "Christian ethics in such a context inevitably tends to be Pelagian; the aim of the Christian life becomes right action rather than the vision of God."[10] This vision of, and intimacy with, God is the end and basis of Christian ethic. Yet through the pursuit of this aim, Christian ethics is also a task involving our own identity. "We know ourselves truthfully only when we know ourselves in relation to God. We know who we are only when we can place ourselves—locate our

---

7. Stout, *Democracy and Tradition*, 141.
8. Hauerwas, *Community of Character*, 50.
9. Hauerwas, *Vision and Virtue*, 31.
10. Ibid.

stories—within God's story."[11] Locating ourselves within God's story is a consistent theme in Hauerwas' ethics. God's story tells us who we are because it tells us through the cross of Christ—the cross through which the love relation with God in Christ is established.

The Christian story is a story of grace, of reconciliation, of redemption, of relatedness to God, and these convictions are necessarily bound to ethical action. This ideal is nothing new, for Hauerwas. For, "once there was no Christian ethics simply because Christians could not distinguish between their beliefs and their behavior. They assumed that their lives exemplified (or at least should exemplify) their doctrines in a manner that made a division between life and doctrine impossible."[12] In Christian theology, as Hauerwas depicts it, the descriptive and the normative happen very close to one another, if not simultaneously. This is another of Hauerwas' great strengths. Christian ethics is not an activity that can be separated from Christian doctrine and, indeed, Christian life as a whole. The story of relation to God through the grace of Jesus Christ is such that the Christian act cannot be treated as isolated from the "love relation" with God. Hence Hauerwas writes critically of any system that looks to treat Christian ethical behavior apart from a treatment of the grace of God through Jesus Christ.[13] Such emphasis on externality cannot avoid the Pelagianism that treats Christian action as its own end and indicates our inability to live as a part of God's story.

The above, of course, hardly summarizes Hauerwas' moral theology. Any such summary would have to include his extensive work on his commitment to pacifism, his long-running engagement with the work of Niebuhr, MacIntyre, Gustafson, and a variety of other theologians, as well as his biomedical ethics and his treatments of ministry to the suffering. Such a summary goes beyond the scope of this current treatment. Still, throughout his theological ethics these foundational patterns persist. Hauerwas consistently offers a picture of the relationship between God's action through Jesus Christ and the formation and sustaining of the Christian moral act. His theological ethics places God's action as its center and strives from this basis to insist on the neces-

11. Hauerwas, *Peaceable Kingdom*, 27.

12. Hauerwas, *Sanctify Them in the Truth*, 20.

13. Katongole, *Beyond Universal Reason*, 36: "Much of contemporary ethical reflection, Hauerwas has consistently argued, assumes a problematic externality of agency and action."

sity of Christian moral action. God's grace transforms the believer and makes the Christian a part of God's story. Hauerwas' theology, thus, radically challenges assumptions that Christian action can be abstracted from Christian existence. He shows that an explanation of moral action follows from the account of the love relationship between us and God through Christ. We cannot, indeed, know who we are apart from knowing ourselves through this relation.

The Self Becomes Permeable to External Determinations

These very positive intentions for the paths along which theological ethics ought to proceed follow the contours of a gradual evolution in Hauerwas' writing. In order for Hauerwas to hold that our moral action is determined by our Christian existence, and to hold that our relations to God, to the Christian narrative, and the Christian community determine our Christian existence, he has to hold that human agency can be determined by something other than itself. This necessity was absent from Hauerwas' earliest writings. But as his writings mature, Hauerwas' depiction of the moral self becomes increasingly permeable to the determination of external forces. Articulating this permeability is notoriously difficult and has been the result of a long progression of conceptual shifts for Hauerwas.

Part of the motivation for the early tendency of Hauerwas to exclude from possibility the potential for any external force to determine human agency was in the kinds of errors he was trying to avoid. Gloria Albrecht nicely summarizes his basic motivations in *Character and the Christian Life* as "(1) to analyze the relationship between an agent and his or her action in order to challenge the emphasis on decision making, or quandaries, in Christian ethical thinking; and (2) to explicate the importance of individual character and the virtues in the development of the moral life."[14] Quandary ethics, according to Hauerwas, claim the center of moral inquiry to be not the way one comes to ethical decision, but merely individual (and typically very tricky) moral problems. While Hauerwas certainly does not deny that we are all faced with difficult decisions, his system, instead, "refuses to make such decisions the paradigmatic center of moral reflection. Morality is not primarily concerned with quandaries or hard decisions; nor is the moral self simply the col-

---

14. Albrecht, *Character of Our Communities*, 37.

lection of such decisions."[15] Allowing moral quandaries to dictate the subject matter of ethics offered no way to treat this "moral self" and confined the moral life to a few paradigmatic instances. Hauerwas, in his early writings, offered a much more holistic picture of the "moral self" in which the shaping of the self to act well was the foundation. "Our moral lives are not simply made up of the addition of our separate responses to particular situations. Rather we exhibit an orientation that gives our life a theme through which the variety of what we do and do not do can be scored. To be agents at all requires a directionality that involves the development of character and virtue."[16] Acting morally was more than just responding to certain difficult problems when they arose. Christian ethics involves shaping the whole self. Hauerwas will retain this instinct throughout his writing career.

Through his efforts to provide directionality to moral action and a way of addressing the moral self as a whole in his early work, Hauerwas chose the concept of *character* as that shaping of self by means of habituation. As Hauerwas writes, "by the idea of character I mean the qualification of man's self-agency through his beliefs, intentions, and actions, by which a man acquires a moral history befitting his nature as a self-determined being."[17] Character was the development of the moral self throughout a life that qualified how we function as moral agents in the world. However, an important characteristic emerges: if one's character determines one's behavior, and one's beliefs, intentions, and actions determine one's character, then one determines one's self, morally. This point is a major pillar of Hauerwas' early ethics of character, and one about which he was by no means timid.[18] The determination of the self, its identity and action, from which moral action springs, is not external. Rather, as Hauerwas writes, "we alone form our character by choosing among the descriptions society offers and deciding how to combine and order them . . . our character is the qualification of our agency."[19] We qualify our agency by our own volition. In fact, our actions shape us habitually and hone our agency to respond to moral situations. "By our actions, we not only shape a particular situation, we also form ourselves

15. Hauerwas, *Community of Character*, 114.
16. Hauerwas, "Self as Story," 76.
17. Hauerwas, *Character and the Christian Life*, 11.
18. Albrecht, *Character of Our Communities*, 37.
19. Hauerwas, "Toward an Ethics of Character," 709.

to meet future situations in a particular way."[20] Hauerwas' opposition to quandary ethics and determinism yielded an ethic in which the moral agent was, for all purposes, entirely self caused. Indeed, this was a key feature of character as depicted in his early writings. For, as Hauerwas writes, "to say someone has character seems, therefore, to imply that in some sense he has control over himself, is a self-master, that through self effort he can regulate his disposition and action by rules, principles, ideals, etc."[21] This set of self-forming actions determines not only our future actions and dispositions, but also the most fundamental level of selfhood: "Character is not a mere public appearance that leaves a more fundamental self hidden; it is the very reality of who we are as self-determining agents."[22] In terms of moral identity (the establishment of which Hauerwas was trying to secure, against attempts to deny its importance, or even its existence), the self and its agency were central. Moral progress is the process of self-formation. The act itself is a sheer product of this identity, and is thus treatable only as it contributes to, or springs from, character. Again, it becomes easy to see one of the great strengths through which the contemporary discourse has so benefitted from Hauerwas. Simply the longevity of his emphasis on grace and his conceptual anxiety about determinism, in its slow evolution, yields a very rich context for a more complex treatment of God's connection with human agency to enter the modern conversation.

Hauerwas has much revised these early notions and identified some problems stemming from a self-determined agency and moral identity in Christian ethics. Years later, Hauerwas writes reflectively on this early work that "I had mistakenly accepted the presumption . . . that a concept of agency could be derived from the notion of action *qua* action. Such analysis presupposes that 'action' . . . is a coherent and conceptually primitive notion, but that was simply wrong."[23] In his later work, Hauerwas leaves behind the idea that action itself determines future action in Christian ethics—that by shaping one's own actions, one could thus determine one's character and one's self.

The reasons he offers for abandoning it, however, will prove important. Hauerwas' later thought allows things other than the self to deter-

20. Ibid., 699.
21. Hauerwas, *Character and the Christian Life*, 13.
22. Hauerwas, "Toward an Ethics of Character," 707.
23. Hauerwas, *Sanctify Them in the Truth*, 95.

mine the specifics of moral action. But in *Character and the Christian Life*, Hauerwas uses the notion of agency as a fail-safe against determinism. If character stands at the basis of the moral act, in every instance, then it is a quick and easy move to add that one is therefore determined by one's character. Whatever goes into shaping and molding this fundamental self determines how one will act. Hauerwas seeks to escape determinism through the simple argument that nothing can determine the self except for the self in any kind of ethical paradigm (Christian or otherwise). As Hauerwas himself writes of *Character and the Christian Life*, "I was trying to find a way to sustain an account of moral continuity while not having our lives 'determined' by our character. After all, it seemed that character had to qualify something, and I took that something to be our irreducible agency."[24] As long as action is treated as a "primitive concept" identical to agency itself, and as long as it remains self-caused, then Hauerwas has effectively refuted the quandary ethics approach while at the same time guarding against determinism. Hauerwas describes this attempt to explain moral action as both determined and undetermined as an attempt to "have my cake and eat it too."[25] Hauerwas' ideas about character and action have developed significantly since *Character and the Christian Life*, allowing a number of factors to determine our moral selves. As he later wrote of this early book, "What MacIntyre helped me see is that you do not need an account of agency in itself to understand our ability to acquire character. Rather character is the source of our agency, that is, our ability to act with integrity."[26] Hauerwas no longer posits an account of being-in-action on both sides of the formation of character. In fact, he contends that an account of being-in-action is no longer needed to have a moral theory centered on character, as character itself constitutes the source of coherent and consistent action. Scrutiny of the Christian moral act is scrutiny of character. What, then, determines action? As Hauerwas wrote in 2004, "the account I had given of human action in *Character and the Christian Life* was inadequate exactly because at that time I did not have the concept of narrative, and in particular MacIntyre's account of intelligible action, as part of my repertoire."[27] Hauerwas no longer treats action as a primitive notion,

24. Ibid., 94.
25. Ibid.
26. Ibid., 95.
27. Hauerwas, *Performing the Faith*, 140–41.

one separate from agency, once he realizes the importance of narrative for the determination of character. The resulting shift in his account of the shaping of agency is precisely what Hauerwas was trying to avoid in 1975, namely, "that men are necessarily determined by their societies in the strong sense of the term."[28]

The development of Hauerwas' thought from these early notions marks a crucial transition in his treatment of the self, character, and that which determines moral action. In his earliest works, coherence and integrity of moral action depended on the irreducible agency of the self. We determine our agency through the shaping of our own character, which, in turn, is the source of our being-in-action. In Hauerwas' developing thought, the question becomes, what categories do we need to understand character, that is, that which founds our being-in-action?

In Hauerwas' developing thought, social practices as shaped by narrative play a role in shaping character, rather than simply through the determination of the self by its actions alone. As Albrecht notes, "for Stanley Hauerwas, the key word is 'determined,' for there are stories we do not choose that shape us in fundamental ways . . . to have a history is to have an identity."[29] In one of the crucial moves Hauerwas makes away from his earlier thought, our stories (and not only the stories of our choosing) determine us to a degree. A great deal of this determination occurs through the power that Hauerwas grants description. The ways in which we are able to narrate ourselves in our context determine our character: "Appeals to agency as a characteristic of the self cannot in principle guarantee our 'freedom' from all determination, since our very ability to know what we have done and to claim our behavior as our own is dependent on the descriptions we learn."[30] The descriptions we apply function much more robustly than simply allowing us to evaluate that which has happened already. In fact, notions of agency cannot be treated in isolation from story. Just as our being-in-action is dependent on our character, the identity of our character, our moral self, depends on our ability to describe. This narrative mode of knowing ourselves and our actions so fundamentally shapes us that Hauerwas calls the narrative character of our knowledge "a reality-making claim."[31] Moral

28. Hauerwas, *Character and the Christian Life*, 103.
29. Albrecht, *Character of Our Communities*, 29.
30. Hauerwas, *Peaceable Kingdom*, 43.
31. Ibid., 25.

growth, the improvement of the well-being of the Christian moral self, is the constant effort of the Christian to act consistently with these reality making claims, these stories.[32] Moral growth is not determined by our selves in action, but rather by our learning to live consistently with that which shapes us: a truthful narrative. Christian character, which constitutes our being-in-action, develops as we better learn and strive to live and act without illusion. In this way, Hauerwas still manages to avoid determinism because our self-applied descriptions shape our character much more than external factors. Our character determines our moral agency, our being-in-action, which is shaped by how we describe our self—that is "story." Again, this does not occur in isolation. For, "to be an agent means I am able to locate my action within an ongoing history and within a community of language users."[33] The coherence of a moral action depends on our ability to descriptively pinpoint ourselves in a context of others. Moral formation is no longer a closed system. We are not self-determined, self-caused, self-masters because our self-applied descriptions are actually an occurrence of community, without which we could not stay true to these "reality making claims."

The usefulness of the concept of story to add coherence to the moral life is not new for Hauerwas, despite its near absence in his earliest work. In one of his very earliest publications, still concerned to argue against the quandary approach to ethics, Hauerwas held that self-examined description, and not merely action alone, helps determine our character. For, to be a moral person "is to allow stories to be told through us so that our manifold activities gain a coherence that allows us to claim them as our own. Our existence itself, if it is to be coherent, is but an incipient story."[34] While this idea had hardly reached its maturity in this early article, Hauerwas held that the storied description of our action gave the moral life its integrity. The absence of story, even inchoate story, is the absence of a category by which we might evaluate and redescribe our actions for the formation of character. Though, again, while his early accounts put the prime emphasis on the self-determining of morality, Hauerwas was clearly aware of the threat present in a moral theology that only turned inward. As he wrote in his first major collection of essays, "Rather than attempting to free each man from his paralyzing pre-

---

32. Hauerwas, *Community of Character*, 132–33.
33. Hauerwas, *Peaceable Kingdom*, 42.
34. Hauerwas, "Self as Story," 76.

occupation with himself, modern moral philosophy has only increased and legitimatized this excessive self-concern. For our self-centeredness it only prescribes further self-reflection."[35] Hauerwas realized, even in his earliest writings, the potential problems of a system of ethics with no point of reference—no broader categories for valuation other than the self. Indeed, he accuses Christian ethics of this very problem, writing, "Christian ethics has succumbed to modern man's one-sided understanding of himself as actor and self-creator. . . . actions must be based on our vision of what is most real and valuable."[36] A separate account to give morality its coherence and bring moral reflection and progress a foundation beyond mere introspection is a need of which Hauerwas was clearly aware long before he placed such an emphasis on story. In *Character and the Christian Life*, however, the notion of description and narration was scaled back considerably, while ideas such as "how consistent our different intentions and projects are within our overall orientation,"[37] took their place.

Even by the time Hauerwas published *Truthfulness and Tragedy*, he had much more fully realized the importance of a thorough treatment of this overarching "orientation"—the same orientation that would become the center of this ethics. As he writes in this transitory period, "character is neither explanatory in origin nor in use, for it cannot be formulated prior to or independently of the narrative which develops it."[38] The notion of character as the basis for our being-in-action is meaningless without the details of the description that gives it integrity and consistency. To argue, as he had previously, that self-determined action forms the basis of our character, and therefore our agency, was to miss the problem that this character is no more than a pile of actions together without some descriptive story to give it meaning and direction. "Stories are thus a necessary form of our knowledge inasmuch as it is only through narrative that we can catch the connections between actions and responses of men that are inherently particular and contingent."[39] The connectedness that produces character and that allows character to, in turn, shape our future action depends on the narration we give as we comprehend

35. Hauerwas, *Vision and Virtue*, 34.
36. Ibid., 30.
37. Hauerwas, *Character and the Christian Life*, 121.
38. Hauerwas, *Truthfulness and Tragedy*, 29.
39. Ibid., 75.

ourselves and our actions. In fact, the intentional nature of our action "creates the space demanding narrative as the necessary form to account for the connection and intelligibility of our activity."[40]

Stories are important in that, according to Hauerwas, our descriptions through that mode can capture the "self." The self is treated as increasingly complex in its formation as Hauerwas' theology progresses. As our being-in-action springs from the fundamental identity of character, the articulation and understanding of the self becomes pivotal. According to Hauerwas, we tell stories because "there is no other way we can articulate the richness of intentional activity. . . . To tell a story often involves our attempt to make intelligible the muddle of things we have done in order to have a self."[41] Still, as in Hauerwas' early writings, the constitution of the self involves the continual incorporation of our past actions. The formation and appropriation of story, at least as much as action, gives coherence to the moral self and the action following from it. As Hauerwas writes in his 1981 reworking of the notion of character in *A Community of Character*, the task of ethics is concerned with the formation of this story. "Ethics is the attempt to help us remember what kind of story sustains certain descriptions. It is, therefore, a discipline rather like history, in that we are forced to tell stories in order to capture our past, sustain our present, and give our future direction."[42] For ethics to preoccupy itself with the analysis of the Christian moral "act" is to miss its primary task. Hauerwas' developing thought has laid aside the necessity of an account of agency and replaced it with the necessity of understanding the notion of character. This self is our agency. The task of ethics is the formation of a coherent self. The direction of our future ethical action is determined (in the strong sense of that word) by our effectiveness in giving voice to the continuity of our past and present. Ethics fails if it turns to the description of the action; it must instead look to the integrity of the self. For, "agency but names our ability to inhabit our character."[43]

Another related but distinct development of Hauerwas' thought on the constitution of Christian self is the inclusion of other people in the reflection upon, and formation of, action. "Human actions become

40. Ibid.
41. Ibid., 76.
42. Ibid., 104.
43. Hauerwas, *Peaceable Kingdom*, 40.

intelligible only as they are set within personal and communal narrative histories."[44] That which gives Christian ethical action its distinctiveness and coherence is not just the individual's ability to render story (and therefore self). Instead, setting one's self in a storied-community, or a community of narrative, holds the potential for identity and coherent moral action. This is, perhaps, not too surprising since, for Hauerwas, the intelligibility of a community (just as for an individual) comes through story.[45] Ethics with regard to community and ethics with regard to self emerge as very similar. The constitution and moral functioning of each depends on its intelligibility through story. The efficacy of this story (and, thereby, the intelligibility of moral action) rests on the formative power of Christian narrative in the ways it shapes communities of faith.

Christian Community Formed by Theological Narrative

As Hauerwas' theological ethics mature, he no longer describes agency as merely the enactment of our self-determined character. Instead, Christian efforts must be focused on becoming a community that can form itself to the story of God. As we are formed by this story, we become capable of rightly ordered ethical action. As Hauerwas writes, "the primary social task of the Church is to be itself—that is, a people who have been formed by a story that provides them with the skills for negotiating the danger of this existence."[46] Forming oneself to accord with the storied account of existence found in Scripture offers tools to avoid the potential pitfalls of life. This sounds like a suspiciously easy task, however, and seems to say nothing to address the plain fact that Christians and their communities continue to sin and fall short ethically, despite having had regular and personal access to this story since Gutenberg (at the very least). Hauerwas does not deny this problem, however: "To be sure, we have often been unfaithful to this story, but that is no reason for us to think it is an unrealistic demand. Rather, it means we must challenge ourselves to be the kind of community where such a story can be told and manifested by a people formed in accordance with it—for if you believe that Jesus is the messiah of Israel, then 'everything else follows, doesn't

---

44. Albrecht, *Character of Our Communities*, 38.

45. Hauerwas, *Community of Character*, 10: "The form and substance of a community is narrative dependent and therefore what counts as 'social ethics' is a correlative of the content of that narrative."

46. Ibid.

it?"[47] Though we have failed to live in a manner true to the story of God (thus shaping our character, thus determining our being-in-action), that is no reason to think that we are incapable of bringing ourselves back to living true to this story (and the resulting character and actions). To ask that we act in non-sinful ways is "not an unrealistic demand." The move from sinfulness to rightly ordered action is a matter of the degree to which we "challenge ourselves" to be a certain kind of community. To place this description of repentance in its proper context, it is important to note both the power of grammar and the origin of this transformative community for Hauerwas. The Church as a community of narrative is deeply connected to God's action in the world, as Hauerwas describes it. For Hauerwas, the Church is God's creation and God's new language for the world. As he writes in a sermon delivered on Pentecost in the late 1980s, "All is finally summed up through God's new creation of the church. By creating this timeful people God has storied the world, as now we have everything necessary to know the time in which we live."[48] Notice here both the power of grammar and the place of the Church with regard to the world. For Hauerwas, to say that moving from sinfulness is to become a certain kind of community of narrative is to say that repentance is becoming a part of the way God stories the world. Becoming enfolded in this narrative community is God's creative action and gift to humanity. At Pentecost, God creates a new grammar, which is a people of story and memory. Moving from sinfulness is to know this grammar and be a part of a practicing community of ongoing linguistic struggle to live the truth.

The community called Church as God's new grammar is deeply bound to the transformation of language, and thus vision, and thus character in the moral life. For Hauerwas, the community lives the truth (or does not) as it lives this new language or, as he writes, "to be a disciple of Jesus means that our lives must literally be taken up into the drama of God's redemption of this creation."[49] The change is not merely cognitive, nor is it merely a shift in how one learns to describe the world. Instead, to be a disciple of Jesus is to be a part of the community which is, at its foundation, God's dramatic grammar. Hauerwas writes that Scripture "not only 'renders a character' but renders a community capable of or-

---

47. Ibid., 34–35.
48. Hauerwas, "Church as God's New Language," 143.
49. Ibid., 148.

dering its existence appropriate to such stories. . . . this narrative does nothing less than render the character of God and in doing so renders us to be the kind of people appropriate to that character."[50] Narrative forms the community and makes the community capable of avoiding sinful behavior by shaping character. Hauerwas holds that the power of these stories changes us, for "the truthfulness of Christian convictions resides in their power to form a people sufficient to acknowledge the divided character of the world and thus necessarily ready to offer hospitality to the stranger."[51] The question is not any longer, "How did one's actions form one's character to shape her agency to yield such a moment of action?" but rather, "What about these individual convictions and the realization of certain truth claims has made the Christian prone to, and capable of, this action?" Character (and, thus, our being-in-action) is no longer self-determined; a communal understanding of particular narratives and convictions determines individual action. We are thus capable of the Christian moral act of hospitality to the stranger, for to be faithful in this way is "not an unrealistic demand." "Everything follows" from the new community of God's grammar in its ability to shape the convictions, vision, character, and truthful living of the individual.

As Hauerwas makes clear (and this point can hardly be overemphasized when examining his work), communal, not individual, reception and understanding of these truthful convictions shapes character, and thus determines action. We cannot cease from sinful action on our own. Christian moral action occurs through interaction in a community formed in this story, and thus capable of mutual instruction.[52] The truthfulness of the Christian narrative, evidently, reveals even to the individual the "what" of rightly ordered moral action, but the "how" comes through following examples. Again, it is easy to underestimate the foundationally transformative grammar even in learning to be a disciple by following our fellow Christian: "The freedom acquired through our reinterpretations is dependent on our having a narrative sufficient to 'make sense' of our lives . . . a story that not only provides the means to

50. Ibid., 67.

51. Ibid., 93.

52. Ibid., 131. We learn what the moral life entails by imitating another. This is intrinsic to the nature of Christian convictions, for the Christian life requires a transformation of the self that can be accomplished only through direction from a master. The problem lies not in knowing *what* we must do, but *how* we are to do it. And the how is learned only by watching and following.

acknowledge the blunders as part of our own story, but to see ourselves in a story where even our blunders are part of an ongoing grace."[53] The moral act, then, is truly ours—a product of an ongoing enfolding in particular stories. Unlike Hauerwas' earlier writings, it is not the power of the agent's act that determines character, and thus determines agency. Rather, it is the power of the agent within a communal setting to describe herself within the narrative—the foundational grammar of the Gospels and God's language of the community called Church. Hauerwas writes that "the 'causation' proper to agents and their actions is not rendered by cause and effect, but by the agent's power of description. My act is not something I cause, as though it were external to me, but it is mine because I am able to 'fit' it into my ongoing story."[54] Christian moral action emerges from the power of description given to those recipients of the foundational and transformative Christian narrative and the training in vision and praxis that this reception entails. Or, as Hauerwas puts it even more potently, "my power as an agent is therefore relative to the power of my descriptive ability."[55] In short, then, the increase in my ability to do the will of God is relative to my power to describe my actions, through community. Christian morality for Hauerwas is the ability of a community of individuals to shape their character through clinging to certain true stories.

Hauerwas solved a number of problems as his treatment of character and Christian action matured. In this way, his thought has moved significantly forward, and the field of theological ethics has greatly benefited from these changes. In his earliest ethics of character, moral identity was entirely self-determined, and this determination was only historically related insofar as it was the product of our past actions. Context for moral decisions was at a minimum. Hauerwas has since realized that "our moralities are historical; they require a qualifier. We are unable to stand outside our histories in midair, as it were; we are destined to discover ourselves only within God's history."[56] Finding ourselves not simply as isolated moments of occasional decision-making, but rather in a larger historical and community context, is certainly a move forward. Related to this change, Hauerwas also seems to have real-

53. Ibid., 147.
54. Hauerwas, *Peaceable Kingdom*, 42.
55. Ibid.
56. Ibid., 29.

ized that Christian moral reflection cannot be done in isolation from a broader narrative and ecclesial tradition. As he writes, "Christian beliefs about God, Jesus, sin, the nature of human existence, and salvation are intelligible only if they are seen against the background of the church."[57] These convictions, Hauerwas asserts, are pivotal to Christian identity and morality, and his reflection on these vital convictions within the "background of the Church" is a significant shift in Hauerwas' theology.

This background is significant not just because it provides a wider context in which to evaluate morality, but functions as a community of witness to a different story, separated from which individual Christian reflections cease to be valid. "The liberal tradition assumed Christianity names insights about 'life' that should be compelling for anyone, but liberals forgot that such 'insights' are empty when divorced from worship of God."[58] The importance of worship and community in Christian moral life is a factor that Hauerwas now rightly sees as indispensable. In fact, much of the force of his later ethics is in trying to prompt Christian theologians to realize that their most valuable contribution is to "capture the significance of the church."[59] Christian ethics in isolation from the community that is uniquely Church, according to Hauerwas, cannot help failing to properly shape us through our stories. Attention to the ways in which our communities tell stories, in Christian moral reflection, is invaluable for developing context—a context that his earlier ethics lacked. Part of this change is due to his realization of the value of a distinctly Christian context-in-practice for Christian moral reflection, but is also due to his attention to the task of description in the moral life.[60] This development is a major change from his early work and shows the great value of his work as a long-term struggle with describing the moral life in such a way that it is community centered and shaped by God's grace.

Whether through his Christology, his ideas regarding sanctification, his notions of character, his emphasis on narrative, or the importance of the worshipping community, Hauerwas has striven to show one

---

57. Hauerwas and Bondi, "On Keeping Theological Ethics Theological," 34.

58. Hauerwas, *In Good Company*, 158.

59. Hauerwas and Bondi, "On Keeping Theological Ethics Theological," 33–34.

60. Hauerwas, *Peaceable Kingdom*, 124. As Hauerwas writes, "the description under which the decision is proposed is as important as the decision itself. For the description frames the decision."

thing: that Christian moral existence springs from the person of Jesus Christ, through whom we witness to and embody God's action in the world. From the beginning of his writing career on, Hauerwas has held that

> while the basis of the Christian life is what God has done his action also includes the reality of human behavior. What God has willed to do for man is not done in such a way that man is excluded from his activity. Soteriologically stated God has acted to save man apart from and in spite of man's unwillingness to turn to God, but while his saving action is not conditional on man's response God has willed to include man's response within his saving action. Thus in a sense God's work is done over and above any decision or activity of man but it also includes and demands a real response from man's side. All attempts to analyze the nature of the Christian life must somehow try to do justice to the dialectical tension between the objective affirmation of God's deed and man's subjective involvement in that deed.[61]

This valuable and important product of Hauerwas' struggle (up to this point, at least) brings Christian ethics to a vital crossroads. His joined commitment to the centrality of the grace of God in Christ in ethics and the safeguarding of human freedom in genuine human involvement in God's action pushes the discourse to the need of concepts and descriptors with which we can frame human action as available for involvement in God's "deed." The bond between God's action in the world and ours, the tension between God's deed and our involvement in that deed, is a crucial feature that touches every facet of Hauerwas' theology. The importance he places on the worshipping community, the emphasis on the story in which we are infolded by Jesus and through which our lives have coherence, the prominence of character as shaped by this narrative, the idea that our knowledge of ourselves is only true if we know ourselves in relation to God, and the recurrent theme of sanctification, all stand in some relation to the general notion that Christian moral action and God's saving action are intertwined.

However, Hauerwas' treatment of the self and her agency has not, itself, realized the important intersection between free human action and involvement in God's deed. While Hauerwas pushes the discourse to pay attention to the potential for a bond between divine and human

---

61. Hauerwas, *Character and the Christian Life*, 130.

action in the moral life, he does not offer (and even in places writes that there is no need for) a sufficiently complex description of agency that would allow for the kind of non-cooperative and participatory connection between God's grace and Christian action his work pushes to articulate. Much of this, I contend, is due to a choice by Hauerwas to treat agency as basically simple. In an ethic relying on the formative power of God's grace in foundational grammar, which transforms a community to, in turn, reshape the vision and character of the individual, there is little need for a complex notion of agency. But this choice has limiting consequences for Hauerwas' ethics. He is only able to speak of the formation of the moral agent by God's grace, as such, in much the same way as a moral agent would be formed by another foundational grammar (shaping vision, character, and so on). One of the great reasons to place Hauerwas in conversation with theologians like Aquinas is to prompt a sufficiently complex description of Christian agency to afford a place for the close connection Hauerwas indicates between God's grace and Christian action.

God's Grace and the Limiting Description of Agency

Stanley Hauerwas, in 1998, writes that he learned from MacIntyre, "you do not need an account of agency in itself to understand our ability to acquire character. Rather character is the source of our agency, that is, our ability to act with integrity."[62] This is certainly correct for all but a few accounts of character in ethics. The formative power of foundational grammar and communities of practice to shape vision, character, and thus action is straightforward enough. Usefully for Hauerwas, as well, a simple account of agency (or even the lack of an account at all) has the additional benefit of further closing the door on the threat of determinism. If the acquisition of character does not require a complex description of agency, then there is little wiggle room for agency to be determined by outside factors. The only problem with this description of agency poses to Hauerwas is that it places unintended limits on the extent to which Christian moral action can be as transformed by God's grace and as drawn through participation into the action of the Holy Spirit as he would like it to be. The case I hope to make is that Hauerwas places unintended limits through this simple description of agency which would

62. Hauerwas, *Sanctify Them in the Truth*, 95.

be much helped by a thicker description of Christian moral agency and the possibility of the non-competitive and cooperative connection with God's agency, as provided by a thinker like Aquinas. Rather wonderfully, Hauerwas' ethics reaches too high for a merely simple description of Christian agency to suffice.

Goals and Limits

Without question, Hauerwas does speak of the importance of God's grace for the moral life, and suggests that the direction his theological ethics means to take is one in which the grace of God transforms the Christian self and the Christian act. "What grace 'transforms,' 'interpenetrates,' 'reorientates,' is not the virtues themselves, but rather the self—our character."[63] Hauerwas strives for a moral theology in which the self is transformed not by the community alone, not by narrative on its own, but by the grace of God. Hauerwas seeks to express that God's grace enfolds us such that our moral action is not just a part of a story, but a partaking in God, God's self: "we participate morally in God's life. For our God is a God who wills to include us within his life. This is what we mean when we say, in shorthand as it were, that God is a God of grace."[64] Hauerwas' theological ethics is not meant to be a system unto itself, but instead speaks about our participation in the life of God through our ethical action. Both the Christian ethical act and our inclusion in God's life are sustained, according to Hauerwas, by the power of the Holy Spirit. For, as Hauerwas writes, the courage of martyrs "is none other than an extension of the daily courage we need to carry on as faithful servants of God, which courage we receive as a daily gift of the Spirit."[65] Hauerwas' theological ethic aims to be Spirit filled, Christ centered, and pointing always to participation in God's life by grace. But with an essentially simple description of agency, the only avenues open to the impact this participation in grace would have on the moral life are those ordinary avenues of character formation through community. His account of formation through foundational grammar, shifted vision, and community stands as the description of every kind moral transformation, including participation in God through grace. Without

---

63. Hauerwas, *Truthfulness and Tragedy*, 68.
64. Hauerwas, *Peaceable Kingdom*, 27.
65. Hauerwas, *Christians Among the Virtues*, 162.

a thicker account of Christian moral agency, such a description places compromising limits on the way his notion of Christian moral formation seeks a connection with God's action.

Ironically, this tendency is nowhere more apparent than in the recurring theme of sanctification. This is not to say, of course, that Hauerwas strives for a treatment of sanctification apart from the grace of God—quite the contrary, in fact. For instance, Hauerwas writes that, for Wesley's theology of sanctification, change in our lives "after all is not a statement about our ability but the sovereignty of God's grace over our sinfulness."[66] What one finds, instead, is that progression in holiness is prompted by one's own perceptions and understandings, rather than the grace of God, in any obvious way.

Hauerwas treats sanctification both in his early and in his later work, and, as there has been a significant transition between his *Character and the Christian Life* and his later writings (especially with the dissolution of the idea that we are self-determined), one might expect an equally significant shift with regard to God's work in the self as treated under sanctification. Rather surprisingly, his treatment of sanctification has not shifted as significantly. In his early writings, God's sanctification largely consists in the ways in which we form ourselves and our actions. When our actions, intentions, and perceptions change, we are sanctified. "The Christian is one so formed as he assumes the particular description offered him through the Church. . . . Sanctification is thus the formation of the Christian's character that is the result of his intention to see the world as redeemed in Jesus Christ."[67] Our shifting in intention yields the result. Our assumption of the description offered through the Church sanctifies us. This is hardly shocking, however, because Christian moral character (and thus action) is so isolated and impermeable in these early writings, despite the claim that Christian sanctification is distinct from other kinds of moral formation. In fact, the means are exactly the same: "What distinguishes Christian sanctification from the way men's lives are generally shaped and formed is not the process of formation itself but the basis and consequent shape of that formation."[68] In his early writings, we are our own masters in sanctification, as one is in any other kind of moral formation. The difference is simply that "we are obliged to a

66. Hauerwas, "Characterizing Perfection," 251.
67. Hauerwas, "Toward an Ethics of Character," 714.
68. Hauerwas, *Character and the Christian Life*, 194–95.

certain 'way' of acting and that this 'way' is the actual determination of our character."[69] Growth in this area, then, is our increasing comprehension of the ways in which we wish to develop our character, and the self-direction of our action. Christian growth, in *Character and the Christian Life,* is an increase in our comprehension of the "requirements of having our agency qualified in relation to this one Lord. . . . a deepening of our self's determination through the testing of our current posture and action against this central orientation and loyalty."[70] While our "central orientation" might be different, growth is just as isolated. In fact, in this early piece, Hauerwas explicitly states that even Christian sanctification is just another form of self-causing character formation. For, "to be formed in Christ, to be sanctified, is to be committed to bringing every element of our character into relation with this dominant orientation . . . [which] is really a way of maintaining the self-mastery of the Christian character."[71] This sanctification, Hauerwas continues in the next sentence, "is an affirmation that the self as agent can impose his particular determination upon the malleable elements of our existence, that we can form the given aspects of our experience through our intentions in new and creative ways."[72] Again, however, little of this is out of character for early Hauerwas.

As his writing matures, Hauerwas displays a transition from relative self-determination, to one's determination in and through the practices and narratives of one's community, especially through grammar and its ability to situate the believer in a truthful story and thereby to live truthfully. For instance, in *Sanctify Them in the Truth*, Hauerwas writes that the practice of the confession of sin to a community is the necessary element for sanctification. He holds that "nothing is more indicative for what it means for the church to be holy, God's very temple, than the privilege we have been given to confess our sins to one another."[73] This practice, indicative of the holiness of the Church, Hauerwas continues, "constitutes whether in faith we can hope to make progress toward holiness."[74] This hallmark of the Church is the lynchpin for sanctification, at least

69. Ibid., 204.
70. Ibid., 220.
71. Ibid., 223.
72. Ibid.
73. Hauerwas, *Sanctify Them in the Truth*, 72.
74. Ibid.

in this instance. However, this is simply one instance. How important, after all, could the confession of sin be? We see just how important when we realize the specific nature of sin for Hauerwas. To confess sin to each other is a way of readjusting perception. "We are not sinful because we participate in some general human condition, but because we deceive ourselves about the nature of reality and would so crucify the very one who calls us to God's kingdom."[75] Redemption from sin, then, is the correction of our misconceptions about the nature of reality. So, to confess one's sins in public is to seek corrections about our self-deception from fellow Christians. Hence the importance of Christian convictions for the transformation of the self: once one has one's convictions rightly shaped about the world, then one can be said to have grown morally. Christian convictions, Hauerwas writes, "transform the self to true faith by creating a community that lives faithful to the one true God of the universe. When self and nature are thus put in right relation we perceive the truth of our existence."[76] The ability to perceive the truth of ourselves and our existence is a gift given by the community and its transformative foundational grammar.

Moral transformation, as Hauerwas describes it, limits connection with God's agency in that it follows the same contours as any other ethical formation through narrative and foundational grammar. The moral act emerges as a product of my truthful understanding of the world as a part of an alternative community of language and practice. It follows naturally, then, that Hauerwas will assert that any kind of encounter with God is a meeting of God through story, and not any other way. For one to "know" God is to have God as a part of a narrative that one utilizes to correct one's perception about the world. "Neither God, the world, nor the self are properly known as separate entities but are in a relation requiring concrete display. That display takes the form of a narrative in which we discover that the only way to 'know' God, the world, or the self is through their history."[77] "Contact" or "intervention" or even the "presence" of God is only relevant in terms of God's role in story—which is to say, God's role in correcting our perception of reality through narrative as communally received. It must be remembered that narrative has extraordinary impact and the mode of God's pres-

---

75. Hauerwas, *Peaceable Kingdom*, 31.
76. Ibid., 16.
77. Ibid., 26.

ence in the community, however. As Hauerwas writes elsewhere, "Jesus is prior to story, though Jesus' life and resurrection can be displayed only narratively."[78] The power of narrative, at least as described in this instance, is its power to display the life and resurrection of Jesus. It may well be, however, that this tendency is what limits Hauerwas' ethics from realizing the very central place he offers God's grace through Jesus that he describes. Such things can only be displayed narratively. Their impact on the moral life is shifting the foundational grammar and vision that was informing the moral life very differently before one becomes a part of this new language.

To grow in holiness is the dramatic transformation of character through the foundational grammar of the Gospels and their shaping of a community of practice. Though Jesus is certainly prior to this grammar, connection with God's grace in the moral life through Jesus is connection with this foundational grammar and the community of language and practice that it forms. So, the emphasis is on the Christian convictions as a "narrative, a language, that requires a transformation of the self if we are to see, as well as be, truthful . . . to learn to grow into the story of Jesus as the form of God's kingdom."[79] Growth in holiness is the process of being infolded by a narrative *actively*. Our actions are the product of character, and character is the product of learning and "growing into" the story of Jesus. The narrative that we learn transforms the moral life. The role of God's grace in the moral life takes the well-worn paths of transformation through grammar and community. Again, such limits are unfortunate only because his ethics pushes the discourse so much further: to an ethic in which grace has concrete efficacy and the Christian is called into participation in the work of the Spirit in the moral life.

Progression in holiness, for Hauerwas' ethics, is linguistic transformation to a new vision of the world. God's involvement in the life of the Christian— or, better still, our "moral participation in God's life"— moves along the same contours as other kinds of transformation of character through grammar and community. The concern of ethics, for this reason, is "how the self must be transformed to see the world truthfully. For Christians, such seeing develops through schooling in a narrative which teaches us how to use the language of sin not only about others

---

78. Hauerwas, "Church as God's New Language," 155.

79. Ibid., 30.

but about ourselves."[80] We are schooled in a narrative. Redemption by God's grace itself is a linguistic shift and how that shift changes our perception of ourselves and the world. For, "To be redeemed, as I suggested above, is nothing less than to learn to place ourselves in God's history, to be part of God's people."[81] This conceptual transformation, this placing of ourselves, limits the impact of the central role that Hauerwas champions for Jesus Christ and the Holy Spirit in Christian ethics. Part of the importance of this disjunction is that it comes in the context of a theology that looks to place God's grace in Christ back at the center of ethics. To meet the desire that Hauerwas has for some real connection between God's grace and human freedom in the moral life, he could much benefit from a thicker description of human moral agency in which this bond transforms the moral life in very different ways than other kinds of ethical formation.

The theme of grammatically driven transformation of vision (and thus character) as either the redemption given to us by grace through Christ or as sanctification extends to Hauerwas' specific moral prescriptions as well. The identity of Christians as peaceable rests very firmly on the foundation of our developing a certain vision and grammar. "Our ability to be truthful peacemakers depends on our learning that we owe our lives to God's unrelenting forgiveness."[82] While the reality of our status as forgiven is certainly an important realization, Hauerwas himself claims that moral action is based on much more. Across his writing career, Hauerwas articulates this perspective change through foundational grammar as the important effect. Thus in his 1988 *Christian Existence Today*, Hauerwas can make essentially the same argument he made in the 1975 *Character and the Christian Life*, as he writes, now thirteen years later, "the church knows that the life of faithfulness is not easily acquired but involves those skills that can be learned only through apprenticeship to a master. Living morally is not simply holding the right principles; it involves nothing less than learning to desire the right things rightly. Such desiring is not so much a matter of choice as it is the slow training of our vision through learning."[83]

---

80. Ibid., 33.
81. Ibid.
82. Hauerwas, *Christian Existence Today*, 93.
83. Ibid., 103.

Moral transformation as the slow training of vision through a community of practice and foundational grammar limits the role of "God's grace which saves us and enables us" in Hauerwas' ethics. The shifting of one's understanding is the pattern of ethical development in his early literature as well as in his more recent work. Writing in 2004, Hauerwas holds that "in short, what it means to be ethically well-formed is having one's imagination trained to regard the world not as a given but truly as a gift from God."[84] The language of God's grace, of creation and redemption, are too quickly relegated to elements of the foundational grammar which shapes the community of practice. "'Creation' and 'redemption' should be taken for what they are, namely ways of helping us tell and hear the story rightly."[85]

While Hauerwas' treatment of Christian agency and its formation through narrative places unfortunate limits on the connection between God's grace and the moral life, he comes much closer to realizing this connection in his work on Christian community, church, and friendship. For instance, in *Christians Among the Virtues,* Hauerwas seems to point to a role for God's grace far beyond mere "secondary theological language." Hauerwas writes that "God is able to love each creature as a friend without His love being diminished for any other creature. It is through our friendships formed by Christ that the Christian learns to participate in that love. Christian friendship, therefore, is dependent upon a source outside itself. . . . it depends on the strength and consistency of the God who has first befriended humans."[86] If the grace of God is not diminished even as it is circulated communally from master to apprentice, from teacher to learner, from friend to friend, then it is truly through the primacy of these friendships that the grace of God comes to us, not diminishing as it does so. In this way, too, the last two sentences might indicate a more robust treatment of grace. If Christian friendship is the primary object of God's grace, which does not diminish as it passes from one friend to another, or from teacher to learner, then the grace of God by which we participate in God's life is truly dependent on these friendships, and does truly depend on God. Once of Hauerwas' greatest gifts to the discourse emerges as the great potential of Christian community to be near-sacramental. God's involvement is nowhere more

---

84. Hauerwas, *Performing the Faith,* 92.
85. Hauerwas, *Peaceable Kingdom,* 62–63.
86. Hauerwas, *Christians Among the Virtues,* 50.

tangible in the ethics Hauerwas describes than in the potential for its inclusion in Christian friendship. The purpose of Christian friendship is "to make possible, under God's gracious favor through the Holy Spirit, friendship with God."[87] Hauerwas' description of the sacramental character of Christian friendship and Christian community leads to exciting new directions in how God might impact Christian life.

The Limiting Description of the Christian Act

So, why do moments such as Hauerwas' treatment of Christian friendship stand in such contrast to the rest of this ethics? Why, given all of Hauerwas' claims about the centrality of God in his ethics, is God's grace often described as effective merely through its place in a foundational grammar in a narrative that shapes a community? The answer, as I will demonstrate, is an uncomplicated one: The Christian act, as Hauerwas describes it, is simple and closed to external determination of any kind. This has the unintended effect of limiting the possibility of a cooperative connection between God's action and free, ethical, Christian action in the moral life. Hauerwas' two equally important and valuable interests in (*a*) guarding against the determination of our moral agency and (*b*) including God's graceful agency in the moral life are butting heads here. Hauerwas is in need of better tools for describing his second concern without compromising his first.

In Hauerwas' early writings, the Christian act is closed to the agency of God as, indeed, how could it not be? The self is closed to all but its own determination. By Hauerwas' own admission, he had still in place the "primitive" conception of the act and the "liberal" notions surrounding the self that would exclude anything but one's own actions and one's own understanding from shaping one's own character, and thereby one's agency. He is decisive in his early writings, refusing even to allow for the notion that the Christian act is something other than uncomplicatedly a product of one's character. "When we force a wedge between thought and action we thereby distort the nature of moral behavior and, more specifically, render impossible an accurate understanding of moral agency."[88] If moral agency finds some source other than how character is shaped, then Hauerwas' entire system would change. If human agency

---

87. Hauerwas, *Better Hope*, 180.
88. Hauerwas, "Self as Story," 80.

were more complex, then Hauerwas would have to allow, in this early work, for a more complicated account of even self-determined character. However, he does not.[89] Agency and character, in an uncomplicated way, form and depend on each other symbiotically. In fact, it is this self-enclosed nature of character and action formation that Hauerwas uses to show the mastery of the self by the self. "As an agent I am not any such event, process, or state that is proposed to be the 'real cause' of my act, such as some intention, motive, or state of willing. . . . I am an uncaused power since no other event is necessary to explain my act other than that I as an agent did it. . . . as the cause of my act nothing further is needed to explain the act's existence beyond the fact that I am the agent of it."[90] The act is closed to any and all kinds of analysis other than that focused on the ways in which I form myself in my previous acts. There is no need for causal language; no needed description of thought, intention, motive, or will. Or, perhaps to simplify the formula even further: as I am, so is my act. There is no room for factors outside of the self. The structure of the Christian act is essentially impermeable, as the Christian self is impermeable. In Hauerwas' early writings, the character is entirely self-determined and one's agency springs entirely from one's character.

Much of Hauerwas' treatment of the permeability of the act to external forces has not shifted since *Character and the Christian Life*. Still, in *Truthfulness and Tragedy*, Hauerwas argues that "an agent is not related to his action as a cause to an effect, but rather as an agent whose description continues to determine what he has done. The 'effect' (act) is not therefore separable from the agent's intentions any more than the agent's intentions are separable from the 'effect.'"[91] There seems to be little change here from Hauerwas' previous writings. Just as in 1975, in 1977, Hauerwas continues to collapse anything like an analyzable structure to the Christian act. The description alone determines the act insofar as description determines one's perspective. Intention and act cannot be plied apart. From 1977 onward, Hauerwas' treatments of action, agency, character, and the relationship between them have grown

89. Hauerwas, *Character and the Christian Life*, 21. A man's agency and his character cannot be thought of as one external cause acting upon a pliable and passive material, for man's agency and character are internally related. To acquire character is to do so by the exercising of his ability to be an agent, but the actual determination of our being by our own agency is not different from our character.

90. Ibid., 88.

91. Hauerwas, *Truthfulness and Tragedy*, 45–46.

few and far between. However, in 1998 (though an earlier version of the article in question was published in 1996), Hauerwas still contends that "agency names those skills necessary to make our past our own though it's often constituted by decisions we thought at the time were 'free' but which from our current perspective we can now see were made without our knowing what we were doing when we made them. In other words, I will argue that our moral lives are more properly considered by retrospective rather than prospective judgments."[92] While this certainly is not as boldly or plainly stated as in either 1975 or 1977, it proceeds along many of the same contours. Our agency, our being-in-action, names a set of skills with a very particular function: to make our past actions and decisions "our own." The specific change he notes in these lines is a change in perspective. Our being-in-action names the movement from an inability to incorporate our actions into our character to the ability to do so. The moral life—the formation of the Christian moral act—then, is about an increase in the ability to incorporate our past actions. Put more succinctly, owning our past actions *is* our being-in-action. The act itself is merely the product. The only analyzable fact of Christian action is how our perspective is shaped to incorporate our past actions. The change is what we learn, and the skills of our description. The act is merely the result. The Christian act can be legitimately scrutinized only insofar as this retrospective scrutiny can rightly shape our perspective for future actions. The Christian act is relevant, because through it we "form ourselves to meet future situations in a particular way"[93]—a summary helpful for Hauerwas' present work, though he wrote it in 1972. The process by which our perspective and description changes must suffice entirely in forming the Christian ethical action. Two important presuppositions emerge: (1) our being-in-action can reliably depend on our power of description, and (2) our being-in-action can be exhaustively discussed by these descriptions. If the structure of Christian action allowed room for external prompting or participation, then our being-in-action could not reliably depend on our descriptions (1), no matter how well they enabled us to make our past actions our own. Further, if the structure of the Christian moral act had the potential to be anything other than relatively simple, then our being-in-action could not possibly be exhaustively discussed by our descriptions (2). If the act is simple, involving no external factors

---

92. Hauerwas, *Sanctify Them in the Truth*, 98.
93. Hauerwas, "Toward an Ethics of Character," 699.

(drawn into participation in God's grace, for example), then one could presume that every retrospective glance at one's actions is a perfect lens through which to make prospective judgments. After all, if such were the case, then one could accurately presume that everything involved in prompting past action would be present in the next action—for the "everything" would simply be the formed self.

If the Christian moral act is simple, not analyzable, then our descriptions of ourselves (with the tacit assumption that we can grasp all that goes into our past and future actions—as such factors are all under our control) will take primacy for examination over either the Christian self or the Christian act. Indeed, this is exactly the case:

> Put simply, story is a more determinative category than self. Indeed, our very notion of 'self' only makes sense as part of a more determinative narrative. We can only make sense of our lives . . . by telling stories about our lives. To be able to 'make sense of our lives' is primarily an exercise, as I suggested above, of retrospective judgement. Such judgements are by necessity under constant negotiation just to the extent we must live prospectively, with a view to the future. We are able to go forward just to the extent we can look back.[94]

The Christian act is uncomplicated, predictable, and a natural outpouring of our apprenticeship in a foundational grammar. The foundation on which rightly ordered Christian action stands is in our ability to make our past actions our own. The faithful act of the Christian martyr is the product of correct description based on a determinative foundational grammar and of retrospective judgment. Faithfulness in action follows well-ordered vision and description. The act itself is uncomplicated.

Hauerwas consistently emphasizes the centrality of Jesus Christ in Christian ethics, the power of the Holy Spirit, and the moral life as a participation in God's grace. However, the means by which he chooses to articulate this transformation, especially through the simplicity of the moral act, limits the connection between Christian action and God's agency. In short, the structure of the Christian moral act simply allows no room for the agency of God. The exclusion of God's agency in the Christian act in Hauerwas' ethics is not purposive. Indeed, he intends a theology that very closely entails the involvement of God's agency in the moral life. But, at the same time, this intention is at loggerheads with his

---

94. Ibid., 101.

safeguarding of our free action. While there is little doubt that Hauerwas leads the discourse in profoundly important ways toward making more feasible a description of Christian ethics that has God at the center, he lacks some important tools to help him accomplish it.

Indications of Change

Excitingly, more recent work offers reasons to believe that Hauerwas' ethics might be moving to a deeper and more complex description of Christian moral agency. Hauerwas' 2004 *Performing the Faith: Bonhoeffer and the Practice of Nonviolence* hints of a change in the permeability and complexity of Christian moral action. Some time ago, Hauerwas began to utilize notions around what he called the "postmodern turn" for its ideas about the permeability of the self. Still, while the community and a variety of narratives could determine the self, only the self determined the act. Hauerwas' recent writings hold the seeds of potential change in this dynamic.

Since at least 1998 (and probably much earlier), Hauerwas has made use of the permeability of the self as prompted in postmodern trends.[95] In *Sanctify Them in the Truth*, for instance, we have a self that can be formed and determined by means of exterior forces. Even further, "just as there is no single thing called the self, neither is there any single thing called body. Our bodies are under constant negotiation, shaped and reshaped by the stories in which we find ourselves."[96] The self, then, in a variety of senses is subject to influence and determination by things outside of it. The "postmodern turn," therefore, represents a significant challenge to the way moral theology is done: "the loss of the 'self' . . . threatens the metaphysical presuppositions on which Christian ethics in modernity has been built."[97] This is not to say of course that Hauerwas is willing completely "to side with the postmodernists."[98] He does, though, look to adapt the idea that "the self, like language itself, is but a sign that gets its meaning from other signs that get their meaning through their relationships of similarity and difference with other signs."[99] The

---

95. Ibid., 78.
96. Ibid., 86.
97. Ibid., 97.
98. Hauerwas, *Better Hope*, 42.
99. Hauerwas, *Sanctify Them in the Truth*, 98–99.

importance of Hauerwas' acknowledgement of the postmodern turn is that, after allowing the usefulness of the permeability of the self to which it points, Hauerwas may grasp the permeability of the act as well. If Hauerwas draws from those who have written about the ways in which the self can no longer be treated as determined only by one's own understanding, it is possible that he might, likewise, realize the potential for such permeability of the Christian act, as well.

Indeed, there are a few moments in his more recent publications indicating that he has begun to treat the Christian act as more than just the natural embodiment of story and the natural consequence of character as acquired through narrative and apprenticeship. In an article comparing Christian ethical behavior to a performance, Hauerwas begins to speak of Christian action with the same permeability as the self. He writes:

> One of the traits of faithful performance is the way in which the performer is drawn out of him- or herself and is "possessed" or "taken over" by the work. This ability to let go of oneself, to dispossess oneself in the very execution of the act, is a skill that is not learned quickly or easily and certainly not on one's own. Indeed, if acquired at all, it is learned in communion and fellowship with others over the course of an entire Christian life. The power of performance, then, originates not so much in the performer but in his or her attunement to the work that is being performed, worked out through and by the performer.[100]

This passage marks a promising direction, namely that the act itself is deeply complicated and occasionally drawn into something outside of it that can fundamentally determine it. While Hauerwas is talking about a "skill" that is "acquired" and is acquired by means of "fellowship with others," it is nonetheless true that the effect desired is that one "dispossesses oneself" in the Christian act. Faithful performance is what it is only because the act is not altogether self-determined—the act is permeable. Now, exactly what it is that the act is permeable *to* is not altogether clear. But nonetheless, this stands as a significant step toward a model of free agency moved by God's grace. Even more promising is how Hauerwas expands this idea, following what was quoted above: "it is a loss of control because the performer gives her- or himself over to the

---

100. Hauerwas, *Performing the Faith*, 101.

drama of God's action, a movement larger than his or her biography."[101] Again, the connection with God's action is not quite clear. Hauerwas does not say that it is God's action that Christian performance abandons itself within, but rather that the *self* is given over into God's action. Still, this permeability of the self is extended to a discussion of Christian action, not Christian identity or judgment. The hint is that faithful performance is a permeable act, that is, a moment in which the self is in part determined by God's agency.

This development is promising for a healthy conversation with Aquinas and others who struggle to articulate a non-competitive bond between free Christian action and God's grace because, just as Hauerwas once began to allow for the permeability of the self, here he seems to allow for increased complexity in the Christian act, especially with regard to God's agency. This signals a rather appetizing potential for the resolution of the tension between his worries about determinism and his desire to show the centrality of God's grace in Christian ethics. This seems all the more true in light of a single passage in which Hauerwas tries to conclude what it means to be performing faith: "[God] has called us into his dance. He has invited us to join with him in the grace of his movements, performing them just as he taught us, that we might awaken bodily and fleshly to a graceful performance that God is enacting in us and through us."[102] In these last lines is the potential that it will not only be in the shape of ourselves that God is enacting through us, but the very shape of our act.

The theological ethics of Hauerwas present some extremely useful promptings to the current discourse, even beyond the very helpful insistence upon the centrality of community and the importance of scriptural narrative. Hauerwas insists upon Jesus Christ as the center of Christian moral life. He champions the importance of sanctification of the Holy Spirit and participation in God's grace, transforming the self. He writes consistently about the grace of God in the moral life, as well as carefully articulating Christian moral action as firmly free. Intriguingly, however, Hauerwas' more recent work seems to treat the structure of the Christian moral act as more permeable. While such a treatment seems to be set in more metaphoric and aesthetic terms, it still indicates the potential for the involvement of God's agency in the Christian moral act.

101. Ibid.
102. Ibid., 109.

Christian ethics, according to Hauerwas' own arguments, is incoherent without the close involvement of God's grace and the action of the Holy Spirit. In this way, he is examined here as the best example of an important trend. His ethics seeks a close involvement of God in the Christian moral life—an instinct that is regrettably scarce in the contemporary discourse. Hauerwas argues not only for the indispensability of the dynamics internal to the worshipping community as the means for moral transformation, but also for the centrality of a connection between God's action and Christian action. The indication of the need for these tools is no small accomplishment, and one that can be realized with the addition of a few concepts about the potential for connection between human and divine agency, which I will describe in later chapters.

First, however, I will point to a theologian with concerns similar to Hauerwas, but discussed in a very different way. The theology of Reinhard Hütter displays a close kinship to Hauerwas in its argument for the need of a close connection between God's action and human agency in the Christian moral life. The same tension that exists in Hauerwas' theology between this involvement and a healthy anxiety about determinism is even more vivid to the reader in Hütter. He just as effectively pushes the discourse toward a thicker description of Christian moral agency and a non-contrastive connection between God's action and the moral life and he, too, could much benefit from a deeper conceptual tools describing moral agency to realize this connection.

2

Reinhard Hütter

The Place of Reinhard Hütter in the Present Treatment

REINHARD HÜTTER, LIKE STANLEY HAUERWAS, is remarkable in the contemporary theological discourse for pushing ethical thinking toward a better-than-cordial connection between divine and human agency in the Christian life. Like Hauerwas, he struggles to maintain the integrity of human freedom in this relationship. Like Hauerwas, as well, he argues for the importance of the very direct influence of God's agency in the shape of Christian moral action. However, Hütter attempts to articulate a resolution to this tension in a way profoundly different from Hauerwas. In Hütter, one finds a theology that wrestles with this tension in a much more dialectical way. In some works, Hütter articulates an ethic that (much like Hauerwas') rests on the formation of the moral self through a narrative-shaped community in which we learn our way into a transformative story. In other works, though, he describes an ethic in which human agency is firmly passive to divine grace. Through this tension, Hütter pushes the discourse to a new cusp of ecumenically expressed, community-based, free, grace-centered explanation of the Christian moral life. Yet, his theology does not resolve this tension. Hütter's struggle with the involvement of God's grace and free human action is a very lively one and has not yet found resolution. What Hütter's theology manages to accomplish has driven the discourse forward, but what it does not yet accomplish pushes the discourse even further. He displays a thorough, deep tension between God's active grace in the moral life and Christian free agency and determinedly pursues a connection between the two.

Reinhard Hütter is very aware of the importance of God's agency in the Christian moral act. He strives for some sort of "conjunction" or "intertwining" that must occur between divine and human agency, aware of the tension this offers between the regulation of human action that is basically responsive to God's action, and passive yielding to God's grace. His writing displays a slowly swaying dialectic between resignation to divine action and careful control of human action. The profound importance of this theoretical motion is its demonstration that one side needs to stand as a corrective over the other. The great weight he assigns to human freedom on the one hand, and the efficacy of God's grace on the other, shows the importance, value, and force of both—God's grace is really that powerful and complete, human freedom is really that central and indispensible.

Hütter offers a better glimpse of the current difficulty of ecumenical Christian ethics in the West to speak coherently about cooperation between divine and human agency. Yet, this is hardly the limit of his contribution to an ecumenical ethic of grace. He consistently centers this grace in the context of the Christian worshipping community, carefully shows the importance of Scripture in the transformation of the moral life, and incorporates the best in ecumenical resources in explaining it. While Hütter demonstrates much that is missing from an ecumenical, community-centered ethic of grace, he puts in place many tools to which this present work will return as these sources are brought together, namely the importance of the Christian narrative and the necessity of the context of the Christian worshipping community.

In his 1993 dissertation, *Evangelische Ethik als kirchliches Zeugnis*, Hütter argues for an ethic that is consistent with Hauerwas in many ways. Like Hauerwas, he certainly strives to articulate an ethic in which divine and human agency intertwine. Christian action, for Hütter, is a response to, and an imitation of, the paradigm of cooperative moments of divine and human action presented before us in Christian worship—most especially in baptism and the Eucharist. This theme of liturgy as a focal point for Christian ethics carries throughout his entire body of work, so far. In this first book, the formation of Christian judgment and the renewal of thinking about action (again with Christian worship functioning paradigmatically) occur through individual and communal conceptual shifts. The agency of the Holy Spirit emerges as a mode in which Christians find some consensus about how to act. Hütter offers a notably Hauerwasian system, but one that even more effectively acknowledges God's work through the Holy Spirit in the Church and the significance of the incarnation, which forges moments of contact between our humanity and God. Nonetheless, *Evangelische Ethik als kirchliches Zeugnis* still stands as a project of the careful regulation of human action, and does not leave a great deal of room for God's grace.

Hütter's second book, his 1997 *Theologie als kirchliche Praktik*, (the title of the English translation is *Suffering Divine Things*), gives his readers a significant reprise on his earlier themes. Christian worship is still notably central, but the description of the role of God's grace is altered. The dialectic between the centrality of divine agency as contrasted with the centrality of human agency dramatically shifts in this second book. In *Suffering Divine Things*, Hütter advocates passivity before God's grace as the key to the conforming of one's actions to the message of the Gospel. Ours is a receptive passivity before the *acting subject* of Christian practice: the Holy Spirit. Though Hütter continues to emphasize the importance of an intertwining of divine and human agency, ours is a purely receptive part of the moral act. The human agent has shifted from active response to divine action, to the passive reception of divine action. The pendulum of the dialectic between emphasis on divine grace and emphasis on human agency in the Christian moral act swings dramatically as Luther's *vita passiva* finds an unapologetic place.

Once more in his 2004 *Bound to Be Free*, Hütter offers a "rearticulation and expansion" of *Theologie als kirchliche Praktik* (*Suffering Divine Things*) but with significant alterations. Again the reader benefits greatly from this non-repetitive rearticulation as Hütter once more struggles with the same basic interactions. However, it is quickly apparent that his views on the relationship between the Holy Spirit, Church practice, and Christian moral action have changed significantly. The pendulum swings back significantly in the dialectic between divine and human agency so that the work of God in the Church now provides us with important bits of knowledge through God's action, and it is our duty to be hospitable to these truths. In *Evangelische Ethik als kirchliches Zeugnis*, God acts in the Church, and then Christians respond to the knowledge of God's saving action. It is this knowledge—the knowledge that is the Gospel—that engages Christians in a personal way. Once more, in a very

Hauerwasian way, Christian action turns on the self-involving character of the Gospel, rather than on the intimacy of God's involvement, or even on a passivity before God's action. That being said, Hütter seems no less aware of the real need for language addressing the close involvement of God in human action. But the action of God is, nonetheless, relegated to truths to which we must be hospitable. While Hütter describes this as a rearticulation of *Theologie als kirchliche Praktik* (*Suffering Divine Things*), it echoes much more truly his *Evangelische Ethik als kirchliches Zeugnis*. His basic purpose has not changed—to strive for a system in which God's agency is indispensably involved in Christian action. But, the tension between human and divine agency is not in any way lessened. Instead, the swinging pendulum has not yet settled, as this final work brings the dialectic back to an emphasis on the careful shaping of human action and away from passivity before God's action.[1]

The Pendulum Swings: Evangelishe Ethik als kirchliches Zeugnis[2]

Evangelische Ethik als kirchliches Zeugnis, while not widely read, is a unique and powerful project that attempts to give full value to the ethical impact of the Holy Spirit's work in the Church. Ecclesiology is so central to Hütter's theology that one might sooner call it (as he does) a "Church ethic" rather than a simply Christian ethic. His starting point in the Church is a fruitful one for him, and one of special interest in the present chapter, in that it is an ecclesial context by which he addresses the importance of both divine and human agency in Christian moral action. This important context is doubly remarkable in that Christian ethical action is, for Hütter, situated in the context of the life of the wor-

---

1. Before proceeding to substantiate the above claims and trace the path of Hütter's developing thought, one quick note: especially in his early work, Hütter makes very frequent use of *italics*. In this chapter, all italic emphases are his and are never supplemented by my own.

2. The reader may notice that the first of the three principle works to be treated in this chapter receives a much longer discussion than the other two. This lopsidedness is intentional and has a simple explanation. Despite its great merits, Hütter's 1993 dissertation is not widely circulated in Germany, and even less so in the United States (untranslated, and with copies available in only seventeen libraries, as compared with the more than four hundred American libraries that carry a copy of Hauerwas' dissertation, or with the 160 libraries that carry the English translation of Hütter's second book). My treatment of *Evangelische Ethik als kirchliches Zeugnis* will therefore not assume a familiarity with the work itself.

shipping community, and yet the shaping of the individual moral agent is still very much at the center of his theology. He poses an inquiry along the following lines:

> How can we approach ethics, coming from ecclesiology in such a way as to take into account the special nature of theological ethics, namely the fact that it does not only have to thematize and consider the action of man, but also the action of God? Since the action of God and the action of man already are in a very specific way the object of ecclesiology, we should ask ourselves if we can look at the overlap between ecclesiology and ethics in a way that we can gain some contours and ideas for theological ethics as Church ethics. In examining the status of discussion of theological Protestant ethics in the last decades we can say that this question has not directly suggested itself as the key question of the discussion. Rather, the impression arises that the connection between ecclesiology and ethics has always been one of the hidden underlying questions that never explicitly found voice in the discourse.[3]

While Hütter sees the connection between ecclesiology and ethics as underexplored, he rightly points out its profound importance in the way that such an ethic makes necessary an account of not only human action but of divine action, as well. The consideration of both human and divine agency marks, according to Hütter, the special character of theological ethics. He asserts that the joint consideration of divine and human agency is already very much in place in the consideration of ecclesiology, and that consideration of the Church, therefore, has much to offer theological ethics.

---

3. Hütter, *Evangelische Ethik*, 7. . . . wie sich von der Ekklesiologie her ein Zugang zur Ethik gewinnen läßt, der dabei dem Besondren theologischer Ethik Rechnung trägt, nämlich daß sie nicht nur das Handeln der Menschen, sondern auch das Handeln Gottes zu thematisieren und zu bedenken hat. Da das Handeln Gottes und das Handeln der Meschen aber schon in sehr spezifischer Weise Gegenstand der Ekklesiologie sind, ist zu fragen, ob das Überschneidungsfeld von Ekklesiologie und Ethik als theologischer Entdeckungszusammenhang so in den Blick gennomen werden kann, daß sich von ihm her Konturen für die theologische Ethik als kirchliche Ethik gewinnen lassen. Blickt man auf die Diskussionslage theologischer Ethik protestantischer Provenienz der letzten Jahrzehnte, so ist festzustellen, daß sich diese Frage nicht unmittelbar als die zentrale Leitfrage der diskussion aufdrängte. Vielmehr ergibt sich der Eindruck, daß es sich bei der Frage nach dem Zusammenhang von Ekklesiologie und Ethik um eine der verborgenen, nie den Diskurs explizit bestimmenden Hintergrundfragen handelte.

However, such an inquiry is not simply an abstract undertaking. Hütter argues that the ethical character of ecclesial inquiry stems from the work of the Holy Spirit in the Church. He considers the Church's affirmation of the work of the Holy Spirit (the third article of faith about which he speaks in the following passage) as the proper object for examination in the connection between the two:

> Proceeding from the reflection upon the *Third Article of Faith* should be a way to open up ecclesiology to the theological ethic. The starting point should be the question about the ethical character of the church, the vocation to be a community of witness and the role that is thereby constitutive for church action. In this context, it is necessary to *pneumatologically* reconnect the ecclesiological reflection in a clear-cut and unambiguous way, so that the ethical speech of church neither decays to flat ecclesial moralism nor is bound in a wrong way to the 'positivity' or 'given reality' of the church.[4]

Hütter wisely realizes that an examination of the connection between ecclesiology and ethic would be misguided without focusing on the subject of the Holy Spirit. To do otherwise would force us to consider the Church as a simple model, which is to say, to consider human action alone. Christian action in the context of ecclesial vocation must be considered with the proper attention to God's action. The ethical speech of the Church is speech that directly connects our moral action to divine agency, in some way. Thus, Hütter continues that he wishes to address this "pneumatological reconnection" in two respects, to be considered one at a time: "first, along the guidelines of the question about the 'conjunction' of God's action and human action in the context of the indicative action of witness of ecclesial operations."[5] Already, in this first respect, Hütter's attention to the need for the consideration of some sort of bond between divine and human action is readily apparent. The term

---

4. Ibid., 19–20. Ausgehend von dem Nachdenken des *dritten Glaubensartikels* soll ein Weg über die Ekklesiologie zur theologischen Ethik erschlossen werden. Ausgangspunkt dafür soll die Frage nach dem ethischen Charakter der Kirche, Berufung zur Zeugengemeinschaft und die dafür konstitutive Rolle kirchlichen Handelns sein. Es gilt in diesem Zusammenhang, die ekklesiologische Reflexion eindeutig und unmißverständlich *pneumatologisch* rückzubinden, um die ethische Rede von Kirsche weder in einen platten ekklesiologischen Ethizismus verfallen zu lassen noch in falscher Weise an die »Positivität« bzw. »Gegebenheit« von Kirche zu binden.

5. Ibid., 20.

"Beieinander," translated above as "conjunction," does not quite reach to the concept of "cooperation," in that there is no operation entailed. Instead we have a joining together side by side or at most an intertwining.[6] An ecclesial context for a consideration of ethics is a backdrop that insists upon some potential for the coexistence of divine and human agency (even though it may not turn out to be an especially efficacious coexistence). Just because the emphasis is not on any cooperative activity (properly speaking) between divine and human action is not to say that Hütter does not emphasize the action of the Holy Spirit. Hütter goes on, "*Pneumatologically reconnecting the ecclesiological and ethical reflection to the Third Article of Faith means that there is no locus for reflection beyond this neediness for God's action.* Approaching this issue from the point of view of the Third Article of Faith also implies a specific, theological problem, namely how theological ethics as church ethics emerges from the gracious actions of God."[7] Such a summary makes plain the value of Hütter's contribution. Hütter realizes the importance of highlighting the worshipping community not just in itself, but as a model for the "conjunction" of God's action and human action in the world, thus upholding a model for the close and intimate involvement of divine agency in Christian ethics.

In his consideration of the pneumatological connection between ecclesial contours and ethical action, Hütter brings two notable Protestant theologians into a useful, though tension-filled, conversation: Karl Barth and Stanley Hauerwas. Hütter's criticism of Hauerwas (a criticism brought in many ways by his rather Barthian perspective) is similar to

---

6. Hütter's "Beieinander" includes none of the agency implied in a "Mitwirking," or a "Zusammenarbeit," but rather a state in which there is a bond in place without any action necessarily implied. This will turn out to be an important subtlety, as it is this "Beieinander" that stands as the model for the actions indicative of Christian witness.

7. Hütter, *Evangelische Ethik*, 20. Deshalb geschieht die pneumatologische Rückbindung in zweifacher Hinsicht, zum einen entlang dem Leitfaden der Frage nach dem »Beieinander« von Gottes Handeln und meschlichen Handeln im hinweisenden Zeugnishandeln der kirchen Vollzüge, zum anderen in der Wahrnehmung der stetigen Bedürftigkeit sowohl der Kirche als auch einer kirchlichen Ethik dem neuschaffenden Handeln Gottes im Geist gegenüber. *Pneumatologische Rückbindung der ekklesiologisch-ethischen Reflexion vom dritten Glaubensartikel aus heißt, daß es für diese Reflexion keinen Ort jenseits der Bedürftigkeit dem Handeln Gottes gegenüber gibt.* Das Ansetzen im dritten Glaubensartikel impliziert also eine bestimmte theologische Fragestellung, und zwar wie die theologische Ethik als kirchliche Ethik vom zuvorkommenden Handeln Gottes her in den Blick kommt.

my own observations of Hauerwas' thought: though God's work in the Church is central for Hauerwas, the Holy Spirit's agency is rather absent from his ethic, and there is little place for God's action and human action finding any point of contact. However, Hütter is not uncritical of Barth, either. While (according to Hütter) Barth is able to offer a way for us to find moments of parallel action between the divine and the human in an ecclesial context that is significant for ethics, he undermines this idea in devaluing ecclesial actions as mere signs giving some exhibition to God's action rather than as a moment in which God's action and human action stand together. While Barth is able to clarify the distinction between divine and human action in an ecclesial context (say, Baptism by water and Baptism by the Holy Spirit), he leaves a gap between God's agency and our own, arguing that ecclesial action witnesses to God's action, and no more. Through his treatment of such ecclesial acts, Hütter argues that Barth demonstrates the dependence of Church action on the Spirit, but does not give adequate voice to the potential for "conjunction." Barth does not go so far as to say that Jesus Christ forges the possibility of (or at least prompts in a useful way toward) the action of the Church to stand as both God's action and human action.

Hauerwas functions usefully at this point, for while Hauerwas does not adequately address God's action in the Church, he certainly does not underestimate the potential to contextualize Christian ethics in Christian worshipping community—Christian moral action as hallmark of the Church. In placing one in tension against the other, Hütter's ambition is a system in which we affirm God's action in the Church and the possibility for the "conjunction" between human and divine action in moral behavior in an ecclesial context, while at the same time identifying the bigger praxis and discourse of Church witness as instances that have the potential for this "conjunction." Hütter goes about this ambition through exploring (though certainly not uncritically) recent treatments striving to address this cooperation, namely, Barth and Gerhard Lohfink. In establishing the potential of moments of conjunctive action to occur in the worshipping Christian community, Hütter utilizes Hauerwas (though even more critically) to show the application of the idea of God's agency through the Holy Spirit in the Church to Christian ethical action more broadly.

Perhaps the most important and valuable characteristic of *Evangelische Ethik als kirchliches Zeugnis* is that it looks, above all, at a way to contextualize Christian moral action in the Church, such that God's action and our action can be seen as joined, noncontrastive, and even intertwined in the moral act itself. Hütter turns, first and foremost, to the Church for reasons that he believes are obvious. As he writes, "the systematic-theological heart of the problem in this question is the 'conjunction', i.e. the togetherness and the difference between God's action and human action. Thereby, the term 'God's action' itself remains, however, in need of *clarification, though not justification*, because a theological discussion about 'God's action' through the promise given to the community that God will act and has acted in that community, has asserted itself as the most obvious explanation."[8] While Hütter wishes to argue for the place of theological ethics in the context of the Church, he does so fully confident that he need not justify God's action in the context of worshipping Christians. In the promise of the Holy Spirit, God acts in the context of Christian community and Christian worshipping action. Hütter looks to clarify the impact of such a promise, but the most obvious source for this conjunction that he sees as so rightly central to theological ethics is Christian worship itself. The achievement of some correct context for the "and" in the conjunction between God's action "and" human action is the value of turning to Christian worship in the context of the promise of the Holy Spirit. "*Worship itself is the model for how we should understand the 'and' in God's and human action. God's action binds itself to particular enactments—theirs is the promise that God will act through them. By people 'doing' these enactments they are in accordance with God's action and stay within it.*"[9] Taking some cues from Barth, Hütter indicates that the enactments of Christian worship stand in the context of the promise of God's action. This is not to say that there is anything occurring in Christian worship that forces God's hand. Instead in Christian worship are some paradigmatic and important in-

8. Ibid., 26–27. Das systematisch-theologische Kern-problem dieser Fragstellung bildet das »Beieinander«, d.h. das Miteinander und Unterschiedensein von Gottes Handeln und menschlichem Handeln. Dabei bleibt die Rede vom »Handeln Gottes« selbst zwar *klärungs-*, jedoch nicht *begründungsbedürftig*, da eine theologische Rede vom »Handeln Gottes« durch die der Gemeinde gegebene Verheißung, daß Gott an ihr handelt und gehandelt hat, sich als das Nächstliegende aufdrängt.

9. Ibid., 200. *Der Gottesdienst selbst ist das Modell dafür, wie das »und« in Gottes und dem menschlichen Handeln zu verstehen ist. Gottes Handeln bindet sich an bestimmte Vollzüge—ihnen gilt die Verheißung, daß Gott durch sie handelt—, und indem die Menschen diese Vollzüge »tun«, entsprechen sie darin Gottes Handeln und bleiben damit zugleich in ihm.*

stances in which not only our actions stand in accord with God's action, but are within God's acting. The waters of Baptism do not constitute the Baptism by the Holy Spirit, but they are closely intertwined in such a way that what we are "doing" is a part of God's action, or at least in conjunction with God's action. Our act and God's action stand together in such a way that this "and" is a paradigm for the ethical life. God's movement in ways that have impact on our action can neither be said to be entirely God's action nor entirely ours. The Spirit's movement of the Christian must be said to be God's work, but it is nonetheless our free action as well. In considering God's action in the context of human life, just as in the waters of Baptism, neither God's agency nor ours can be neglected.[10] "In other words, ecclesial ethics has to ask about 'good works,' that can be described as works done 'through the Holy Spirit.' These are works that bear the promise that God in his actions will bind himself to them."[11] Moments such as Baptism offer a lens through which to view other "works" to which the promise of God's presence applies. The "Church ethic" that he proposes asks questions of any human act that stands alongside God's agency—questions that are more usually asked of moments like Baptism. Church action is more than a model. Church action, in the sense in which Hütter considers it, is the core moment of beginning, "*initium*" of God's action in the world in a broader sense. Christian moral action or "deeds of the kingdom" is a joining in to God's agency that proceeds from the critical context of "Church action": "By church action, again and again and in new ways, joining in this '*initium*' as testimony to God's action, God's action becomes 'powerful' in the world and the 'deeds of the kingdom' are enacted. The enactment of the church service is—as a common joining in God's action—the heart of both the action and the power of the Church."[12]

---

10. Ibid., 101–2. Indem der *Creator Spiritus* in die Umkehr ruft, schafft er zugleich die Möglichkeit zu dieser Umkehr. Selbst die Wirklichkeit der Umkehr muß strikt genommen dem Werk des Geistes zugeschrieben werden—anderweitig würde der Mesch über eine »Möglichkeit« verfügen, deren »Verwirklichung« ihm zur Disposition stünde. Der *Spiritus Creator* schafft jedoch beides, die Möglichkeit und ihre Inkraftsetzung zugleich. Aber eben—und das ist das Entscheidende dieser theologischen Handlungslogik—nicht derart, daß der Mensch als Handelnder dabei ausgeschaltet würde.

11. Ibid., 281. Kirchliche Ethik hat m.a.W. nach den »guten Werken« zu fragen, die als die gelten dürfen, die »aus dem Heiligen Geist« sind, d.h. denen die Verheißung gilt, daß Gott sich in seinem Handeln an sie bindet.

12. Ibid., 283. Indem kirchliches Handeln immer wieder neu als Bezeugng des Handelns Gottes in dieses »initium« einstimmt, wird Gottes Handeln in der Welt

In order for the context of church action to have application to other realms of human agency, Hütter recognizes the importance of the possibility for a relationship between human and divine action, described in such a way that human action need not be contrasted with divine action, but not in such a way that confuses the two. Though his depiction of such a relationship cannot quite be called cooperative, his description of "conjunction" comes quite close:

> God's action is entirely different from human action, in so far as it does *not* compete with it. By God working in the human being through the Holy Spirit, the human being stays a human being, also by staying an agent. God's newly creating action through the Holy Spirit is a "restoration" that does not turn the human being into a dead product, but that leaves him be an acting subject. The human being not only remains an agent in God's action, but is also restored anew through God's action as an agent by being led into the freedom of allowing God to work on him and by agreeing to this action. By God creating man anew, man himself acts. Man believes, confesses, prays. As God works in all things, i.e. creates all things new and in doing so proves to be God, man acts holistically as well, and thus, may remain a human being in this "conjunction."[13]

The categorical difference between divine and human agency is used here as a factor that helps, rather than hinders, our conception of a relationship between divine and human action that need not be in competition. While it may be true that another agent acting within human agency would entail a compromise of human freedom, God's action

»mächtig«, vollzieht sich »Tun der Basileia«. Der Vollzug des Gottesdienstes ist als das gemeinsame Einstimmen in Gottes Handeln der Kern sowohl des Handelns wie auch der Macht der Kirche.

13. Ibid., 102. Gottes Handeln ist darin vom menschlichem Handeln grundverschieden, daß es *nicht* zu diesem in Konkurrenz tritt. Indem Gott am Menschen im Geist handelt, bleibt der Mensch Mensch, auch indem er Handelnder bleibt. Gottes neuschaffendes Handeln im Geist ist ein »Herstellen«, das den Menschen nicht ein totes Produkt verwandelt, sondern ihn in seinem Sein als Handlungssubject beläßt. Der Mensch bleibt nicht nur Handelnder in Gottes Handeln, er wird vielmehr als solcher durch Gottes Handeln an ihm neu in Kraft gesetzt, indem er in die Freiheit geführt wird, Gott an sich handeln zu lassen und dieses Handeln selbst handelnd zu bejahen. Indem Gott den Menschen »neuschafft«, handelt der Mensch selbst. Der Mensch glaubt, bekennt, betet. Wie Gott alles wirkt, also im vollen Sinne neuschaffend handelt und sich darin als Gott erweist, handelt auch der Mensch *ganz* und darf in diesem »Beieinander« somit Mensch bleiben.

through the Holy Spirit is more restorative of our agency than limiting. Our action that follows from divine action is no less our action for doing so. Divine and human agency work in "Beieinander"—in, by, and with one another—which in itself is a greater freedom in that human beings "allow" God to work in them. While Hütter is, by mere conventions of language if for no other reason, compelled to give a progression (our action follows a restoration, we are lead into freedom, etc.), his depiction still reaches for a noncompetitive relationship between divine and human action that does not diminish human freedom. That which proceeds from a "Church" action is brought into the context of God's agency through the Holy Spirit and, as such, is an anticipation of the potential for intertwining. "As a Church action, [imitation of Christ] comes from the action of God and remains *within* it. It thus conforms to his action by imparting it in a way such that it requires completion through God's action. In this it is and remains, as the witness of God's action, a prayer that prays for God's action."[14] God initiates an action, renews us for it, completes the action, and then the action itself occurs within this agency, though Hütter is careful always to qualify that our agency is just as involved. A witness of God's action in the world is the fulfillment of the promise of the Holy Spirit and involves a noncompetitive, "conforming" effort that, while initiated and completed by God, remains both human and divine.

Hütter gains this important position (most especially his position regarding conjunctive conforming) through a critical interaction with the theology of Karl Barth. Barth, according to Hütter, offers what he calls a theological action theory that seeks to outline this conjunction between human and divine agency, and does so both in the context of the Church, and in such a way as not to imply any equality or likeness (beyond the analogical) between the two. Barth begins from a doctrinal standpoint as well, using the Chalcedonian definition of the two distinct and unconfused natures of Christ, fully human and fully divine: "In order to describe the *unique unity* of this 'conjunction,' Barth—in a very open way—goes back to the conceptualization of the Chalcedonian

---

14. Ibid., 203. Nachahmung Christi als Mitteilung des Handelns Gottes geschieht in bestimmten Vollzügen und muß als ganz von Gottes Handeln umgriffen gedacht werden. Als kirchliches Handeln kommt es aus dem Handeln Gottes und bleibt *in* ihm, indem es diesem Handeln darin entspricht, dieses so mitzuteilen, daß es selbst wiederum der Vollendung durch Gottes Handeln bedarf. Darin ist und bleibt es als Zeugnis von Gottes Handeln zugleich Gebet, das um Gottes Handeln bittet.

logic. God's action and human action are to be strictly distinguished, because there is an infinitely qualitative difference between the *creative* action of God and the *created* action of human beings. This means that we must neither think of an identity nor a mixture, nor are they allowed to be separated. They remain 'a unity emphasizing their differences,' a 'connection,' an 'event.'"[15] Hütter, like many others, finds that Barth places such a heavy emphasis on the separation that the "event" itself becomes meaningless. God's action and human action are distinguishable elements in Church action, but this infinite qualitative difference is such that the moment of a Church action like Baptism fails to be a "connection" and appears as a nearly dispensable sign of something accomplished entirely by God, both prior to and outside of human action. While Barth's theology does have its strengths, "the togetherness in the 'conjunction' is undermined in a certain way by Barth's interpretation of the teaching on Baptism. By interpreting Baptism and the Lord's Supper as mere sign action by men, he misses the reference point of the unity of 'conjunction' of God's action and man's action."[16] Where Barth succeeds in differentiating between the divine and human agency at work in the action of the Church, he fails to depict any real connection between the two. Despite these significant weaknesses, in the context of ethics taking its foundation in ecclesiology, Hütter does identify some very helpful elements. He writes that "the advantage of Barth's diastatic version of the Chalcedonian logic . . . lies in its implicit reference to the 'missing middle,' which originates where the Chalcedonian logic is transferred

---

15. Ibid., 103. Um die *differenzierte Einheit* dieses »Beieinanders« zu beschreiben, greift Barth in recht offener Weise auf die Begrifflichkeit der chalcedonensischen Logik zurück. Gottes Handeln und menschliches Handeln sind streng zu unterscheiden, da ein unendlicher qualitativer Unterschied zwischen dem *schöpferischen* Handeln Gottes und dem *geschöpflichen* Handeln des Meschen besteht. Das heißt, weder eine Identität noch eine Mischung beider darf gedacht werden, noch aber sind sie voneinander zu trennen. Sie bilden eben eine »differenzierte Einheit«, einen »Zusammenhang«, ein »Ereignis«.

16. Ibid., 103–4. Beschreibbar ist allein der handelnde Mensch, der »je und je« betet, bekennt, lobt und ein bestimmtes Zeugnishandeln vollzieht. Zu reden ist andererseits von Gottes neuschaffendem Handeln an diesem Menschem. Die *Unterscheidung* beider in ihrem »Beieinander« leuchtet ein und wird von Barth in jeder Hinsicht durchbuchstabiert. Das *Zusammen* im »Beieinander« beider wird jedoch durch Barths Fassung der Tauflehre selbst in bestimmter Weise unterlaufen. Indem er Taufe und Abendmahl als reine Zeichenhandlungen des Menschen verstanden wissen will, fehlt ihm der Bezugspunkt der Einheit des »Beieinanders« von Gottes Handeln und menschlichem Handeln.

from its original reference to the person of Jesus Christ to the context of a theological action-theory. In this version, it is God's acting in the Spirit that steps in this hidden middle and establishes the 'connection' between God's action in terms of creating something new and the ecclesial action that testifies to this action. That means, God himself redeems this connection and makes it 'visible.'"[17] While Barth's particular approach to the qualitative difference between God's action and human action leads him to compromise the importance or relevance of Church action itself, his theology does offer Hütter a fruitful starting point by implying the necessity of some sort of intermediary between the human and the divine, despite the fact that his system fails to provide it. Hütter argues for an implication that, for Barth, the outward action is but a witness—a testifying to God's action—there is implied some connection between the two. Just as God, through the Holy Spirit, made the connection visible in the person of Jesus, so, too, God makes the connection visible in the actions of Christian worship. Barth emphasizes that in ecclesial life, diastatic logic means that we are not forced or obliged to produce or achieve the action of Christian witness. Instead this freedom carries an implication that we can freely, then, expose ourselves as agents to God's witnessing action and that God, through the Holy Spirit, provides the connection between the two.[18] This gap and failure on the part of Barth's description of the "connection" and "event" of ecclesial moments of "conjunction" between God's action and human action actually gives Hütter a point of focus as to where that connection ought to be and the

---

17. Hütter, *Evangelische Ethik*, 281. Der Vorzug von Barths diastatischer Version der chalcedonensischen Logik . . . liegt in deren impliziten Verweis auf die »fehlende Mitte«, die dort zustandekommt, wo die chalcedonensische Logik von ihrem ursprünglichen Bezug auf die Person Jesu Chrisd auf den Zusammenhang einer cheologischen Handlungstheorie übertragen wird. In dieser Version tritt Gottes Handeln im Geist selbst in diese verborgene Mitte und stellt den »Zusammenhang« von Gottes neuschaffendem Handeln und dem dieses Handeln bezeugenden kirchlichen Handeln her; d.h. Gott selbst löst den Zusammenhang ein und macht ihn »sichtbar«.

18. Ibid. "This diastatic logic uses the ecclesial witness-action in its freedom from works, that is, in the freedom in which the ecclesial action does not have to 'produce' anything, 'put anything into practice,' 'achieve' anything and, thus, in this freedom can completely expose itself to the action of God, so that it testifies to it in a free and, at the same time, more defined manner." Diese diastatische Logik setzt das kirchliche Zeugnishandeln in seine Freiheit von den Werken ein, d. h. in die Freiheit, in der das kirchliche Handeln nichts »herzustellen«, nichts zu »verwirklichen«, d. h. nichts zu »leisten« hat, und in dieser Freiheit sich dem Handeln Gottes ganz so ausserzen kann, daß es dieses in freier und zugleich bestimmter Weise bezeugt.

agency that ought to provide it: "It is God's action in the Spirit itself, that steps in to fill the 'missing middle' in order to establish the connection between God's new-creating action and the church action that testifies to this action."[19]

Hütter utilizes another German theologian, Gerhard Lohfink, to complete this guideline, as Lohfink is able to achieve the unity of this "conjunction," which Barth's system implies but lacks. Lohfink rejects the synergist model (that is, part of the work is done by God and part of the work is done by us) as a potentially helpful metaphor, because the implication is that we accomplished something that is (at most) prepared by God. Lohfink focuses the discussion on the cooperation of God's work in faith, rather than on an explanation that would have God's action and human action running parallel, but remaining distinct. According to Hütter, "while Barth considers the 'and' as an unconnected parallel—God, in his action, leaves it entirely to man to freely decide to act toward God—Lohfink emphasizes the intertwining of the two, without admixture—i.e. on the one hand an active allowing oneself to be drawn into God's action (man acts by allowing God to act), and on the other hand, God's action through man actively allowing God to act (God acts through man's action)."[20] Lohfink's approach to "conjunction," while lacking the kind of parallelism in Hütter's account of Barth, at least offers a picture in which both divine and human agency are given indispensable places. While, from Barth, he gains the important point of the incommensurable and categorical difference between created action and the action of Creator, Hütter's incorporation of Lohfink brings the possibility of an intertwining of agency without forgetting this difference. "The question about the understanding of the 'and' in the *context of God's action 'and' human action* is a central problem when talking about the ethical character of the church. Lohfink's solution construc-

---

19. Ibid., 104. ist es dann Gottes Handeln im Geist selbst, das in die »fehlende Mitte« tritt und den Zusammenhang von Gottes neuschaffendem Handeln und dem dieses Handeln bezeugenden kirchlichen Handeln herstellt.

20. Ibid., 184. Während Barth das »und« allerdings als ein unverbundenes Nebeneinander denkt—Gott setzt in seinem Handeln den Menschen frei, ganz als Mensch auf Gott hin zu handeln—, betont Lohfink die Verschränkung beider, ohne sie jedoch zu vermischen—also einerseits ein aktives sich-in-Gottes-Handeln-hineinziehen-Lassen (der Mensch handlnt, indem er Gott handeln läßt) und andererseits das Handeln Gottes durch dieses aktiv Gotthandeln-lassen des Menschen (Gott handelt durch das Handeln des Menschen).

tively helps us look in a direction that will allow us to develop an ethical ecclesiology as the basis for church ethics which will neither fall victim to the Pelagian heresy nor to the subtlety of Semi-Pelagianism,"[21] or at least the strange Barthian version of Pelagianism in which God's action in the Church is not quite a necessity, simply because it has no contact with human action beyond a sort of parallel. The ethical character of the Church depends, as Hütter argues, upon a coherent conception of this "and." While Barth refuses a strictly cooperative picture that would confuse the difference between God's action and our own, Lohfink (while lacking the emphasis on the explicitly ecclesial context) attempts to find contact between the work of God and the work of people in the context of the realization of God's kingdom.[22] Like Barth, Lohfink looks to a christological paradigm for treating moments he judges ought to involve an intertwining of God's action and human action. Hütter certainly does not follow the application of this model toward a Lohfinkian realization of the kingdom of God on earth. However, he does take from Lohfink this insight about a unity without admixture as a corrective to Karl Barth's discussion. Hütter writes,

> a Church ethic that orients itself to the narrative of God's action (which asks about the action of the Church that testifies to God's action) requires a theological action theory that considers the "conjunction" of God's action and human action within the Church's witnessing action in a way that both, each in its own way, are taken into consideration. Both Barth's as well as Lohfink's *Chalcedonian Logic* serve as a guideline for this theological action theory, with Barth emphasizing the difference in

---

21. Ibid., 185. Als zentraler, für die Rede vom ethischen Charakter der Kirche konstitutiver Problemzusammenhang erweis sich erneut die Frage nach dem genauen Verständnis des »und« in der *Rede vom Handln Gottes »und« dem Handeln des Menschen*. Lohfinks Lösungsvorschlag weist konstruktiv in eine Richtung, die es erlauben wird, eine ethische Ekklesiologie als Grundlage einer kirchlichen Ethik zu entfalten, die weder der Gefahr des Pelagianismus noch der subtileren des Semipelagianismus verfällt.

22. Lohfink, "Der Not der Exegese mit der Reich-Gottes-Verkündigung Jesu," 12. Das Kommen der Basileia is ganz und restlos Werk Gottes, und es ist ganz und restlos Werk des Menschen. Dieses Sprachmodell läßt sich freilich nur dann durchhalten, wenn in ihm das Werk Gottes und das Werk des Menschen nicht unverbunden nebeneinander stehen, sondern wenn der Mensch ganz das Werk *Gottes* tut und wenn umgekehrt Gott *sein* Werk ganz durch Menschen tut. Mann könnte dann, in Analogie zu dem christologischen Modell Chalkedon, von *unvermischter Einheit* sprechen.

unity, i.e. the diastatic unity, and Lohfink emphasizing the unity in the difference between them.[23]

While Lohfink (as his conclusions indicate) fails to sufficiently regard the difference between the action of God and that of human beings, and Barth (while succeeding on that point) fails to sufficiently regard the potential for God and human beings to act in "conjunction," Hütter's juxtaposition of the two theologies offers the potential for a conjunction that distinguishes divine and human action while combining them in a noncompetitive way such that neither is compromised.

Hütter's interaction with Barth, along with the minor corrective pulled from Lohfink, leaves his reader with optimism about the potential for the interaction of God and human agency in the action of the Church in a way that neither confuses nor compromises the two, but still describes them as being in genuine interaction. However, the application of such a notion to ethics still remains tangential at best. If, in an ecclesial setting, there can be some sort of conjunction between God and human beings in a way appropriate to both, what relevance does this have for an ethical life? To phrase it differently, what is meant by a "Church ethic"? Enter Stanley Hauerwas. Hütter's extensive (and not uncritical) treatment of Hauerwas provides the application for this "conjunction" to the minute-to-minute ethical life of the Christian. Starting from an examination of Hauerwas' description of human action, Hütter's treatment of Hauerwas is much like his treatment of Barth: The flaws and gaps in Hauerwas' theology (most especially regarding an absent, but assumed, pneumatology) prove as valuable as the more sound elements. Upon the heels of demonstrating the possibility of, and need for, a "Beieinander" between God's action and our own in the ecclesial ethical life, Hütter scrutinizes Hauerwas for the application of such an interaction beyond the walls of the Christian sanctuary.

---

23. Hütter, *Evangelische Ethik*, 279. Eine sich an der Geschichte des Handelns Gottes orientierende kirchliche Ethik, die nach dem kirchlichen Handeln fragt, das Gottes Handeln mitteilend bezeugt, bedarf einer theologischen Hanlungstheorie, die das »Beieinander« von Gottes Handeln und menschlichem Handeln im kirchlichen Zeugnishandeln so bedenkt, daß beidem in je einiger Art Rechnung getragen wird. Dabei hat sich sowohl von Barth als auch von Lohfink her die *chalcedonensische Logik* als Leitfaden für die in den Blick zu nehmende theologische Handlungstheorie nahgelegt, wobei Barth die Unterschiedenheit in der Einheit, d.h. die Diatase, und Lohfink die Einheit in der Unterschiedenheit beider betont.

Hütter rightly recognizes that, for Hauerwas, the "self" and the "agent" are identical notions. The selfhood of a person lies in that person's actions, which are the materializations of that person's intentions. The action of the self-causing human agent, for Hauerwas, emerges from the rationality of that person—that is, the reason that person gives for one intention over another. Hütter notes that for Hauerwas, "the 'proprium' [that is, the core, defining character—the essence] of a human action is the intention personified in it, which in turn presumes the possibility of communication, i.e., speech. The moment that is crucial for the action in this context is the fact that it only becomes understandable to the agent as well as the observer through the description of the intention(s). In other words, a certain behavior is an action when the question 'why' appears to be meaningful and is answered."[24] For Hauerwas' acting agent, rationality, perspective, and description stand as indispensable categories for the coherence of the moral act. The perspective and description of the acting agent define the human action for Hauerwas. But these things do not happen abstractly. The description provided by Hauerwas' moral agent, as Hütter reads it, is just as much a description to one's community as a description to one's self. Likewise, the rationality and perspective of the moral agent proceed from their communal setting.[25] Such facets of Hauerwas' theology mean that, for Hütter, notions of story and the shape and character of community make a tremendous difference to the shape of moral action.[26]

---

24. Ibid., 136, 137. Das Proprium einer Handlung ist demgegenüber die in ihr verkörperre Intention, die selbst wiederum die Möglichkeit der Mitteilung, d. h. die Sprache voraussetzt. Das für diesen Zusammenhang nun entscheidende Moment an einer Handlung ist, daß sie sich sowohl für den Handelnden als auch für einen Beobachter nur durch die Beschreibung der Intention(en) erschließt. Mit anderen Worten, ein bestimmtes Verhalten ist dann eine Handlung, wenn die Frage »warum« sinnvoll erscheint und beantwortet wird.

25. Ibid., 138. [D]ie Perspektive des Handelnden, die in Hauerwas' Überlegungen im Vordergrund steht, zwar durchaus norwendig ist, alleine aber nicht ausreicht, um die Verständlichkeit einer Handlung zu gewährleisten. Vielmehr kommt den Beschreibungen, die die handelnde Person von ihren Intentionen macht, ein grundlegender *sozialer Charakter* zu. Sowohl die Sprache, in der die Erklärung abgegeben wird, als auch die Begriffe, mit denen dies geschieht, sind sozialer Natur.

26. Ibid., 140. Die Art der Ordnung oder Rationalität, die den Bedürfnissen und Eigenschaften des »intentional agent« am meisten entspricht, ist . . . eine narrative/story. Sie stellt eine Form von Rationalität dar, eine Weise, die Intention des Handelnden zu verstehen, die instrumentaler Abstraktion schlicht überlegen ist, d. h. der Erklärung von Verhalten in Ursache-Folge-Schemata.

For Christians (according to Hütter), such a system of moral action is not without its flaws. Hauerwas argues that we only know ourselves as we are able to place ourselves, which is to say locate our stories, in the context of God's story. "With this, Hauerwas, in a not unproblematic way, replaces pneumatology with the concept of narrative/story. That is, he obstructs the approach to pneumatology in such a way that God's action is still thematized through the medium of a remembered story of God's action."[27] Hütter recognizes that for Hauerwas, rationality, narrative, perspective, and description obstruct the need for the agency of God itself. Following, as this does, so closely on the heels of Hütter's work on Barth, the reader is led to see some parallel between the two theologians: both treat moral action through the context of Church community such that God's action and human action do not meet but, at best, exist side by side. "However," as Hütter continues, "Hauerwas' statement that true self-realization is based on locating one's own story within the story of God's action, presumes the *Spiritus Creator*, God's action through the Holy Spirit that creates things anew, if we do not want to declare this locating as an action of the human being."[28] Hütter, here, argues that Hauerwas fails to provide a system in which God's action stands as central because Hauerwas *presumes* a basic pneumatology. Hütter takes Hauerwas at his word—that God truly is central to the Christian life, so God's action through the Holy Spirit must stand in the gap between divine and human action. Again, following as this does on Hütter's treatment of Barth, the reader sees a parallel in the handling of the two theologians—both have significant holes in their respective systems, but these flaws and their presumptions are helpful and illustrative in leading to a more coherent proposal for ethics. Hütter goes on: "thus the crucial point that if God's action is not to be replaced through the simply human (at least not allowing for the theological action of God), it must be thought of as action that anticipates all human action. If God's action is in the center of all Christian convictions, then we have

---

27. Ibid., 149. Damit Tritt bei Hauerwas in nicht unproblematischer Weise die Konzeption von narrative/story an die Stelle der Pneumatologie, bzw. verstellt den Zugang zur Pneumatologie dadurch, daß Gottes Handeln zwar im Medium der erinnerten Geschichte des Handelns Gottes noch thematisiert wird, . . .

28. Ibid. Hauerwas' Aussage jedoch, daß wahre Selbsterkenntnis darin gründet, die eigene Geschichte innerhalb der Geschichte des Handelns Gottes zu verorten, setzt geradezu den *Spiritus Creator*, Gottes neuschaffendes Handeln im Geist voraus, will man diese Verortung nicht zur Tat der Menschen deklarieren.

to first and foremost consider this and explicate it in a theological way. And there likewise it belongs to the center of Christian convictions, that God's action meets with human beings and thereby God's work always anticipates human actions."[29] It is difficult to argue with Hütter that, if Hauerwas is to be coherent, then one must say that God's agency must stand somewhere, tacitly, behind the dynamic Hauerwas describes. If one begins with the basic conviction with which Hütter ends his treatment of Barth—namely that in the ecclesial context there is the possibility of a conjunction between human and divine agency—then Hauerwas' theology proves pertinent and useful. If God's action anticipates and stands behind Church action, and the action of the worshipping community— its narratives, descriptors, and rationality—stands behind Christian moral action, then God's agency works in conjunction with Christian action. Hütter writes about Hauerwas that "his approach would be misunderstood, if we understood it as an effort to find a 'point of contact' for God's action in the Spirit. *What is important to him, however, is the far more radical insight that God's action has to be thought of as twofold: in the pneumatological way, that it is entirely God's action, and in the action-theoretic way, that it is also the action of human beings.*"[30] Hütter does not argue that Hauerwas provides the necessary arguments for a theology that incorporates the conjunction he seeks. But, for Hauerwas' theology to be coherent, Hütter argues that it *has* to be thought of as twofold: the work of the Holy Spirit and the work of human beings. To accomplish this, Hütter imposes the pneumatology that he feels to be implicit in Hauerwas' system. Through Hauerwas, Hütter expands the potential of the conjunction of divine and human agency beyond a moment of Christian worship to, instead, the much broader formative in-

---

29. Hütter, *Evangelische Ethik*, 130–31. . . . somit an entscheidender Stelle wenn nicht Gottes Handeln durch menschliches schlicht zu ersezten, so doch zumindest dem Handeln Gottes theologisch nicht so Rechnung zu tragen, wie es als allem menschlichen Handeln zuvorkommendes gedacht werden muß. Steht Gottes Handeln aber selbst im Zentrum aller christlichen Überzeugungen, so gilt es, zuerst und vor allem dieses theologisch zu bendenken und zu explizieren. Und da es ebenfalls zum Zentrum der christlichen Überzeugungen gehört, daß Gottes Handeln auf den Menschen trifft und damit seinem Handeln immer zuvorkommt, ist die Ansicht.

30. Ibid., 145. Dabei wäre sein Zugang allerdings durchaus mißverstanden, würde man ihn als Bemühung um einen anthropologischen »Anknüpfungspunkt« für Gottes Handeln im Geist verstehen wollen. *Es geht ihm vielmehr um die weit radikalere Einsicht, daß Gottes Handeln zweimal zu denken ist, einmal eben pneumatologisch ganz als Gottes Handeln und das andere Mal ganz handlungstheoretisch als das Handeln Menschen* (CCL 206f)!

fluence that Hauerwas grants *every* moment in Christian worship. In the combination of his conclusions following his Barth treatment and the expansive applicability of the activity of the Church to ethical behavior, Hütter binds the shaping of the Christian character by the community with the sanctifying action of God. Our actions and God's actions are, thus, intertwined in every ethical moment. *"It is the 'story of Jesus' which defines how God reigns and also how such a reign can create a corresponding 'world' and a 'society.' Worship is the place where the church's 'discipleship to Christ' is at its center and from which it must proceed. Only in this place does the society that conforms to God's actions have its origin."*[31] Just as God forms the Church through the Holy Spirit, so Christians and their actions are formed in the Church.

Through his harmonization of Hauerwas and Barth (a harmony that occurs only through much improvisation and transposition), Hütter gives a setting to the "Beieinander" of God's action and human action. Through the distinct enactments of the Christian Church, divine and human agencies not only occur in parallel, but find a meeting point—a conjunction. As everything that the Christian does is the result of the effect of the Christian worshipping community, and as it is, therein, that Christian intentions, perspectives, rationalities, and descriptors are shaped, the "Beieinander" is applicable to the whole of the Christian life. While the alterations of the theologies of Barth, Lohfink, and Hauerwas are significant, they are done openly and with careful explanation. Hütter provides a framework that in some ways follows the contours of a Barthian or Hauerwasian solution, but in the end, this framework derives from what the writings of these theologians lack as much as from what they contain.

Pointing to the necessity of describing this "conjunction" in the Christian moral life is doubly valuable in Hütter's theology in that he, through Barth, chooses a liturgical framework to explain it. His "Church ethic" beautifully shows the inseparability between the Christian moral life, the Christian doctrinal life, and the Christian worshipping life. God's grace is not only central in what such an ethic would be, but intertwined with God's grace in many facets of Christian existence. In this

---

31. Ibid., 200. *Es ist die »Geschichte Jesu«, die sowohl definiert, wie Gott herrscht, als auch, wie eine derartige Herrschaft eine ihr entsprechende »Welt« und »Gesellschaft« schafft. Dabei ist der Gottesdienst der Ort, in dem die kirhliche »Nachahmung Christi« ihr Zentrum hat und von dem sie ausgehen muß. Denn allein hier hat die dem Handeln Gottes entsprechende Gemeinschaft ihren Ursprungsort.*

way, Hütter perceives and helps realize Hauerwas' ethic—one in which Christian ethics always and everywhere depends upon, and interacts with, Christian history, Christian doctrine, Christian Scripture, and Christian liturgy. Such a task is of inestimable value to the discourse as a whole.

Nevertheless, the "conjunction" that Hütter seeks is not yet realized. His theology wrestles mightily with the bond between human freedom and a grace-centered Christian ethic, and yet he lacks the tools necessary to describe that bond. In this first book, Hütter still articulates a Church ethic that, in the end, relies primarily upon the careful shaping of perspective and judgment. The Christian moral act is the result of the "renewing of the mind" by the Holy Spirit more than it is the illusive moment of "Beieinander" to which he seemed to be leading his reader. Though he lifts up the conjunction between human and divine action as proceeding from the Church, he holds its realization in reservation for the *eschaton*. The actual work of the Holy Spirit in the Church (and thus in Christian life as a whole) is a formation of judgment such that the ethical life is a "narrative casuistry" based on our reshaped minds. Our perception is altered such that the enactment of Church is that activity that is based on our convictions of God's sanctifying work. Despite Hütter's significant strides, his conclusions take a step backwards, ending in a system in which the work of the Holy Spirit shapes our judgment through Church enactment as a model that impacts the rest of our lives because it is so influential to our perception and judgment.

The first indicator that Hütter is balking at the conclusions offered in his innovative treatments of Hauerwas and Barth is his return to the actual bond between God's action and our own. He describes not a conjunction, finally, but an anticipation. "*Thus, church action, with its focus on God's promise, means to practice the patience of hope. It means practicing active waiting on God's action,* which positions the eschatological existence of the Church between the quietism of internalization and the conservatism of the uncritical legitimization of any status quo on the one hand, and the utopianism bound to the category of innovation, on the other hand."[32] Such an instance on its own is not terribly worrisome,

---

32. Ibid., 282. Kirchliche Ethik bleibt dem »Tun der Basileia« auf der Spur, indem sie den Weg kirchlichen Handelns begleitet. Sie tut dies, indem sie kirchliches Handeln von der Berufung der Kirche her unter Ausrichtung an den Kennzeichen der Kirche parakletisch so ausbuchstabiert, daß es in der Nachfolge der bezeugenden Entsprechung an der Verheißung ausrichtet bleibt, daß Gott mit seinem Handeln hinzutritt und

but it does give the reader pause. Since Hütter has carefully led his readers to the potential for the Holy Spirit to have intimate involvement in the Christian ethical life, we are, perhaps, surprised to learn that our ethical activity is waiting for God's agency—even though he describes this waiting as active. The position of the Church is safeguarded from error by its anticipation of God's agency, rather than a conjunction with it. Hütter finally articulates a "Church ethic" as an anticipation held in a long-term, eschatological reservation. "Church ethics is entirely an eschatological ethic, for it lives as a church enactment—embraced by the narrative of God's sanctifying action—entirely from God's action which remains different from all other human action and which anticipates it. It remains in anticipation of the creative action of God in his creation. This is the reason for hope and patience of Church action."[33] In this lifetime, the *narrative* of God's sanctifying action in the Church embraces us and our agency, rather than God's sanctifying action in itself. Our action remains an anticipation of, not a conjunction with, God's action. God's action is shown to be more relevant to us than perhaps one might have thought, but no more involved in the ethical life of the Church.

Hütter uses Romans 12:1–2 as a model for how this is meant to work—that is, how the agency of God in the Holy Spirit ends in an ecclesial ethic. He writes, "Romans 12,1–2 is the paradigmatic New Testament text in comparison to which this Paraklete language of the Church should stand, because in this text the logic of the intended '*paraklein*' or Paraklete action is exemplified."[34] The Romans passage reads:

dieses Zeugnis zur Mitteilung bringt. *Kirchliches Handeln in seiner Ausrichtung an Gottes Verheißung ist somit zugleigh Einübung in die Geduld der Hoffnung, Einübung in das tätige Warten auf Gottes Handeln,* das die *eschatologische Existenz* der Kirche zwischen dem Quietismus der Verinnerlich und dem Konservatismus der unkritischen Legitimierung jeglichen status quo einerseits und dem an der Herstellungskategorie verhaften Utopismus anderseits markiert.

33. Ibid., 282–83. Kirchliche Ethik ist . . . ganz eschatologische Ethik, da sie—umgriffen von der Geschichte des heilgeschaffnenden Handelns Gottes—als kirchlicher Vollzug selbst ganz aus dem Handeln Gottes lebt, das von allem menschlichen Handeln unterschieden bliebt und ihn zuvorkommt. Sie bleibt in Erwartung des schöpferischen Handelns Gottes an seinem Geschöpf. Dieses ist der Grund der Hoffnung und der Geduld kirchlichen Handelns.

34. Ibid., 269. Rm 12,1–2 is der paragmatische neutestamentliche Text, an dem sich diese parakletische Rede von Kirche zu messen hätte, denn in ihm wird die Logik des hier intendierten {parakalein} exemplarisch vorgeführt: Ich ermahne euch nun, Brüder, durch die Erbarmungen Gottes, eure Leiber darzustellen als ein lebendiges, heiliges, Gott wohlgefälliges Opfer, was euer vernünftiger Gottesdienst ist. Und seid

"I appeal to you therefore, brothers and sisters, by the mercies of God, to present your bodies as a living sacrifice, holy and acceptable to God, which is your spiritual worship. Do not be conformed to this world, but be transformed by the renewing of your minds, so that you may discern what is the will of God—what is good and acceptable and perfect."

The model for our regard of the application of the Holy Spirit to the ethical life is a renewal of the mind. This, in itself, does not seem to directly address his momentum in seeking a conjunction of God's agency and our own, but it certainly does not conflict with it either. However, this "renewal of the mind" does not turn out to be a field in which this conjunctive action happens, but is rather an indication of where *our* attention ought to be drawn in forming Christian action. This is nowhere more evident than when Hütter summarizes the importance of the "language" of the Holy Spirit as "Comforter" in the Church: "The language of Paraklete determines Church ethics as comfort in two ways: First, as the language that characterizes Church praxis discourse, which places it in the reality of God's sanctifying action and thus puts the cultivation of judgment in the realm of what is self-evident through God. Second, as the reflection of church ethics, that is characterized by the *ethical language of the Church*. This reflection of church ethics develops the vocation of the church towards its true form, its enactments and its church action."[35] The language, more than the Spirit, has the effect of comfort. Even further, the language of the Holy Spirit in the Church places our discourse and our action in the context of God's sanctifying action, but hardly into contact with it. The cultivation of our judgment happens through the task of language and understanding rather than through any direct "conjunction" with divine agency. The Holy Spirit seems to be more involved in reflecting what the Church is actually doing through language than the Spirit is in shaping that action itself.

---

nicht gleichförmig dieser Welt, sondern werdet verwandelt durch die Erneuerung des Sinnes, daß ihr prüfen mögt, was der Wille Gottes ist: das Gute und Wohlgefällige und Vollkommene. (Rom 12:1-2)

35. Ibid. Parakletische Rede bestimmt kirchliche Ethik als Trost in zwiefacher Weise: Zum einen als die die *kirchliche Diskurspraxis* prägende Rede, die in die Wirklichkeit des heilschaffenden Handelns Gottes und damit die Urteilsbildung in den Raum des von Gott her Selbstverständlichen stellt, zum anderen als die die *ethische Rede von Kirche* prägende Reflexion kirchlicher Ethik, die die Berufung der Kirche auf ihre Rechtgestalt, ihre sie kennzeichnenden Vollzüge und das kirchliche Handeln hin entfaltet.

In turning to a consideration of Hütter's later writings, however, this is hardly his last word on the matter. His initial concerns will remain the same, as will the basic loci of the origins of Christian moral action. However, God's agency becomes central, and the greater role that his description offers to God's agency means a less vital, less free role for human agency in the moral life. In this first book, Hütter is able to (rather accurately) demonstrate the genuine onus of moral theology to articulate an ethic that shows a close, noncompetitive, conjunctive, and even intertwining connection between divine and human agency, but lacks the tools to describe that connection and its efficacy in the moral life.

The Pendulum Swings Again: Theologie als kirchliche Praktik

Hütter's 1997 *Theologie als kirchliche Praktik*[36] likewise addresses the necessity for attention to the discourse praxis of the Church, but (at least on the surface) toward an entirely different end. Hütter frames his project as an attempt to solve for a crisis in the activity of theology with regard to the identity of the Church and its relevance, rather than as an explicit approach to Christian ethics. Bemoaning the modern eclipse of the public character (and therefore relevance) of the Protestant Church, he draws attention to the nature of the Church and the self-understanding of theology. Given the postmodern setting where theology can no longer be viewed as an activity stemming from reason, Hütter argues that the current crisis of relevance and authority is actually a question of the relationship between ecclesiology and binding doctrine. Reflection upon the task of theology needs to be a reflection upon the place in which it occurs—the self-reflection of the Church. Hütter argues, however, not only for the relevance of conceptual adjustments for the task of theology, but offers a much larger treatment on the disposition of humanity before God, both with regard to the shaping of language and the shaping of one's life and actions. He places the task of the production of theology in basic passivity before the grace and agency of God. As the argument unfolds, however, one finds that this foundational passivity before the grace of God extends to the broader "praxis" of "Churchly" existence in much the same way that it did in *Evangelische Ethik als kirchliches Zeugnis*. The difference between the basic approach of his 1993 book

36. All quotations, except where noted, are taken from Doug Stott's 2000 translation, *Suffering Divine Things: Theology as Church Practice*.

and that of this 1997 effort is that in the former he advocates a careful control of understanding, perception, etc., and in the latter a yielding passivity to God's agency in the Church.

Hütter, in this second book, turns his focus from a project of careful regulation and control of moral action through narrative to an emphasis on the Holy Spirit as the acting subject in matters theological and ethical. True to form, Hütter's attempt to address the place and task of theology ends up addressing the ethical activity of the Church in the world as much as it addresses the linguistic activity of theology in the Church. Nonetheless, at the outset, Hütter's *Suffering Divine Things* addresses the loss of the public character and relevance of the Protestant church by addressing its strictly theological (that is to say, linguistic) activity. In the modern crisis of theological discourse, Hütter says the practice of theology is reduced to two basic alternatives: "It can continue to take its orientation largely from a comprehensive concept of reason . . . or theology can understand itself directly and explicitly as 'poiesis,' that is, as a 'construction,' its creator being the religious subject who within the framework of its theological constructions conceptualizes certain, in the comprehensive sense, religious experiences and makes these experiences communicable."[37] Neither of these alternatives is viable, Hütter argues. The basic paradigm of the alternative between proceeding from the framework of reason and proceeding from the context of the more organic "construction" lived through the life of the believer seems unavoidable enough. But, he holds, the notion of this constructive "poiesis" is conceived of wrongly. While it is true that "theology has the opportunity of understanding itself as a poietic undertaking instead of viewing itself exclusively within the historical paradigm,"[38] as compared to other sorts of historically oriented disciplines, such an activity would seem to compromise the very identity of the Church—turning into a mere setting for the free reign of the creative human impulse.

However, as Hütter writes, the activity of theology is profoundly misunderstood unless it is contextualized in the setting in which it is made public—the Church. In fact, Hütter intertwines the practice of the one and the existence of the other. "Understanding theology properly as a discursive church practice requires understanding the Christological and pneumatological disposition of its corresponding public, namely,

37. Hütter, *Suffering Divine Things*, 22–23.
38. Ibid., 33.

the church. . . . *The church as public and theology as discursive church practice mutually imply one another.*"[39] Theology is not to be conceived of (strictly speaking) either under the rubric of an expression of the context of reason or as a product of the creative human impulse, but in the framework of a specifically Church practice. It is as Church practice that the public character of theology escapes the threat of being merely a human expression. Instead, "*as the public of the Holy Spirit, the church is constituted not through 'boundaries' but through a 'center' that in the core practices creates 'space' and 'time' and is expressed authoritatively in doctrina.*"[40] The public nature of the Protestant church and its relevance is not the range of its reach, but in that which makes up its "center." The Church practice of theology is not a public expression of the creative human impulse, but rather of the activity of the Holy Spirit. That which theology offers is the articulation of the creative action of God in the Church, rather than of the cognitive theoretical core of human creativity. As the critique of modernity and the project of postmodernity makes the "framework of reason" option untenable, Hütter holds that the constructivist option is left with two alternatives. Either we look to the intersubjective activity of the individual religious person for some sort of articulation of faith, or "the other alternative would be *explicitly pneumatological* as well as *ecclesiological* prolegomena to Christian theology, that is, a development of the pathos that makes Christian theology plausible as a distinct church practice."[41] Again, Hütter opts for the ecclesial context of the practice of theology since the first option is perfectly free to exist in isolation from the "core acts" and practices of the Church on which he feels the dogmatic discourse of theology is dependent. Hütter feels that the Protestant church tends to choose the first, untenable option of looking to the intersubjective individual religious experience for the "center" of Christian theology. The alternative he pursues places the activity of the Holy Spirit in the Church and the core Christian practices. The activity of the Spirit in Church practice constitutes the public character of theology, and the resulting (recovered) relevance of the Church.

Thus, theology, as a practice, is not an activity of innovation or cognition as much as it is a reception of some other activity of innovation and creativity—a *pathos*, a suffering, an undergoing of the action

39. Ibid., 166.
40. Ibid., 165.
41. Ibid., 23.

of the Holy Spirit in the Church. The practice of theology addresses this basic reality and points to its own origins beyond itself. The creativity to which the practice of theology yields is not the cognitive theorizing emerging from our rationality or our experience, but the "poieses," the creative action, of God through the Holy Spirit. If theology emerges from anywhere else it is simply an activity embodying idolatry; that is, if the practice of theology is anything but a reception, a suffering, an undergoing, a pathos, it can only speak to the human: "theological discourse not shaped by this specific notion of divine poesis and thus not pathically constituted can only 'objectify,' that is, idolize God by producing conceptual products through poietically argumentative and imaginative power, products which conceal God and justify the theological subject controlling this discourse."[42] The authenticity of the Church practice of theology and the relevance of the public character of the Church, thus, must rest on a creative power beyond human imagination and creation, stemming neither from reason nor intersubjective experience. The freedom and creativity of theology only expresses its object through a yielding to God's creative activity. Thus, "*Only in the Holy Spirit and its genuine poiesis of communion does theology as a church practice participate in God's liberum arbitrium. Only by remaining bound to God's economy of salvation does it step into the 'freedom of the children of God,' becoming thus a discipline commensurate with its object. For only within its distinct pathos does it become capable of truth.*"[43] The creative capacity of the practice of theology is, therefore, not of human making at all, but rather in its ability to voice the creative action of God in the Church. The core of the identity of theology as a practice is its suffering, its pathos, of the sanctifying action of God in the Church. Hütter does not want to deny, however, that the activity of theology can be creative (in a more conventional use of that term). The Church practice of theology is not limited to rearticulation. Instead, the creative, poietic capacity of theology emerges from that which it suffers and undergoes. Its poiesis, its creative capacity, is determined by its pathos, that activity which it undergoes. So, "if pathos itself remains determinative of poiesis . . . and if the poiesis of theology remains strictly oriented toward this pathos, then one can derive poiesis from pathos in a twofold manner: first as the poiesis of God underlying the pathos of both faith and theology; second as

42. Ibid., 31–32.
43. Ibid., 157–58.

the poietic pathos of theology as a communicative-presentative church practice."[44] While complex, such a statement nicely summarizes Hütter's ambition for a framing of the activity of theology as a Church practice. That which happens to the Church and thus to the practice of theology determines what theology articulates. Theology's innovative character must remain fundamentally oriented to that activity of God that "happens to" the Church. Thus, the creative, innovative capacity of theology emerges from the creative action of God, which underlies the receptive, suffering, pathos disposition of the life of faith.

Church action in its pathos of the action of the Holy Spirit gives authenticity and relevance to the activity of theology. Hütter describes the connection between theology as a practice and the actions of the Church as accomplished by the Holy Spirit in terms of the conceptual shaping power of narrative and action. His exploration of this notion is largely through an interaction with George Lindbeck. According to Hütter, Lindbeck's understanding of religion depicts a specific relationship between practice and the use of language that "always precedes the individual subject and unavoidably shapes that subject's experiences. This brings into structural focus the pathos of theology as a distinct practice between concrete life-acts, on the one hand, and the doctrine that articulates the grammar of faith on the other."[45] Always before the subject in a linguistic activity like theology is the dynamic between language and ceremony in the Church. Expanding from his earlier treatment of thinkers like Hauerwas, Hütter explores Lindbeck's work not only to address the formative power of narrative, but the specific importance of practice that shapes it. Through his treatment of Lindbeck, Hütter argues that it is "possible to understand theology as a distinct practice shaped by the central acts of language and ceremony of the church, acts with which it remains inextricably related."[46] The practice of theology itself is shaped by the action of the Church, both in a linguistic sense as well as in moments like the sacraments. For Lindbeck, a setting like Church, as a cultural-linguistic model, is a matrix constituting a comprehensive reality through "an indispensable network of language and ritualized activities."[47] According to this model, the content of faith is

44. Ibid., 34.
45. Ibid., 25.
46. Ibid., 26.
47. Ibid., 45.

actualized through the content of the Church from which it emerges. The linguistic activity of theology undergoes the "pathos" of the active content—that is, the action—of faith.[48] Lindbeck offers a model in which the activity of the Church (and most especially the linguistic activity of the Church) is a "poietic pathos," innovating insofar as it suffers, undergoes, another kind of activity. The poietics of theology are an outpouring of the practice of the life of faith.

Of course, a cultural-linguistic matrix is not the same as the action of the Holy Spirit in the Church, as Hütter is well aware. The problem with applying Lindbeck's ideas to a setting like Church is that, while in the practices of the Church (and theology in particular) our "poiesis" only comes through "pathos," this does not imply that there is any poiesis occurring besides the dynamics of the cultural-linguistic network. Rather, in the context of Christian poietic pathos, "one must inevitably inquire concerning *the poiesis that is the determinative ground of the pathos of the praxis of faith and of theology. This raises the question of the Spiritus Creator, the presence of God in his creative activity, and activity that in its own turn creates its own recipient.*"[49] For the practice of faith and the practice of theology the creative activity of God is to be borne, suffered, undergone. The practice of the Church undergoes, suffers this poiesis, and it is from this poiesis that our own poietic content emerges in the practice of theology itself. The creative activity of God in the Church (which also constitutes the Church) is that which stands behind theology to be suffered (and indeed, constitutes the practices of the Church, the practice of theology included). Even further, "because both faith and theology are grounded in God's salvific action, and in the strict sense are his works,"[50] they are bound to the action and timing of God's creative agency in the Church.

The bond between practices of the Church like theology and the action of God stem from the specific relation of "pathos" that Hütter wishes to offer. In the conception of pathos, "the reference is rather to the 'other' of action, that which determines or defines a person prior to all action, in all action, and against all action, that which a person can only *receive*."[51] The activity of the Church, insofar as its innovative

48. Ibid.
49. Ibid., 63.
50. Ibid., 36–37.
51. Ibid., 30.

poiesis rests on a basic pathos to the activity of God, is "passive activity." The "other" of action—the presence of the Holy Spirit in the Church—is definitive of the person and of the action. The Christian in the practice that constitutes faith can only receive.[52] Our existence, our activity as Christian, is an active passivity. We are determined by God's action, and our response of pathos to that determining (poiesis) is the "core" of our action. Christian activity emerges only from the passive life of faith before God. "The *vita activa* then emerges from the *vita passiva* of faith; pathos issues in poiesis and practice while never really leaving the horizon of pathos."[53] Our existence and our action, as Christian, is an action of passivity, a suffering of the action of God. Hütter would not have his reader believe that this means our activity is forced or bound. Instead, this passivity before the action of God entails a greater freedom: "Precisely the *vita passiva*, however, is free in that it is qualified by the core practices of the church and by *doctrina*. It enters into God's freedom, to use Luther's expression, by being 'rapt' into it by the core church practices and by *doctrina*."[54] The unique qualification of poiesis by God's action in the Church incorporates a unique freedom because it is, in some way, only to our own activity that we are bound.

The Christian life of passivity before God, insofar as it leads to certain human practices, is receptive equally to our actions (as expressions of God's) and God's action (considered as such). In this way, Hütter describes the Christian life as a *bios sui generis*—it is a life that takes itself up and generates itself, in that it has its foundation in passivity before the poiesis of "other." Because it is bound to this activity, "faith is to be understood . . . as *vita passiva*, as a *bios* grounded in God's salvific activity."[55] The Christian activity that constitutes faith is brought about only by its passivity before God. Christian "faith is pathos precisely because its actualization is utterly determined by the work of the Holy Spirit and receives its 'form'—which is its object—precisely from that determination, that is, it is 'sanctified.'"[56] The sanctifying action of the Holy Spirit is the object before which the activity of the Church is passive.

52. Ibid., 30–31.
53. Ibid., 31.
54. Ibid., 151.
55. Ibid., 37.
56. Ibid., 137.

Even before looking more closely at how Hütter treats Christian action in a more explicit way, some important differences between *Theologie als kirchliche Praktik* (*Suffering Divine Things*) and *Evangelische Ethik als kirchliches Zeugnis* emerge. In the earlier book, Christian practice, the practice that stemmed from the promise of God to work in the Church, was shaped by perception and understanding emerging from narrative and the conviction that God works in the Church. In *Suffering Divine Things*, that is certainly no longer the case. God's action is already shown to be the primary and determinative factor before which Christian practice must be first and foremost passive. Our activity, as Church, is constituted by and formed by God's action through the Holy Spirit and our agency is passive to such work. In his first book, the ambition of "Beieinander" is not realized in Hütter's description of the Christian moral act because God's agency was estranged from human action. In *Suffering Divine Things*, exactly the opposite is the problem: God's agency stands as the singular determinative factor in the form of the Christian life and in the actualization of Christian practice. However, the place given to God's agency is so central that human agency seems to get in the way. The "poiesis" that would emerge from the Christian moral agent is seen as in competition and conflict with the "poiesis" of God. Our "pathos" before God's agency as contrasted with the poiesis of our own agency shows the dramatic shift between Hütter's 1993 book and the 1997 work. As in his earlier book, Hütter is in conversation with Karl Barth, and this conversation looks, as it did in 1993, to the Chalcedonian logic Barth employs to talk about the parallel work of God and human action that constitutes action in the Church. In *Evangelische Ethik als kirchliches Zeugnis*, Hütter concluded that the "missing middle" of this logic proved a useful flaw. While Barth's theology failed to achieve an actual connection between divine and human action, it nonetheless showed the need to address this connection and indicated the power of God to do it. Likewise in this piece, Hütter looks to Barth for at least the broad framework demonstrating the necessity of a meeting point between divine and human action to fill this "missing middle." For Barth, "the consequence of this diastatic determination of the relation between God and human beings within the framework of a comprehensive logic of action involving two irreducible subjects is precisely this 'absent center,' a center that can be filled only again and again in the joint acting of these two subjects."⁵⁷ The importance of a "Beieinander" still seems to be at stake. Yet Hütter shifts from his earlier work in seeking more than the internal conviction of God's action in the Church and more than the shift of perspective, descriptors, and understanding forged by God's action. Such conceptions mean that the locus of faith is exiled from the life of the Church to the intersubjectivity of the individual believer, which is precisely the problem he claimed to be at the root of the loss of the public character and relevance of the Church at the beginning of the book. Writing against Barth, "if indeed all human action *per se* can at best refer either anticipatorially or in response to this event, and yet if God's action in principle has never nor will it ever tie itself to any human action, then God's actions can be conceived only as becoming evident as God's self-manifestation in the interiority of the believer."⁵⁸ Such a bond between divine and human action is an ambition falling far short of Hütter's goal, as it means the loss of the public character and authority of the Church. The meeting of divine and human action takes place as a part of the living practice of the Church, and not simply as a premise in the heart of the individual believer. He argues that for Barth, the action of the Church does not constitute a "conjunction" but is rather an obediential yielding to the action of God. "The concrete obedience of the church is a human action, a 'responding' action of the church toward Christ and the Spirit, for according to Barth, the word and Spirit together constitute the concrete point at which the mediate authority of the church subordinated itself visibly and concretely to the immediate authority of Christ."⁵⁹ Again, Barth, even in his mistakes, turns out to be a useful lens. As in *Evangelische Ethik als kirchliches Zeugnis*, in which Hütter takes issue with Barth's failure to find a genuine bond between divine and human action, in this book the same failure is noted, but in a different way. Barth's notion of a "response" proves a useful mistake, in that (especially for the activity of theology) it is meant to be some connection between God's action and our own in the ecclesial setting that produces some authority. Again, though, Barth's theology fails to provide this connection: The problem of the "missing middle" remains. The "center" that is meant to be the connection between divine and human action, "lacks any unequivocal referent, quite unlike the origi-

57. Hütter, *Suffering Divine Things*, 109.
58. Ibid.
59. Ibid., 105.

nal Christological 'life setting' of the Chalcedonian definition. . . . The construction does not provide for the Holy Spirit to tie itself to such a confession or for such a confession to express human action 'in' the Spirit such that the confession itself might be understood as a work of the Holy Spirit."[60] The crucial difference between his critique of Barth in 1993 and in 1997, however, is that in the latter instance, he advocates a bond between divine and human agency in which we passively receive God's action, and thus Church action is forged. Instead of a connection in which our action connects to God's promise of action, his more recent critique of Barth looks for a way in which our action finds its place "in" God's action and thus is understood more as God's work than our own. Again, a competitive treatment of divine and human agency is at work here. Our action is inversely proportional to God's action in Church practice, just as much in this book as in the last. But the difference here is that Hütter asks his reader to view Church practice as a moment in which our activity is more properly called passivity to God's action. We undergo God's creative activity as pathos: this is our action. Hütter's primary pursuit in this work is to show the application of this passivity before God's agency to public character and authority of the Church in its practice of theology.

However, Hütter does not confine this passivity to the authenticity of theology with regard to the category of revelation. Theology is too connected to the practices of the Church for that to be the case. He writes that "theology as a church practice needs the horizon of canon, the core practices, and doctrine. . . . The object of discursive theological practice is thus never immediately accessible; it is accessible only through the biblical canon, the core church practices, and the tradition of church doctrine."[61] The unique "Beieinander" that Hütter seeks in this later work is notably public. The practice of the Church and the object of this practice meet in the public action of the Church itself. The activity of theology is intimately bound up with the practices of the Church. "The soteriological mission of the church as the public of the Holy Spirit must be understood as the specific nexus of church practices and church doctrine within which theology is to be situated as a distinct church practice itself, indeed, as an aspect inhering within the

---

60. Ibid., 106–7.
61. Ibid., 141.

telos of this public."⁶² The Church itself is the public of the Holy Spirit and the setting of the meeting between divine and human agency. While the particular activity of theology is a quintessential instance, the path by which Christians are sanctified occurs through the larger context of "core" Church practices, and not just the activity of theology. "Although [these practices] do indeed refer to human activities, through them the human being 'undergoes' or 'is subject to' the actions of the Holy Spirit."⁶³ Only in this context does theology have its true character. The practices of the Church are the public expression of the action of the Holy Spirit in which our agency is caught up, overwhelmed, redeemed, and before which we are to be passive. These practices are the poiesis of the Holy Spirit before which our agency must remain captive: "the *vita passiva* of faith and then also of theology is a participation in God's freedom insofar as it is rapt into that freedom by allowing itself to be 'taken prisoner' by the work of the Holy Spirit."⁶⁴ Our freedom in these practices is in the imprisonment of our agency. For the life of faith, as with the activity of theology, the work of the Holy Spirit contests with our agency, and our passivity before God's action is the meeting of divine and human agency.

In *Suffering Divine Things*, Reinhard Hütter interacts a great deal more with Martin Luther than he did in his previous work. In articulating the Church practices in which our agency is "taken prisoner" and "subject to," or "suffering," the action of the Holy Spirit, he looks to the "core" Church actions articulated by Luther. These actions speak to the moral life of every Christian, and not just to priestly and theological activities. According to Luther, these are the core Church practices: "(1) the external, orally preached word of God (which includes believing, confessing, and acting in accordance with it); (2) baptism; (3) the Lord's Supper; (4) the office of the keys as church discipline; (5) ordination and offices; (6) public prayer, praise, thanksgiving, instruction; and (7) discipleship in suffering. The economic mission of the Holy Spirit, its soteriological work of sanctification and renewal, is performed *through* these seven activities."⁶⁵ Numbers one and seven ought to catch our attention most particularly. Acting in accord with the word of God is a part of that which the Holy Spirit accomplishes in us, before which our

62. Ibid., 126.
63. Ibid., 131.
64. Ibid., 152.
65. Ibid., 129.

agency is captive and passive, "rapt" into God. As it turns out, Hütter's 1997 book applies to conceptions of Christian moral action as much as does his 1993 book, despite his major shift in position. The (every-) Christian practices of acting in accordance with the word of God, the actions of public prayer, and the practice of discipleship in suffering are just as much the context of the nexus producing theology as are the Eucharist or ordination. The meeting between human and divine action that is the task of passivity, of yielding to and suffering God's action in the Holy Spirit, encompasses our moral action and our discipleship. In fact, their very capacity to be passive moments before God (in the seeming competition between God's agency and our own) sets them aside as "core" practices. "These practices are thus distinct activities whose point is precisely their *passivum*.... They are *core* practices because other practices unique to the church can certainly also be enumerated alongside them, albeit practices in contradistinction to which these *core* practices remain constitutive for the mode of enactment of the Holy Spirit's economic mission and thus for the church itself."[66] The actions of Eucharist, Baptism, acting in accord with God's word, discipleship and the rest, are the modes of the Holy Spirit's enactment and are the content of the public character of the Church. Discipleship in suffering and action in accordance with the word of God are only *what they are* in their passivity before God's action. They are much more properly God's action than our own. It is important to note that in this work, instead of aspiring to argue for a "Beieinander," Hütter uses the metaphor of "enhypostasis"— a post-Chalcedonian Christology concept treated extensively by Barth, though Hütter cites Pannenberg as his primary modern source for the notion. Enhypostasis, at least according to Pannenberg, is a way of speaking about the reliance of Jesus' human nature on the existence of his divine nature. In the Chalcedonian definition a hypostasis that is manifest in the incarnation could not be attributed to the human nature of Jesus. Without the divine nature, Jesus' human nature would not exist (orthodoxy would not say the same thing of Jesus' divine nature, the Logos, with regard to his human nature).[67] Hütter locates the practices

---

66. Ibid., 132.

67. Pannenberg, *Jesus—God and Man*, 338. "Hence, it can be conceived by itself only by abstracting from the actual reality of Jesus' existence. In his concrete reality, the man Jesus has the ground of his existence (his hypostasis) not in himself as man but 'in' the Logos."

of the Church using this exact paradigm. They exist in the Spirit as the human nature of Jesus was incarnate of the Logos. Without the action of the Spirit, the practices of the Church would not exist, whereas without the core actions of the Church, the agency of the Holy Spirit is still a coherent idea. While Hütter is still looking for some sort of bond between divine and human agency in the Christian moral life, he now is saying that these practices "subsist enhypostatically in the Spirit. Whereas person and work are certainly to be distinguished in the case of human beings, precisely the opposite is the case with regard to the person and work of the Spirit. The *poiemata* of the Spirit, however, the core church practices, inhere the salvific-economic mission of the Spirit. This is why the reference here is to the *pneumatological enhypostasis* of the core practices."[68] The eschatological postponement of the realization of the binding of divine and human action that Hütter seemed to hold in 1993 is done away with in this later work. The creative action of the Spirit is that which the core practices undergo, and it is that which defines them. The Holy Spirit's action constitutes the foundation and the realization of Christian moral action.

But at what cost? While Hütter is able to forge some kind of contact between divine and human agency in the Christian moral act, God's action and our action are shown to be treated competitively and in inverse proportion. In this way, a notion like "enhypostasis" can be addressed using terms like "rapt," "taken prisoner," "subject to," and others. If the term "enhypostasis" is meant to speak to the twofold nature of Christ—fully human and fully divine—it is hard to see how Hütter's treatment parallels that model. According to the above material, the ecclesially contextualized Christian moral act is only fully human when it ceases to be properly free and is "taken prisoner" by the action of God, while in a theology of the incarnation, the notion of "enhypostasis" is meant to address a relationship that refuses competition between divinity and humanity (while at the same time not denying the primacy of God's causality in the matter). Hütter's adaptation accentuates the dualism and treats God's poiesis and human poiesis as inversely proportionate in the Christian moral act. The Christian moral act as existing "in the Spirit" is what sets it aside from other sorts of action, *not* as a cooperation of human and divine agency, or even an equal Beieinander (itself a perversion of the incarnation), but as an *operation of divine agency*.

68. Hütter, *Suffering Divine Things*, 133.

While in both his 1993 and his 1997 work Hütter seeks an ecclesial context in which to address the bond between human and divine agency in the joint moment of the Christian moral act, his approach changes between the two. In 1993 Hütter wrote that moral action occurs through an ecclesially situated understanding, in which description and perspective is based on the conviction of God's action. In 1997 he writes that human action must be held captive to, be passive toward, suffer, undergo, the action of the Holy Spirit. Christian moral action is no more a matter of conjunction than it was before, but this time the approach to a "Beieinander" is from the opposite end. It is only in the binding and limitation (even if this limitation is self-imposed) of human agency that the conjunction occurs. "A human being *undergoes* God's actions, is radically qualified anew through these actions, is justified and sanctified, and is permanently relationally shaped in substance."[69]

Just as in his first book, Hütter's ambition is to show the relevance of the action of the Holy Spirit to Christian ethics. He seeks to articulate the involvement of both human and divine agency in the act itself. However, his contrastive view of divine and human agency forces him into an either/or exhibited by both of his books. In both books he offers a kind of joining of divine and human agency, but one that is competitive and that leads him into dramatic shifts in argument and emphasis. Hütter is as careful in this book as in the last to speak of the importance and the need for the bond between human and divine agency in these practices. His ambition, no less than in 1993, is for the conjunction between God's action and human action in the moral act, but his contrastive tendencies mean that just as he excluded the involvement of divine agency in *Evangelische Ethik als kirchliches Zeugnis*, he does so now as well: "Although the human being is always *present* in these activities, and is always and especially *actively present*, listening, receiving, responding, praising, and rendering obedience, still this human activity does *not* constitute these practices. Human activity is indeed always an inherent part of them, but never more than that. The disposition of all seven practices is rather such that in them the human being is always the *recipient*."[70] Human agency does not constitute the Christian moral act as a part of the core practices of the Church. Ours is the part of passivity, receptivity. Hütter's own italicized emphases here could not have been

---

69. Ibid., 125.
70. Ibid., 132.

better placed. Human activity does *not* constitute these practices. If they did, they could not be actions of the Holy Spirit. The human being is always the *recipient*, for if the human being was the active agent, then the Holy Spirit would be excluded.

Hütter champions the need for a close bond of divine and human action at the foundation of Christian ethics in this second book, as he does in the first. But, in an ironic similarity to his first book, he presents a "Beieinander" in which divine and human agency run a parallel course related to one another in inverse proportion: an inclusion of one consistently accompanies an exclusion of another. In the end, while both divine agency and human agency play some part in the Christian action, their contrastive, dualistic conjunction is a far cry from the "poietic pathos" he seeks. While the "missing middle" may have narrowed, the parallel lines on either side have been drawn that much more heavily.

The Pendulum Swings Back—Bound to Be Free

In his most recent book, *Bound to Be Free* (2004), Hütter indicates just how aware of this tension he is. *Bound to Be Free* is an eclectic collection of material, the first half of which is meant to be a rearticulation and expansion of his theology as found in *Suffering Divine Things*. However, what one finds in these first six chapters is, once again, a shift in his theology. Though he pursues the same project of showing the close bond between divine and human agency in the formation of the Christian moral act as in his 1997 work, and does so using the same principal characters of the Holy Spirit and the worshipping community, he carefully and subtly alters the specifics of the relationships between the Holy Spirit, the community, and Christian action so that the end product much more closely resembles his 1993 *Evangelische Ethik als kirchliches Zeugnis* than it does his 1997 *Theologie als kirchliche Praktik (Suffering Divine Things)*. Though he does change his approach considerably in this "rearticulation," he does not come any closer to a noncompetitive bond between God's agency and human agency. If anything, the alterations of this chapter even more poignantly emphasize his difficulty in addressing this bond and the need for different conceptual tools for doing so.

In *Bound to Be Free*, Reinhard Hütter offers the first six chapters as a rehearsal of the argument as expressed in *Suffering Divine Things*, and then devotes additional chapters to "pushing this argument further."[71] Just as in his earlier work, Hütter hopes to indicate how he might return to the unapologetically public nature of the Church, but he begins (again, just as before) with the lens of the linguistic activity of theology; the genuinely and necessarily cataphatic, affirmative linguistic activity of theology. However, Hütter confines the conjunction of divine and human agency to this linguistic and intellectual activity, much more so than in his earlier work. Once again, it is public action of the Church that reasserts its genuine identity.[72] Also, just as in his previous work, Hütter puts a heavy emphasis on Martin Luther in defining just what the actions of the Church are, even offering a similar list of practices.[73] Thus, through Luther, Hütter affirms (just as he did in 1997) that the marks of the Church and the action of the Holy Spirit find their expression in the Christian ethical act.

Hütter makes it apparent very quickly, however, that he means something very different by "the Spirit's concrete work" than he did before, and instead of an inherently passive stance before the Spirit, ours is an active shaping of perspective based on the *knowledge* of the action of the Spirit, rather than the action of the Spirit itself. In what is meant to be a repetition of his earlier arguments, Hütter writes, "The church is gifted with a promise that it carries in its very way of being the church. This promise is nothing less than a knowledge of God that both saves and transforms."[74] This "saving knowledge" of God is quite a far cry from the moments of human action in which our agency was held captive in passivity to the real acting subject of the Holy Spirit. In a return to his much earlier tendencies, Hütter moves the identifying marks of the Church from passivity to the action of the Holy Spirit, to that which

71. Hütter, *Bound to Be Free*, 3.

72. Ibid., 5.

73. Ibid., 50. "Luther identifies a set of particular practices as the church's constitutive marks. In them, we encounter not only 'church' but also the Spirit's concrete work, through which he fulfills his own sanctifying mission in the triune economy of salvation. These constitutive marks, or core practices, include the proclamation of God's word and its reception in faith, confession, and deed; baptism; the Lord's Supper; the office of the keys, or church discipline; ordained ministry; prayer, doxology, and catechesis; and the way of the cross, or discipleship. What we find in Luther's account is a way to conceive these distinct communal practices as concretely enacting and thus mediating the Holy Spirit's sanctifying work."

74. Ibid., 44.

comes from the knowledge of this action. Hütter continues, "Yet it is a knowledge that depends on the church's practices and in this significant sense antecedes us as individuals. Only by being drawn into those practices that in their very core are the church's makeup do we come to a knowledge of God that we do not own—a knowledge that ultimately will own us. In this specific way *the church will turn out to be the end of the subject*—precisely in its modern sense, where knowledge presupposes the subject's self-positing and, ultimately, the subject's will to power."[75] In what is meant to be a repetition of the 1997 approach, the reader finds a return to the response of 1993. Though it may be that (just as before) the knowledge of God comes to us from outside of us, there is no sense here that the Holy Spirit is the acting subject. Instead of God's action, it is *our* knowledge of God's action that antecedes us and our actions. Hütter continues to employ the imagery of "suffering" and "undergoing," but this time it is our own knowledge of God (granted that it comes from outside of us) that we are "suffering." "The knowledge of God that we suffer in faith—embodied in and lived through the core practices—as the Holy Sprit's sanctification can ultimately be reflected only in a theology of the cross. Because only here, in the cross of Christ, do we find the immoveable difference secured between the love that is God's full knowledge of us, achieved in Christ's cross—when we were still sinners, radically estranged from God—and our love, the full knowledge of God that is the completion of the Spirit's sanctifying work."[76] Again, though his arguments are cast in the language of his second book, the change is significant. We do not suffer the poiesis of God through the Holy Spirit, but rather the *knowledge* of God. This knowledge is lived through the core practices of discipleship and acting in accord with the Word of God, not through the agency of the Holy Spirit suffered in a *vita passiva*.

The human actions about which Hütter does speak are not those that follow from the revealed truths, but those that would best prepare us for the reception of revealed truths about God, namely, the practices of hospitality and the honoring of truth. These two practices intertwine to reveal the knowledge necessary to form these core practices that constitute Church and, consequently (according to Hütter), Christian moral action. He writes, "the practice of hospitality is the very training ground for honoring the truth. Only by letting ourselves be welcomed

75. Ibid.
76. Ibid., 55.

by the greeters of heaven and by ultimately welcoming them, by accepting heaven's hospitality and by extending it, can the truth about our own lives and pasts be truthfully faced—and thus forgiven. In welcoming others into our lives, especially strangers and the needy, we have to face the truth about distinct persons, about the state of the world and society, and—not least—about ourselves."[77] In a way that is extremely difficult to reconcile with his 1997 work (but fits well with his 1993 work), we prepare ourselves for this "saving knowledge of God," which is to say that we prepare ourselves for the reception of that which we "undergo." But we prepare ourselves not for a conjunction with the action of the Holy Spirit, but rather with the truth revealed by the Holy Spirit. The idea of the "concrete action" of the Holy Spirit in discipleship is only explained as those actions that follow from revealed knowledge. The Spirit is involved in revealing truths, but is, again, separated from a connection with human agency in the act itself. Hütter thus significantly limits the extent to which "the way of the cross" is a work of the Holy Spirit, as he says it must be.

Here, just as in 1993, Hütter argues for a "conjunction" of divine and human agency. God acts to reveal knowledge; we practice hospitality and honor the truth as it comes to us, and then our moral action follows from our reception of truth. While one would not go so far as to say that God is inert, here, God is nonetheless distant, active only in revealing those reorienting truths that prompt certain actions from us (and from us alone). This presents a significant clash with Hütter's earlier work in which Christian moral action is meant to be an action by the Holy Spirit as well as an action of ours. For Hütter, our hospitality to truth is meant to model itself upon God's hospitality toward creation. Hütter indicates that our reception of God's activity (even though it seems to be limited to a reception of particular knowledge that precedes action) is accompanied and made possible by God's reception of humanity.[78] Hütter still maintains that the basic ambition of a Christian moral act like hospitality is caught up with, and mirrored by, God's own action toward humanity. Even better, Hütter indicates that because of this connection, an act such as human hospitality is rightly conceived of as God's action as well as our own. Hütter argues that, rather than resting in abstractness, "truth rests in the threefold identity and agency

77. Ibid., 63.
78. Ibid., 67.

of the triune God as these identities unfold in creation, the election of Israel, the life, death, and resurrection of Jesus Christ, and the calling of the many into a communion in the life of the triune God through the Holy Spirit. The practice of hospitality is therefore rightly both a reflection and an extension of God's own hospitality—sharing the love of the triune life with those who are dust."[79] Following Hütter's argument here, both his goal and the problems with its realization are made plain. Ours is the practice of hospitality to the truth, which is the saving knowledge of God. But, rather than being stagnant, God's truth is God's activity unfolding in God's action toward humanity. Instead of speaking of receiving God's agency, Hütter prefers to use the buffer of receiving the truth of God's agency that is revealed in God's agency. Our practice of hospitality is both a reciprocation and an extension of God's hospitality. Again, one can see the general direction Hütter pursues: God's agency and our agency in an intertwining relationship in the Christian life of discipleship—our action and God's action are connected, or at least conjoined. Yet Hütter argues that the identity and agency of God, which has such bearing on us (and is an extension of God's own reception), is the truth of God's action through Jesus, the truth of God's action through the Holy Spirit, through creation, the truth of God's action in calling humanity to join into the divine perichoresis. It is the truth of God's action, rather than God's action itself.

These limitations are confirmed as Hütter makes clear that, just as in *Evangelische Ethik als kirchliches Zeugnis*, the conjunction between the truth of divine action and human agency (which has such an impact on moral action) occurs in our reception of God's actions in the Church. "Christian knowledge of God can be gained only by suffering God's saving activity as it engages us in word and sacrament as well as the rest of the church's core practices and as it commits us to preaching and teaching (*doctrina evangelii*) through those normative formulations (*doctrina definita*; doctrine) that help us hold on to the gospel in the face of its distortion."[80] We receive God's action (indeed, suffer God's action) through our experience of the Holy Spirit in its concrete enactment in the core Church practices (of which discipleship and acting in accord with the Word of God is one). Thus (just as Hütter says it must be) our reception of the truth of God is our reception of God's action. In short,

79. Ibid., 68.
80. Ibid., 45.

just as before, a "core Church practice" is a moment of the conjunction of human action and divine action. We are hospitable to the truth of God's action—we suffer God's action—and thus discipleship is accomplished. Yet, the same questions persist in this book that the reader was left asking of the other two: How can we say that both God's agency and human agency are at work in discipleship? If discipleship (as one of the core practices) is an action of the Holy Spirit, then how is our agency engaged in the process? Do we merely passively receive God's agency? If discipleship is an action that follows from the reception of the saving knowledge of God imparted in the life of the Church, then how is God's agency involved at the level of the individual? Hütter makes clear that "participating in these [core] practices provides the ongoing occasion for 'suffering' the Spirit's sanctifying work, for growing in faith.... Thus saving knowledge of God entails being engaged and transformed by the Spirit's sanctifying work and thereby increasingly drawn into God's triune life."[81] Yet his theology lacks the tools to explicate just what it means to be "engaged by the Spirit's sanctifying work." Is it a reception or an action? Hütter insists that, through reception and participation in God's knowledge via the core practices, we "suffer" the Spirit's work. How is human action in discipleship a suffering of the Spirit's work? There can be little doubt that Hütter's ambition is to show a very close connection between what it means to receive God's work in the Spirit and to be active within God's work in the Spirit, yet the specifics of his treatment lead at best to a conjunction, as they did in 1993 and in 1997. Ultimately, he offers a theology that strives to show the way in which human agency is "increasingly drawn into God's triune life," but unable to provide any noncompetitive connection between the two.

Just as in *Evangelische Ethik als kirchliches Zeugnis*, Hütter explains this connection as our bond with God's truth through the revealed narrative, rather than with God's agency itself. "In the proclamation of God's word, in baptism, in the Lord's Supper, the gospel addresses and claims us in tangible and specific ways; in ordained office, prayer, doxology, catechesis, and the suffering walk of discipleship, the gospel engages us in a personal, intellectual, and most deeply existential way."[82] Hauerwas' notion of a narrative that encompasses and shapes the Christian life echoes loudly here. In the worshipping life of the Church, the truth of

---

81. Ibid., 53.
82. Ibid., 50.

the Gospel encounters us in an active way and engages us on an individual basis. Yet, once more, tools to talk about why this engagement is so "personal, intellectual and most deeply existential" are fairly thin. We are embraced by the truth of the Gospel (and thus engaged by the action of God) through our connection to God in worship and doctrine alone.[83] In such a profound limiting of our modes of reception of God's truth (which he himself says is God's triune agency as well), it becomes even more difficult to see the coherence of the idea that discipleship is a concrete action of the Holy Spirit. Unless the whole of our moral life can be confined to our time in worship or our active contemplation of narrative or doctrine, it is extremely challenging to see how acting in accord with the Word can be said to connect to God's agency at all, except through knowledge that precedes the moral situation.

Reinhard Hütter's treatments provide crucially important promptings to the contemporary ecumenical ethical conversation. He indicates morality as an enactment of the Holy Spirit. He speaks to the necessity of a conjunction between divine and human agency as a crucial subject in what moral theology must address. He pursues a theology in which we rely on God's action, and that reliance is exactly what makes our own free agency to be what it is. He lifts up the dynamics internal to the Christian worshipping community as the setting for moral transformation. He, too, highlights a "missing middle." His work shows the need to expand language and thinking about the bond between divine and human agency in Christian ethics because despite addressing these same issues for the third book in a row, internal tension persists. Hütter's long struggle with these issues remains invaluable to the discourse. His writing exhibits both the importance and the difficulty of describing Christian ethics in such a way that free human agency and divine agency both have genuine, efficacious roles. Even more beneficially to those who read his work, he shows the importance of this relationship in concert with the centrality of Scripture (and the transformation it offers), and the context of the Christian worshipping community. God's grace is central in his account of ethics, and is inseparable from God's grace in the liturgy, Christian community, and the Christian narrative. These strides push the discourse into new and important territory, making the lack of a description of a noncompetitive bond between divine and human agency in the moral life that much more poignant.

83. Ibid., 77.

Promising Trends in Recent Literature

Reinhard Hütter's more recent works seems to be conscious of this tension, and even conscious of the potential sources of its solution. In his 2007 "St. Augustine and St. Thomas on Grace and Free Will in the *Initium Fidei*," Hütter sets himself about the ambitious task of articulating the relationship (if any) between divine and human action in the first act of the beginning of faith. The piece looks most especially to show (in a way very unlike his earlier treatments) that in this singular moment, God's grace is deeply connected with human freedom. He stages this inquiry in the interpretation of Augustine by the Reformation theologians, especially Erasmus and Luther. Finally, he lifts up Thomas Aquinas as the best interpretation, to date, of Augustine's anti-Pelagian arguments about grace and free will.

Some passages in this article not only qualify the arguments examined in his previous writings but in some cases entirely reverse them. In framing the misinterpretation of Augustine by Reformation theologians, he condemns Martin Luther for the exact argument that he championed in *Suffering Divine Things*. He says that Luther's interpretation of the place of human freedom in the beginning of faith was reactionary. He writes, "Luther's corrective move veered to the opposite extreme: God is not merely the first but the sole agent of the act of conversion, with the human in a state of utter passivity."[84] As he articulates again, further into the piece, "In an effort to set the record straight once and for all, Luther went too far: God is not merely the first and final agent of human salvation but its sole agent, with the human remaining purely passive."[85] While in 1997, Hütter argued for the importance of the *vita passiva* of the Christian before divine agency in the moral life as articulated by Luther, he here sees Luther's solution as excluding a necessary connection between divine and human agency in the single moment in which the sinner is turned to God. A gap opens in Hütter's treatment of the structure of Christian action in which there must be an actual bond between God's action and human action in at least this one instance.

As he goes on to articulate the importance of this bond, he offers thorough treatments of several metaphysical points from the theology of

---

84. Hütter, "St. Augustine and St. Thomas on Grace and Free Will in the *Initium Fidei*," 526.

85. Ibid., 529.

Thomas Aquinas. Most especially he centers on the natural relationship between God's causation and human, secondary causation, and God's causation of secondary, contingent effects. As he explains the first of these two points, he highlights arguments from Aquinas that stand quite antithetically to his previous works. For instance, he writes that "God as external cause is in no way extrinsic to the creature's nature or existence but external only to the creature's proximate causality."[86] In this instance at least, Hütter does not qualify this statement as applying only to the *initium fidei*. Framing human causality, as he does, in the context of a metaphysic of being, Hütter argues that God's causation of human willing constitutes a harmonious bond since God is the cause of all that is and all that moves. With this new approach, Hütter finally articulates an idea toward which his writing career has gestured, but never managed to achieve. From Thomas Aquinas, he gains the notion that "God's external causality remains transcendent causality all the way down and hence is not competitive with the internal proximate causality of the will—whose first universal mover is also God."[87] Hütter, in his more recent writing, begins to realize the importance of articulating a bond between human and divine agency that is connected in an interactive and noncompetitive way. Again, such an articulation is centered primarily around treating the singular moment of the *initium fidei*, rather than tracing its broader implications to the larger context of the Christian moral life. Even so, the notion of a noncompetitive bond between divine and human agency in the Christian life is a new one for Hütter. This exciting new direction, and the impact of a source like Thomas Aquinas has obviously had on his thought, has brought Hütter to the brink of realizing the direction in which the rest of his earlier literature has already pointed: a noncompetitive relationship between divine and human agency in the Christian moral life as a whole, as well as in particular actions.

In another 2007 article, "The Christian Life," written as a part of a larger collection on systematic theology, Hütter offers some similarly promising remarks about the place of divine grace in the moral life. While they are not nearly as striking as those found in "St Augustine and St. Thomas on Grace and Free Will in the *Initium Fidei*," Hütter does offer a corrective to another of the key authorities his books have cited: Karl Barth. In this second piece, Hütter writes, "divine and human

---

86. Ibid., 545.
87. Ibid., 545–46.

agency stand in a differentiated, dialectical unity of infinite qualitative difference: two comprehensive, mutually non-exclusive and non-competitive causal agencies. However, Barth neither offers an integrated account of the two agential causalities nor draws upon the notion of operative qualities, that is, accounts of acquired or infused virtues."[88] While Hütter still argues that Barth offers an account of the bond between divine and human agency that is noncompetitive, he begins to realize that the basis of this lack of competition is that the two never actually meet. He argues, here, what he neglected in *Evangelische Ethik als kirchliches Zeugnis*, which is that Barth does a very adequate job of describing the fundamental difference between God's action and human action, and even places them running in a useful parallel at times, but does not offer what Hütter's ethics seek: a relational bond between divine and human agency, in at least some small part of Christian life. These trends are a new step in Hütter's long-term struggle with the relationship between God's grace and human action in the moral life. They set the stage for tools that will help realize the description of that connection.

---

88. Hütter, "Christian Life," 296.

3

Common Threads

STANLEY HAUERWAS AND REINHARD HÜTTER point the contemporary discourse in theological ethics into important new territory. In different ways, they both highlight God's grace in Jesus Christ as the cornerstone of the Christian moral life. They both do so in impressively concrete and practical terms, describing an ethic that springs from the praxis of daily Christian existence. For both Hütter and Hauerwas, Christian ethical existence is inseparable from Christian liturgical life, Christian encounter with Scripture, and God's work in the Christian worshipping community. They both refuse the division between individual and community Christian ethics and blur the lines between Christian doctrine, Christian narrative, Christian community, and Christian ethics. As this treatment puts them in conversation with Aquinas, their great strengths in these areas will be even more apparent. While they are theologically "thick" in these areas (a "thickness" that is much-needed in conversation with Aquinas), they are "thin" in describing the bedrock of their ethics—a cooperative, noncompetitive connection between God's grace and free human agency in the moral life. This chapter will lift out some of the consistent themes in their areas of great strength and (in tandem with the next chapter) show how Aquinas can be useful for filling out their weaker areas.

Theologians like Hauerwas and Hütter push the contemporary ethical conversation toward a community-centered, historically and liturgically contextualized ethic in which God's grace and human agency have a noncompetitive connection. To aid in realizing this description, I offer a conversation with Thomas Aquinas, especially his descriptions of God's grace, the New Law, and the Gifts of the Holy Spirit. Thomas has a unique and striking ability in describing free human agency as naturally created to be permeable to the saturation of God's grace. To Hauerwas, Hütter, and the contemporary ethical conversation as a whole, Thomas can offer a few tools for articulating a noncompetitive bond between God's agency and human action. Though his description of the Christian ethical life can benefit from interaction with contemporary sources, his theology offers much-needed tools for an ecumenically expressed, community-centered ethic of God's grace.

Before turning to Thomas for these tools, however, two steps are necessary, the sum of which will constitute the content of this (in many ways preliminary) chapter: First, I will trace some common threads in the ways that Hütter and Hauerwas point to the efficacy of God's grace in terms of the moral life. As it happens, it is precisely along the contours of these patterns that Aquinas can be the most help, and from which his system can draw the most benefit, as well. Second, I will explain some of my boundaries and parameters in the chapter treating Thomas Aquinas. As will be shown, the themes on which I will focus—the New Law, the Gifts of the Holy Spirit, and the divisions regarding grace—are integrally connected and solve for many of the same problems. These three themes enjoy a very diverse treatment across Thomas' writings, and simply pulling bits of ideas without regard for the evolution of his thoughts on these matters (which was considerable) would result in a very scattered and internally consistent treatment. Therefore, it is necessary to speak very clearly about the writings from which I will be drawing and where those writings fit in the larger picture of the development of Aquinas' thought.

In the next chapter, with those two preliminary steps in place, I will demonstrate what Thomas' ideas about the New Law, the Gifts of the Holy Spirit, and the divisions regarding grace might have to offer the specific directions and laudable instincts of strains in the contemporary theological-ethical discourse aiming at a close involvement of God's agency in the moral life, especially as represented by Hauerwas and Hütter.

Promising Patterns

Rightly ordered Christian moral life, as described by Hauerwas and Hütter, proceeds along patterns that are remarkable not only for their similarity with one another, but in their fruitful compatibility with a much older attempt at a similar project—Thomas Aquinas. Though explained in quite different ways, both Hauerwas and Hütter tend toward three common patterns when explaining the involvement of God's grace in the moral life. These three patterns are themes that Aquinas will take up as well, but with different strengths and different weaknesses, and using somewhat different terms. Hauerwas and Hütter have opened space in the contemporary discourse for some sophisticated descriptions of free human agency and God's grace, and it is, therefore, their terms and their patterns that help enfold these tools into modern Christian ethics. In their respective attempts to show how close the involvement of God's grace in the moral life really is, Hauerwas and Hütter tend toward three themes (all three of which will prove remarkably compatible with Aquinas): (1) The indispensability of the Gospel narrative and the connection of that narrative with the effect of God's agency in the Christian moral life; (2) God's resituating of our character by gift as the starting point for the impact of God's agency in the moral life; and (3) the necessity of God's agency as being intimately involved in the moral life, proceeding from a connection that is noncompetitive and cooperative between human and divine action. Hauerwas and Hütter share these three means of describing the involvement of God's agency in the Christian moral life, and it is along these contours that Aquinas best contributes to their trajectories.

The Indispensability of the Gospel Narrative

Hauerwas, in particular, gives quite a heavy emphasis to the first theme, the centrality of the Gospel narrative, and the connection between this narrative and God's role in the moral life. As shown in an earlier chapter, Hauerwas tended in his earliest publications to argue for a picture of the Christian character that was completely self-determined and a Christian agency that was, basically, self-caused. As his thought developed, however, he began to speak of the ways in which Christian character and the Christian moral act were in fact determined by the worshipping community, which in turn was profoundly shaped by the Gospel narrative. The history of the Christian community constitutes its identity, and that history and identity center on the revealed Gospel narrative. God's impact on the moral life occurs through community and individual reception of Scripture (and more specifically, the Gospels). Hauerwas writes that Scripture "not only 'renders a character' but renders a community capable of ordering its existence appropriate to such stories. . . . this narrative does nothing less than render the character of God and in doing so renders us to be the kind of people appropriate to that character."[1] The transformative power of receiving the biblical narrative is very closely connected with (if not, in fact, constitutive of) God's impact upon the Christian moral life. The Gospel narrative is central to his Christian ethic, connecting, as he does, the efficacy of the Gospel narrative with God's agency in the moral life.

Reinhard Hütter's theology exhibits a surprising oscillation between the careful shaping of a self-determined Christian action and the *vita passiva* of careful hospitality to God's action. Still, the Gospel narrative operates centrally and irreplaceably in his Christian ethic, and is very closely connected with how God's agency is involved in the Christian moral life. This was certainly true with his 1993 *Evangelische Ethik als kirchliches Zeugnis*, in which he articulated a system that has a great deal in common with Hauerwas, especially with regard to the Gospel narrative. In this early piece, innovation in Christian ethics "anticipates the renewal of the Holy Spirit in the place of the worship service and . . . proves itself in the Church discourse praxis of narrative casuistry."[2] The casuistry of the narrative functions for Hütter in a way is very similar to that in Hauerwas' theology. But, even more than for Hauerwas, this early work of Hütter's exhibits an even closer connection between the action of the Holy Spirit in the Church and the shaping power of the Gospel narrative. The impact of God's agency upon the moral life finds specific moments of Christian moral action through the shaping power of the Gospel narrative. Hütter's second book is considerably different, employing the terms "suffering" and "undergoing," "pathos" and "poiesis," in explaining the connection between divine and human agency in the moral life. However, in his 2004 "rearticulation" of this earlier book, it becomes the knowledge of God that is "undergone," and "suffered," rather than God's agency. Our bond with God's agency is through the revealed narrative. "In the proclamation of God's word, in baptism, in the Lord's Supper, the gospel addresses and claims us in tangible and specific

---

1. Hauerwas, *Community of Character*, 67.

2. Hütter, *Evangelische Ethik*, 278. Im *Entdeckungszusammenhang* kirchlicher Ethik geht es dann um die eine vom Begründungszusammenhang her informierte *Urteilsbildung*, die die Erneuerung des Geistes am Ort des Gottesdienstes erwartet und sich in der kirchlichen Diskurspraxis narrativer Kasuistik bewährt.

ways; in ordained office, prayer, doxology, catechesis, and the suffering walk of discipleship, the gospel engages us in a personal, intellectual, and most deeply existential way."[3] For Hütter as well, then, the encounter with the Gospel narrative is an indispensable part of Christian moral existence, and is very intimately bound up with the impact of God's agency in the moral life.

For Hauerwas and Hütter, then, an initial theme emerges in the ways they have addressed the connection between God's agency and the Christian moral life: the Gospel narrative is very closely bound with the ways in which God's agency impacts the moral life. It must be admitted that these theologians do not hold such a theme consistently in each work, nor do they speak about the content of the Gospel narrative and its impact in the same way. However, the centrality of the Gospel is an often repeated theme, and is consistently connected with the relationship between Christian action and God's agency.

God's Resituating of Our Character by Gift

The second theme that appears with consistency in these thinkers as the starting point for the Christian moral life is a fundamental resituating of our character by God's gift. The initiating point of contact between God's agency and the moral life is, for Hauerwas, God's gift of a foundational grammar and narrative, forming a community of practice and story. This resituating of our character yields a different vision of the world, and makes us amenable to living, as he puts it, the truth of the Gospels. This resituating is the gift of God's new language: the Church. The fundamental resituating of character and agency described by Hütter is a formation of conviction and perception in God's gift, renewing the mind and making one hospitable to the praxis discourse of the Christian narrative. Though these two theologians treat God's fundamental resituating of character and agency as the initial starting point in the moral life, this tendency will prove an important contact point with Aquinas.

For Hauerwas, the centrality of narrative and the God's resituating of character as a starting point of moral transformation are very closely connected, and both notions are integral to the ways in which he points to God's agency connecting with Christian morality. The Gospel narrative and Christian community—both rightly named as God's language for

---

3. Hütter, *Bound to Be Free*, 50.

Hauerwas—provide a fundamentally new context for character development. Through these gifts, one's descriptions of one's self, one's world, and one's vision of that world are profoundly reframed. This foundational grammar and changed vision is the starting point of character in the moral life, for Hauerwas. The "language" of the church, as well as the Christian narrative, "requires a transformation of the self if we are to see, as well as be, truthful . . . to learn to grow into the story of Jesus as the form of God's kingdom."[4] Christian transformation begins by God's gift of resituating character in a new grammar and a new vision. These gifts make one amenable to formation by apprenticeship and practice in the worshipping community. This resituating is a potent meeting place (or at least the potential for a potent meeting place) between divine agency and free human action in the moral life for Hauerwas' theological ethic.

Through slightly different paths, Hütter comes to a similar framework and common point of potential contact with Aquinas. As a starting point for the moral life, Hütter names transformation of concept and perception under the heading of a "renewal of the mind." In his first book, he adopted a role for narrative in the moral life, as does Hauerwas. The focus on transformation of concept and perspective finds its most potent setting in his most recent book, however, in which he not only emphasizes the role of the Church as providing important conceptual models for the moral life with God, but also emphasizes the necessary Christian disposition of hospitality to these truths. God acts in the Church, and Christians are drawn into these practices and thus receive the gift of a "saving knowledge" that fundamentally resituates and ultimately "owns" us. Further, for Hütter, the actual work of the Holy Spirit is the shaping of conviction and perception, the formation of judgment through narrative casuistry, which he calls a "praxis discourse." He uses Romans 12:1–2 as a paradigm for the work of the Holy Spirit in the Christian moral life, a passage that ends with the words, "be transformed by the renewing of your minds, so that you may discern what is the will of God—what is good and acceptable and perfect." The gift of the Holy Spirit fundamentally resituates Christian character and agency, making them amenable to the will of God, or as he frames it in 2004, hospitable to the truth. In patterns similar to Hauerwas, Hütter describes an ethic in which God's gift deeply transforms the context of one's character and action. Like Hauerwas, too, this is a potent meeting point (or, again,

---

4. Hauerwas, *Peaceable Kingdom*, 30.

the potential for a potent meeting point) between God's agency and free human action in the Christian moral life.

Divine and Human Agency in the Christian Moral Life

The third and final theme common to Hauerwas and Hütter as they write about the role of God in the moral life has been treated extensively already, but bears brief repetition: they both champion (though imperfectly) an intimate, noncompetitive bond between divine and human agency in Christian action. More precisely, they talk about the importance, not just of divine agency as the *sine qua non* of Christian moral action, but of a connection between God's agency and our own in the Christian moral act. Hauerwas speaks consistently of the grace of God and the action of the Holy Spirit "saving and enabling us" in the Christian moral life. For Hauerwas, the Christian moral life is not meant to be isolated, but joined with (indeed, a partaking of) God's life.[5] Not only does God's grace stand at the foundation of Christian moral existence, but the bond between God's grace and human action constitutes the uniquely Christian moral act. Hütter's work valiantly strives for an articulation of this connection. In his first book, the bond of "Beieinander" with God's agency was the important category for Christian moral action. In his second book, the Holy Spirit was explained to be the acting subject in Christian moral action, and the bond between our agency and God's was one of receptivity. By his final treatment, it becomes the knowledge of God that saves and transforms, but it is no less our connection with the saving actions of God in the Church that remains the foundation of Christian moral action.

These three tendencies exhibited by Hauerwas and Hütter are promising patterns for a contemporary recovery of a grace-centered ethic, and a sound foundation for dialogue with a thinker like Aquinas. These three themes of (1) the irreplaceable Gospel narrative and the connection of the effect of this narrative with the impact of God's agency in the Christian moral life, (2) God's resituating of our character by gift as a starting point for the Christian moral life and as a meeting place of God's agency and free human action in the moral life, and (3) the necessity of not only God's action, but also of an intimate connection between

5. Ibid., 27. For Hauerwas, in Christian moral action, "we participate morally in God's life. For our God is a God who wills to include us within his life. This is what we mean when we say, in shorthand as it were, that God is a God of grace."

God's action and human action in the Christian moral life, are all very important instincts.

Thomas Aquinas, in treating the importance of divine agency in Christian moral life, begins in very similar places. His treatments of the New Law, the Gifts of the Holy Spirit, and Grace exhibit very similar themes in articulating the importance of God's action to Christian action, and the connection between divine and human agency in the Christian moral life. Before turning to such a treatment, however, I offer some brief remarks on the parameters of this treatment and the organization for lifting up the tools Aquinas can offer to help the contemporary ethical discourse better articulate a bond between divine and human agency in the Christian moral life.

Thomistic Promptings

In proposing tools for an ecumenical ethic of grace in community, it is worth taking some cues from Hauerwas and Hütter, especially in the ways each has argued for the importance of Christian ethics as a meeting point between divine and human agency. I have indicated some patterns in their arguments for this meeting point, specifically (1) the intimate, noncompetitive bond of God's grace and human action, (2) Christian ethics beginning with God's gift fundamentally resituating character and agency, and (3) the close connection between the work of the Holy Spirit in Christian community and the transformative power of the New Testament narrative. I have also indicated that these important trajectories are in need of additional tools. In the next chapter, I will offer an in-depth treatment of some potentially useful tools from the theology of Thomas Aquinas, particularly his distinctions regarding the effects of grace, the Gifts of the Holy Spirit, and the twofold sense of the New Law. Given the detail in which Aquinas presents these ideas, however, it is worth pausing for a moment to consider the application of them (along with a few resources from Aquinas' modern readership) to the contemporary discourse.

The application of the theology of Thomas Aquinas onto a particular strain of contemporary theological ethics might strike some as not particularly harmonious. Styles of argument and use of sources differ considerably. Both Hauerwas and Hütter (unlike Aquinas) use a minimum of scriptural interpretation and relatively little contemporary philosophy in their writing. This is not to say, of course, that such interpretation and such philosophical tools fail to inform their theologies—quite the opposite, in fact. Nonetheless, some flexibility and adaptation is necessary. In offering articulations of Aquinas on Grace, the Gifts, and the New Law, I speak more directly to how these ideas, at their core, might help prompt an ecumenical ethic of grace in community. Rather than insisting upon each detail of these concepts, as explained by Aquinas, I seek a broader application of these tools. In the paragraphs that follow, I will use the specific contours of the contemporary discourse (especially the patterns from Hauerwas and Hütter) to show the usefulness of the conceptual tools provided by Thomas Aquinas and the great benefit of including even a broad application these tools.

The Usefulness of Thomistic Distinctions on Grace

The distinctions Thomas provides in his treatise on grace offer fruitful and useful tools for prompting a wider ethic of grace in community. The strains of the contemporary ethical discourse outlined in this work demonstrate just how important it is to find a way of describing a bond between God's agency and human agency in Christian ethics, as well as the difficulty of finding a means to do so. In their own ways, Hauerwas and Hütter have tried to show the importance of pointing to moments of contact between divine and human agency in the moral life. Both, too, show just how hard it is to articulate this bond in a way that does not compromise descriptions of God's transcendence or bow to the threat of determinism.

Thomas can be of significant help here. An ecumenical ethic of grace that takes the tools within his treatise on grace into account gains deeper concepts for addressing just what it means to be engaged in properly Christian action. Christian moral action has God's grace as its center, as Hauerwas and Hütter rightly emphasize, but an ethic that relies on this bond must make a number of important distinctions, even at the most elementary level. Foundational questions about the origin and purpose of moral action help sharpen the problem: Am I supposed to behave ethically because it is natural to me? If ethical behavior is natural, does that mean I can do it without God's help? Does God ask me to do things that are beyond my natural capacity? If ethical behavior is not natural, then is it fair that God asks me to do it? Does a person need some kind of healing from God to act ethically? Are there moral actions that God simply accomplishes through me in which I am merely a recipient? Are there Christian moral acts in which God invites me into cooperation? The risk of despair on the one hand or a flat-footed Pelagianism on the other demands a way to differentiate frameworks for the bond between human and divine agency in different sorts of moral action that involve a bond with divine agency. It would be ludicrous to suggest that in each instance of moral action, Christians would have to know the exact details behind the bond between divine and human agency—most of those men and women praised as moral exemplars in the Gospels and the Christian tradition were not systematicians. Still, being aware of the differences in this bond between divine and human agency is extremely instructive in recovering an ecumenical ethic of grace. Awareness of the difference between Christian ethical action that must be accomplished through us and action in which we are cooperative and between the role of sin and the healing of justification is a must, if only done in the abstract.

As I will discuss in detail in the next chapter, Thomas offers some division in the effects of God's grace in the Christian moral life in the *Prima Secundae*. Each division offers some useful precision in better articulating what a grace-centered ethic might be, and in exactly what ways God can be said to be involved in the moral life while safeguarding human freedom. These distinctions will be examined at length in the next chapter, but their great potential for fruitful inclusion in the contemporary discourse can be seen even before the detail he provides is introduced. Aquinas argues for a difference between an effect of God's grace that results in a change in habit (having a continual effect on the moral agent in ways that he will explain), and a more immediate effect of "*auxilium*" or "help" (more oriented toward distinct moments of action, rather than longer-term shaping of ethical character). In short, Thomas prompts his readers to think about the difference between an effect of grace oriented toward *all* moral acts and an effect of grace oriented toward *only one* action. Additionally, Thomas articulates a difference between grace that is operative (purely a gift from God, operative upon us without any involvement of our agency) and grace that is cooperative (no less a pure gift from God, but in which God draws our free agency into cooperation in such a way that God's act and our act result in a single act). In short, Thomas again leads his readers to a useful distinction, this time between those effects of grace that are accomplished in us, but without our action, and those effects in which God invites us into a cooperative involvement. Thus, Thomas enumerates four "types" of effect in and from God's grace: operative and habitual, cooperative and habitual, operative *auxilium*, and cooperative *auxilium*.

Theologians like Kobusch, McGrath, and Rogers[6] have indicated a degree of discomfort with the specific language Thomas adapts to address these differences, particularly with regard to habit and the problems of a system in which someone can "have" some quality that leads to meritorious action. Alternatively, Tanner, another Protestant theologian, sees the category of habit as a very useful concept for detailing Christian moral action. She writes that "an infused created habit sufficient for further increases in the gifts of God's grace heads off the idea that God's power becomes the creature's own, and makes clear that the human free will unrevised by grace is not a principle factor in God's salvation of us."[7] The key word, of course, is "infused." While Kobusch, McGrath, Rogers, and others object to the use of the particularly Aristotelian term "habit," there is much to be treasured in the kind of shaping that Aquinas tries to indicate with it, and the distinction he explains within it. Aquinas offers a distinction between the kind of disposition, or habit, or character, or shape-of-the-person-in-her-action that is the result of human practice or acting, and that habit or character or shape-of-the-person-in-her-action that is the cause of practice or acting. The former is something we do without the involvement of God's justifying and sanctifying grace—we can cultivate bravery, for instance. The latter is something different. While those dispositions (character, shape-of-the-person-in-her-action, or whatever version of this category is most comfortable), like those we cultivate ourselves, can be at the foundation of action, this is quite different from an equally real habit, disposition, etc., which is purely gift. The infused habit of grace of which Thomas speaks in the *Prima Secundae* is of the second kind. God heals human nature by the grace of Jesus Christ through the Holy Spirit and inclines us toward obedience to God and the leading, guiding, directing agency of the Holy Spirit dwelling in the Christian heart. We do not "possess" or "own" or "control" or "cultivate" this kind of habit. It is the pure gift of the groundwork that makes us amenable to God's agency through the Spirit, healing us of the rebellion that we chose. As Sokolowski explains, "Aquinas makes use of the category of habit to explain how we are made able to 'act' in the super-

6. See my introduction.
7. Tanner, *God and Creation in Christian Theology*, 118.

natural context; we must receive these habits and virtues to be able to do anything at all, so they cannot be the result of our earlier performance."[8] Christian moral action is utterly dependent upon the pure gift of God's grace, even if a part of that pure gift is a lasting disposition. The usefulness of the term "habit" and the division between an infused and an acquired habit, helps move toward a description of Christian moral action as dependent upon the grace of God. We are healed of our sinfulness and made amenable to God's guidance by God alone. This healing and making-amenable is not begun anew in every moment, but is rather the gift of a lasting disposition.

However, this disposition is far from enough to end in Christian moral action. If Thomas stopped after articulating the infused habit of grace, then one might rightly accuse him of simply saying that God enables us to act well, and does so apart from God's intimate involvement (even if God does so by means of a gift). The usefulness of the distinction between grace that is habit and grace that is "*auxilium*" or "help" begins to emerge. The relationship between habit and *auxilium* is the relationship of a healed disposition, ready to be guided by God, and God's moving of such readiness into action. These are not merely academic distinctions. Thomas draws out the difference between God's healing of human moral agency, and God's actual, intimately transcendent prompting and moving of that disposition into Christian moral action. Again, the point here is that Christian moral action is utterly dependent upon the intimate involvement of the grace of God through Christ in the Holy Spirit, both in the shape of its agency and in the accomplishment of Christian moral action.

Thomas' distinction between habit and *auxilium* is the distinction between God's grace that heals us and readies us for Christian moral action, and God's grace that accomplishes that action through an intimate bond with our agency. Rogers helpfully points out that

> God's intervention is constant, unceasing, and eventful. Aquinas signals this fact with a much controverted word, *auxilium*. Non-latinist Protestants see this word translated as God's "help" and imagine that *auxilium* is a matter of God and the human being engaged in Pelagian or semi-Pelagian collaboration, God and the human being pulling on the same rope. Catholics see the same word and think of sixteenth-century controversies about the

---

8. Sokolowski, *God of Faith and Reason*, 80.

mechanics, physical or otherwise, of God's intervention. Neither the Protestant reduction nor the sixteenth-century inventions are helpful.... Like "infusion," [*auxilium*] always marks the spot where God intervenes—powerfully, sovereignly, redemptively—in human acting. But also, like "infusion" it is an *x* that marks the spot where God intervenes ... a theory would only obfuscate the simplicity of the claim, Here God acts.[9]

While such language might be a little misleading in the way it speaks of "intervention," Rogers points out that the gift of a disposition is not the same as the intimacy of God's guidance, causing, and prompting. Through this distinction, Thomas treats the difference between God's gift of healing and God's intimate presence in acting. Christian moral action depends upon both, which is to say that Christian moral action depends upon God's healing grace preparing us, and the wholly transcendent and wholly intimate action of the Holy Spirit. As Rogers continues, "God acts in us in such a way that we act. It is part of God's mercy and justice, that God gives us to participate in good works—all God's work—so that we are not left out of our salvation, but are involved in it. In *auxilium*, God bears, carries, moves, engages our wills."[10] The close and harmonious bond between God's action and our own redeemed human nature is the core of Thomas' distinction between infused habit and acquired habit, and between the habitual gift of grace and the grace of God's *auxilium*.

The same truth lies behind the distinction Aquinas makes between habitual grace that is operative and habitual grace that is cooperative. The distinction makes clear both the overabundance of God's gift (and our total reliance on that gift for Christian moral action) as well as the intimacy of the bond God establishes with our own fallen, now healed, moral agency. The one who receives the gift of operative habitual grace receives something that she could never gain on her own: the perfection that turns her core orientation to God as her true end and happiness. This is a pure gift, and it is done through us, but without us, for this is too great a task for us—we simply receive.

The gift of cooperative habitual grace does not imply the opposite, however—that we begin, side by Pelagian side, with God to "pull on the same rope" (as Rogers puts it). Rather, cooperative habitual grace is the

---

9. Rodgers, "Faith and Reason Follow Glory," 453.
10. Ibid., 453–54.

agency of God *cooperating with us* to incline us towards certain actions. Our human capabilities are extended to a new potential (not binding this word to its strict relevance for Aristotelian physics) so that we may be prompted and moved by the Holy Spirit to actions that, before this gift, were far out of our reach, and even out of our inclination and desire. It is called cooperative because our own agency is involved—not because we have muscled our way into God's action, but rather because God elects to cooperate with our willing and our acting such that our own created human agency is a part of our justification and redemption.

Thomas' distinction between the operative and cooperative *auxilium* offers similar promise to the contemporary conversation. *Auxilium* is the active, intimate, helping, engaging grace of God moving us to Christian moral action. In the distinction between operative and cooperative, Thomas allows some conceptual space between those actions that God accomplishes as gift, in which we are purely recipients, and those actions that God accomplishes through gift in which we are invited into participation. But, at the same time, even our healed agency is not enough without this intimate engagement of our agency by the Holy Spirit. Even with this habitual healing by God's grace, our sinfulness persists. We still live in a fallen reality, and as St. Paul writes in Romans 7:15, we do not do those things that we want, but the very things that we hate. This is why the indwelling involvement of God's grace in the Holy Spirit is so necessary. The Holy Spirit is the root of the action in our sanctification. Even once our agency is healed and inclined toward God in the habitual gift, God operates within us a perseverance in this readiness of human disposition and will. In short, by the gift of operative *auxilium*, God sustains what we cannot: our readiness for the prompting guidance of the Holy Spirit. Even our readiness in this healing we cannot sustain on our own. Rather, our perseverance comes from this constant bond with God's action. While we are healed, we are still fallen. For this reason, we must rely on God to do what we cannot—hold us in readiness for God's guidance. This is an operative gift, which means it is done without us.

In the gift of cooperative *auxilium*, we are moved to accomplish the good Christian moral act by the grace of God. Again, this is not a picture of the human being and God "pulling on the same rope." This particular effect of God's grace is no less a gift than the other three that Thomas names. In this gift, God catches up our agency, in harmony with the causation with which we were created, and moves, guides, and cooperates with us for the realization of the Christian moral act. The gift of God in cooperative *auxilium* is the accomplishment of good works with our hands and feet, our lips and voices, our heads and hearts, but, nonetheless, entirely by the Holy Spirit, in the noncompetitive, transcendent intimacy that is our connection with the grace of God.

Even if some wish to drop a few of the tools with which Thomas describes this bond by means of Aristotle or others, these core instincts can be vitally useful to contemporary ethics. Stanley Hauerwas and Reinhard Hütter have rightly pointed the contemporary discourse in the direction of the centrality of God's agency, Christ's presence, and the work of the Holy Spirit in the Christian moral life. Adopting (or at least adapting) the conceptual tools such as the distinctions on grace (described in full in the next chapter) opens the door not only to deeper ecumenical dialogue regarding frameworks for Christian ethics, but also helps realize the important trajectories toward which Hauerwas and Hütter direct the discourse.

The Usefulness of Thomas on the Gifts of the Holy Spirit

Like Thomas' description of the effects of God's grace, his brief treatment of the Gifts of the Holy Spirit offers important conceptual tools for an ecumenical description of God's grace and Christian ethics in community. One of the consistent patterns between Hauerwas and Hütter is their emphasis upon the foundation of the Christian moral life (and God's grace at work upon it) as a fundamental resituating of character and agency by God's gift. Aquinas shares this instinct with them, but offers a useful set of tools in the Gifts for a deeper description of this fundamental resituating of our agency by the Holy Spirit. While perhaps, in pursuing an ecumenical ethic of grace in community, it is too much to advocate the adoption of each of the details of these tools (as they will be described in the next chapter), improvising on these details and the direction to which they point can be very useful to modern theological ethics.

The shaping of big-picture disposition or character, especially dispositions concerning the intellect, is a big part of what Hauerwas and Hütter have in common, and one of the important facets of how they argue for the involvement of God's agency in the moral life. In Hauerwas' "character" ethics, and in Hütter's "disposition of hospitality to the truth," a much deeper transformation takes place than merely learning a set of ideas. Both theologians engage virtue ethics and seek to describe the foray into Christian moral life as a foundational shift—a shift that is firmly situated in the natural dynamics of our character, vision, and intellect. God is at work in this shift, but each seeks a way to describe such work in a way that stands firmly against determinism.

For Aquinas, the threat of determinism is always imminent in treating divine agency and the moral life. One cannot say that God simply acts upon us, as if we were instruments who did not have free will. God's action in the context of our action cannot be approached in such a way that Christian ethical action is no longer human action, nor can it be approached in such a way that God's agency is entirely separated from it. Hauerwas and Hütter have addressed this problem, rightly, by closely associating the involvement of divine agency in the free Christian moral act with a transformation of understanding, judgment, perception, and so on. Aquinas answers this problem by offering a category by which we are not simply made puppets of God's action, but in which God offers a gift whereby our capacity to judge, to understand, to perceive that which we are to do (and every capacity of ours to do it) are made amenable to the prompting of the Holy Spirit. Rather than being an imposition upon a pattern of cognition and action that is already fundamentally separated from God, these gifts, as habits, enable a perfection in which our patterns of cognition and action are *more naturally* (and not less) joined to God, so as to be better moved by the One who first moves, and still moves, our agency. The notion of the Gifts as habits that lay out a supernatural framework for a closer connection between what we know we are to do, and that which we are prompted to do by the leadership of the Holy Spirit, yields a possibility for Christian action that is no less free, no less ours, but more naturally inclined to the movements of divine agency.

Aquinas' description of the Gifts of the Holy Spirit offer a way to talk about the perfection of the dynamic of our own natural agency and action through the action of the Holy Spirit, making our agency amenable to God's prompting, while still preserving our action as our own. The virtuous action that follows from such promptings follows from a perfection of our agency, but it nevertheless (as Anthony Kelly writes) "goes beyond a deliberative mode of activity. Man is said to be moved by a principle greater than his reason to higher activities, as by a divine instinct. To this divine instinct he is attuned by the Gifts."[11] In order to speak in such a way about movement by a higher principle, Thomas rests on the larger framework of human causation in the context of divine causation. But here Thomas offers, in a very intimately individual way, a means by which God both works through and perfects a transformation of our character in such a way that our actions are better "attuned" to divine agency. This perfection and transformation of character, and its close association with the impact of divine agency in the moral life, is very similar to the dynamic that Hauerwas and Hütter consistently pursue. However, Thomas manages to contextualize this transformation in the involvement of the Holy Spirit in a way that makes moral action receptive to divine agency, but not in such a way that the action is any less our own. Aquinas' explanation of the Gifts rests on the idea that the principle of all human movement (especially the movement of human reason) is God. Since God moves everything that is in us anyway, the principle of the movement of the reason was never reason itself, but God.[12] But especially in the Gifts, we are presented with the capacity of the Holy Spirit to perfect our own patterns of cognition and action, according to the modes natural to us in a way that we are, without being any less free, better disposed to be moved by the guidance of the Holy Spirit.

As Bernard Lonergan helpfully points out, the violence implied in the idea of external intervention being added to an internal change, such as the one we find in Thomas' treatment of the Gifts, ought to give pause. But Lonergan finds that in the mature expression of his theology of the Gifts in the *Summa*, Thomas offers "a very adequate answer to the objection that external intervention is violent, or as we would say, unnatural."[13] In Thomas' treatment of the Gifts, the external action of the Holy Spirit

---

11. Kelly, "Gifts of the Spirit," 196–97.

12. Horst, *Die Gaben des Heiligen Geistes nach Thomas von Aquin*, 76. Wie man sieht, nähert sich die Argumentationsfolge einer Frage, die so lautet: Welches Prinzip der Bewegung ist in der Seele? Es ist offensichtlich (palam), daß es—ebenso wie im "Ganzen" (im Universum)—Gott ist. Das Göttliche bewegt in irgendeiner Weise alles, was in uns ist. Das wiederum heißt: Das Prinzip der Vernunft ist nicht selbst wieder die Vernunft, sondern "etwas Besseres." Was aber ist besser als Wissen und Erkennen— wenn nicht Gott? Darum wurden einst die vom Glück Begünstigte genannt, denen das Überlegen nicht förderlich ist und die der Vernunft nicht bedürfen, da sie ein besseres Prinzip haben als Vernunft und Erwägen: nämlich die divinos instinctus.

13. Lonergan, *Grace and Freedom*, 43–44.

is given a framework within which to operate in our operation. We are given a gift by God, perfecting the dynamics of our own cognition and action and, at the same time, enabling a natural connection between the action of the Holy Spirit and our own action. As Lonergan continues, "the gifts of the Holy Spirit make connatural to the creature the external guidance and aid of the Spirit of truth and love. . . . the gifts of the Holy Spirit bring us into the region of pure supernaturality, a region that lies beyond the bounds of all created perfection."[14] Such a bond is made "connatural" to us by means of making us habitually suited to warmly receive God's promptings to virtuous actions through the Gifts.

In attempting to frame an ecumenical approach to God's grace in Christian moral agency, it may be overburdensome to ask for the adoption of the Gifts in the sevenfold manner in which Aquinas presents them, just as it may be overburdensome to ask that this same discourse adopt the ways in which Thomas divides different kinds of cognition and different kinds of action. But, the idea that through the Gifts of the Holy Spirit, God's agency not only perfects the dynamics of our character and action (whatever we explain this dynamic to be), but also makes a union between God's agency and our agency natural to us is an important idea from which the contemporary ethical discourse could significantly benefit. Tools like those offered by Aquinas in the Gifts can help bring the contemporary conversation about the framework of Christian ethics closer to an articulation of free human agency, healed by God, and made amenable to the promptings of the Holy Spirit.

The Usefulness of the Twofold Sense of the New Law

As with Thomas' distinctions between the effects of grace upon human agency and Thomas' account of the Gifts of the Holy Spirit, his description of the twofold sense of the New Law has great potential for use in contemporary attempts to describe God's intimate involvement in the Christian moral life. One great service rendered to the contemporary discourse by Hauerwas and Hütter is their emphasis on the importance of Christian scriptural narrative and the close bond between its transformative influence upon worshipping Christian community and God's transformative influence upon that community. Hauerwas and Hütter have tried to describe the change in the shape of Christian moral agency

---

14. Ibid., 44.

that results from an individual and community identity formed by the Gospel narratives. Thomas' account of the twofold sense of the New Law can help considerably to realize this direction.

The New Law, for Aquinas, is an extrinsic means by which God directs human action, leading to our eternal happiness (an end beyond our natural capacities), shaping our interior thoughts/feelings/unspoken-and-unseen-workings-that-lead-to-moral-action, so that we might know without a doubt what to do. The New Law (in its most primary sense) is the grace of the Holy Spirit, given to those who believe in Christ, according to Aquinas. But it also (in its secondary sense) rightly names the writings of the New Testament. This pairing is not accidental for Aquinas, since he argues that the New Testament contains things that dispose us to receive God's grace and direct us as to its use. The New Law is inscribed upon our hearts and inscribed upon the pages of the New Testament in a complementary way.

The importance of this complementary pairing in the overall picture of God's grace and Christian ethics has been painted differently by different readers. Servais Pinckaers, for instance, champions the twofold sense of the New Law as "the high point of all legislation issuing from the wisdom of God and communicated to human beings. . . . this is the treatise that demonstrates most clearly the fundamentally Christian character of St. Thomas' teaching."[15] He praises Aquinas for his "audacity" in emphasizing the action of the Holy Spirit, and the chiefly interior dimension of this New Law,[16] calling the twofold sense of the New Law one of the "three towering peaks, which almost seem to touch the heavens," of his theology.[17] While this may seem, perhaps, overly enthusiastic, such an evaluation is nothing compared with the words of Heinrich Christmann in the introduction that he wrote for the fourteenth volume of *Die Deutsche Thomas Ausgabe*—a series that presents the Latin text of the *Summa* with a parallel German translation. Christmann writes of the twofold sense of the New Law: "Thus law becomes grace, and grace becomes law—such is indeed a bold equation, probably the boldest equation that was ever set up in the history of mankind for the moral sphere."[18] In this series, the editors grouped the treatise on the New Law

---

15. Pinckaers, *Sources of Christian Ethics*, 172.
16. Ibid., 174.
17. Ibid., 172.
18. Christmann, "Einleitung," 10. So wird Gesetz Gnade, und Gnade wird Gesetz—

and the treatise on grace in the same volume, rather than placing the New Law together with other elements of the treatise on Law. Given such choices, Christmann's comments are hardly surprising (though such comments actually neglect that Thomas accomplished this pairing in the introduction to the Treatise on Law, as quoted above). To place the twofold sense of the New Law not only as the capstone of Thomas' morality but also as the greatest thought in the history of moral theology, is perhaps difficult to justify. Christmann's evaluations prompt more caution as he goes on to indicate that the New Law is not an external principle by which God directs action (the category, as argued above, into which Thomas places both law and grace); he seems to see this transition as placing the law not simply as efficacious with regard to internal principles, but itself an internal principle: "in effect, the law stops ranking among external assistance."[19] In contrast, Joseph Wawrykow downplays even the importance of the twofold sense of the New Law in terms of its place in the scope of moral theology. In 2005, he writes, "That I-II 106–108 are important and provide the link between what comes before—on law and its various manifestations, including the Old Law—and what comes after—grace—is beyond question. Nonetheless, those questions add little to the presentation of grace itself; and their main insight—the interiority of the New Law, as the inward prompting of the Holy Spirit—is adequately advanced by Aquinas in the course of his detailed teaching on grace."[20] While certainly not discounting the importance of the twofold sense of the New Law for the overall picture of Thomas' moral theology, Wawrykow does indicate here that the insights of *ST* I-II 106, while vital, are adequately articulated in his treatise on grace, and the pairing of God's agency with the Gospel narrative, as such, is not a particularly vital moment.

Whatever importance one assigns to the twofold sense of the New Law in the larger context of Thomas' moral theology, especially with regard to grace, I propose that the insight is a vitally important tool for the contemporary ethical discourse. It not only refuses a dualism between

---

wahrlich eine kühne Gleichung, wohl die kühnste Gleichung, die je in der Geschichte der Menschheit für die Sphäre des Sittlichen aufgestellt wurde.

19. Ibid. Eigentlich hört nun das Gesetz auf, zu den äußeren Hilfen zu zählen. Gesetz und Gnade sind nur noch insofern "äußere" Hilfen zu nennen, als ihr Ursprung außerhalb des Menschen in Gott und in Christus liegt.

20. Wawrykow, "Grace," 192.

the efficacy of the Gospel narrative and the efficacy of divine agency, but also rightly places the emphasis on the latter without dismissing the former. Hauerwas and Hütter laudably place the Gospel narrative as vitally important for Christian ethics, and seem to consistently relate this importance to the transformative power of God's grace; the conceptual tool of Aquinas' twofold sense of the New Law offers the contemporary ethical discourse a prompting by which they can continue to rightly emphasize the importance of the Gospels, while still pointing, in a deeper way, to God's agency in the Christian moral life.

The notion that the New Law is twofold, and that its efficacy is based on the primary sense of its being "instilled" in our hearts in the grace of the Holy Spirit, is a tool that would much aid contemporary ecumenical discourse. Hauerwas and Hütter consistently lift up the centrality of Jesus Christ in the moral life, but still place most of the onus of moral transformation on the Gospel narrative. The kind of "narrative casuistry" indicated by Hütter, or the kind of spontaneous moral "improvisation" described by Hauerwas, addresses the transformative power of the Gospel narrative as it adapts to specific moral moments, thus being the kinds of "reality making claims" that can rightly lead us to well-ordered Christian action. As Servais Pinckaers notes, Aquinas argues for this same kind of flexibility and adaptability of the New Law, but only because the grace of the Holy Spirit is the primary sense of the New Law. Pinckaers writes, "the action of the Spirit through the virtues creates within us a spontaneous, personal movement toward good acts. This in turn allows for a reduction of precepts to the minimum, so as to open up a wider field for freedom's initiative."[21] The New Law is not flexible in its direction of us because of the great adaptability of the category of narrative (or even revealed narrative), but because the Spirit works within the individual Christian, in the exact circumstances in which she finds herself. "This point is repeated time and again by Thomas in his treatment of the New Law: it is not a set of laws governing external behavior but instead an internal prompting to God directly."[22] The narrative is a part of the efficacy of God's more direct internal promptings. To speak about the New Law without this dimension is to speak about it without *quod in ea est potissimum*. Pinckaers phrases it this way: "the principle of the New Law, and consequently of Christian ethics, is not

21. Pinckaers, *Sources of Christian Ethics*, 185.
22. Hall, *Narrative and the Natural Law*, 69.

the Gospel viewed as a text or an eternal word, comparable to a physical body, but rather the life principle, the breath of God that animates this body. Without it would have only an inert material object. We hasten to add, however, that the body formed by the Gospel texts is indispensable if we are to receive the breath of the Spirit."[23] The transformative power of the New Law is this "life principle" of the Spirit, while the text is indispensable as well. The New Law is most certainly a written law, but that is not its chief sense. As Isabelle Chareire helpfully summarizes in her *Éthique et grâce*, "in its essential principle, the New Law is interior. It is the grace of the Holy Spirit that comes to us by faith made operative through charity. In its secondary element, the New Law is external, the Scripture (i.e. the letter of the Gospel), that prepares us to receive the grace of the Spirit."[24]

Boiled down, perhaps the most essential insight Aquinas can offer regarding the shaping power of the New Testament upon Christian agency through community is that the transformative power of the Gospel narrative is integrally related to the transformative power of God's grace. The important contemporary trajectory to place the New Testament writings back at the center of Christian ethics need not (cannot, according to Thomas) compete with the centrality of God's grace in the human heart in Christian ethics. The New Law is both interior and external, but the same New Law, inscribed by the same one God. Hauerwas and Hütter strive (in very different ways) to tie God's transformative influence on Christian morality with the shaping of this particular narrative. Through the conceptual tool of the twofold sense of the New Law, Thomas helps the contemporary discourse toward an ecumenical account of the importance of this narrative and its connection with God's grace in Christian community and in Christian moral action.

---

23. Pinckaers, *Sources of Christian Ethics*, 176.

24. Chareire, *Éthique et grâce*, 156. "En fait, dans la Loi nouvelle, il y a deux éléments: dans son principe essentiel, la Loi nouvelle est intérieure, elle est grâce de l'Esprit Saint qui nous vient par la foi et rendue opérante par la charité; dans ses éléments secondaires, la Loi nouvelle est extérieure: l'Écriture (c'est-à-dire la lettre de l'Évangile) nous prépare à recevoir la grâce de l'Esprit en la portant à notre connaissance, et les sacrements nous disposent à mettre en œuvre la grâce."

Parameters, Focus, and Organization

The next chapter will offer detailed treatments of some of the tools that Thomas Aquinas uses to explain this bond of joint action between the Christian and the Holy Spirit in the moral act. The depth and interconnectedness of individual concepts in the theology of Thomas Aquinas can easily lead his modern readership to a kind of irresponsible "sampling" in which a concept or a passage is used without regard to its context, the history of its development, or the ways in which it depends on other ideas. In some ways, such "sampling" is unavoidable, as the reader must find a point of entry into this text. However, in an attempt to limit this problem in the current treatment, I wish to present, very clearly, the boundaries of this examination. Thomas' ideas about the connection between divine and human agency in the Christian moral act have undergone a great deal of development across his writing career. Without speaking, at least briefly, to that development, a thematic, *ad hoc* sampling has the potential to fall to pieces in trying to connect ideas from different points in Thomas' writing career in which his treatments of these issues differ considerably from one another. The next chapter will focus (1) on the treatment of the New Law, (2) on the treatment of the Gifts of the Holy Spirit, and (3) on the distinctions he makes with regard to the effects of grace. Thomas' writing on these three issues has undergone significant evolution, and limiting the scope of the texts upon which I will focus will be important in looking to draw consistent ideas from Aquinas for contemporary ethics.

Thomas offers a twofold sense of the New Law: the written Gospel and the action of the Holy Spirit in the heart of the believer. While these two elements find separate treatment throughout his writing career, the notion of the New Law as twofold does not receive systematic treatment prior to the *Summa*.[25] The passage from his commentary on Romans that was examined in the introduction is certainly an instance in which he explains the action of the Holy Spirit as closely bound to what it means to be a Christian under the New Law, but does not explicitly join such an idea with the written Gospels. In that passage, he joined it with notions of adoption. There are also moments, such as in the *Summa contra Gentiles*, in which Thomas treats the action of the Holy Spirit within

---

25. Pinckaers, *Sources of Christian Ethics*, 177.

the believer as related to the infused virtue of charity,[26] and then later on speaks about the "New Law, as being more perfect, is called *the law of love*, whereas the Old Law, as being less perfect, is called *the law of fear*."[27] Again, the implication here is that there is a connection between being ruled by the "law of love" in two ways: in the explicit terms offered in the written Gospels, and in the action of the Holy Spirit as a part of the virtue of charity, in which we are moved by means of God's love to virtuous acts. Once more, however, the New Law is still not directly treated as twofold, though the pieces are certainly all in place to do so. As it happens, the significant change in Thomas' treatment of the New Law (as twofold) in the *Summa theologiae* represents a disjunction not only with his earlier works, but with Thomas' predecessors, as well. As Ulrich Kühn notes, it was the general opinion in the scholastic tradition that the New Law was granted for the fulfillment of the commandments and the sufficient corresponding help of the grace of God. But the idea that the New Law was an internal, indwelling or instilled law (*lex indita*) was absent from Peter Lombard, Albert the Great, and the Franciscan school, and therefore (perhaps not surprisingly) it was absent from Thomas' early writings.[28] In most of the instances in which he treats the New Law or the Law of Christ, he treats it (and the Gospels) as a particular written collection and an oral tradition of commandments—especially in the terms presented in the Sermon on the Mount. While Thomas and his scholastic contemporaries certainly present grace as the requirement for the fulfillment of these commandments, in the end the commandments of the New Law are treated as regulating external actions.[29] The natural

---

26. Aquinas, *Summa contra Gentiles*, bk. 4, ch. 21. "Now, the divine effects not only have their beginning in the divine operation, but also are upheld in their being thereby, as proved above. Again, nothing can work where it is not, because worker and work must needs be actually together, even as the mover and the thing moved. Hence, wherever we find a divine effect, God must be there as its efficient cause. Therefore, since charity whereby we love God, is in us from the Holy Ghost, it follows that the Holy Ghost is in us, so long as charity remains in us."

27. Aquinas, *Summa contra Gentiles*, bk. 3b, ch. 116.

28. Kühn, *Via Caritatis*, 194. Es war zwar allgemeine Meinung in der scholastischen Tradition, daß im neuen Gesetz zur Erfüllung der Gebote auch die entsprechende zureichende göttliche Gnadenhilfe gewährt würde—daß aber das neue Gesetz eigentlich eine lex indita sei, wird weder von Petrus Lombardus noch bei den Franziskanern noch auch bei Albertus Magnus gesagt und ist selbst im SK des Thomas noch nicht zu finden.

29. Ibid. [Ü]berall heißt es nur, daß das neue Gesetz oder das Gesetz Christi bzw. des Evangeliums, das selbst als eine Sammlung bestimmter schriftlich und

law was treated as "instilled," or "internal," but not the New Law. Kühn argues that Aquinas is deeply indebted to Augustine's *On the Spirit and the Letter* for the notion of the New Law as an instilled divine law. The innovation in the *Summa* is that the core of the New Law is no longer the grace of Christ making possible the external obedience of the commands of the New Law, but rather, the foundation of the New Law is rightly understood as the internal agency of the Holy Spirit in the heart of the Christian, moving the believer to God, prior to any external regulation.[30] Again, while one sees implications of the New Law as the "Law of Liberty" in the biblical commentaries (particularly Galatians and Romans),[31] Thomas does not treat the New Law as both the written Gospel commands and as the internal agency of the Holy Spirit until the *Summa*. In short, it is not until the *Summa* that Thomas' mature and full treatment of the New Law emerges. While each of the twofold senses of the New Law is treated in isolation in a variety of other loci, the New Law as both God's grace working through us and the commands of the

---

mündlich vorliegender Gebote vorgestellt ist (im wesentlichen die Bergpredigt und die Anordnungen über die Sakramente umfassend), die Gnade zur Erfüllung dieser Gebote mit sich bringt und dadurch vor dem alten Gesetz ausgezeichnet ist—aber es bleibt doch letztlich sein Wesen als äußeres Gebot bestehen, und in der Summa fratris Alexandri wird das Gesetz Christi ausdrücklich mit dem menschlichen und dem mosaischen Gesetz als geschriebenes Gesetz der lex naturalis als der eigentlichen und einzigen lex indita gegenübergestellt.

30. Ibid. Es ist aus den vielen Zitaten bei Thomas offensichtlich, daß er sich in seiner neuen Sicht der Dinge stark Augustin, insbesondere dessen Schrift "De spiritu et littera" verpflichtet wußte, die zwar auch von den anderen Scholastikern herangezogen wurde, bei Thomas aber eben diesen Durchbruch zu der Erkenntnis des Wesens des neuen Gesetzes als lex divinitus indita mit ermöglichte. Von diesem Durchbruch her wird im Innersten eine letzte Gesetzlichkeit im Verhältnis Gottes zum Menschen überwunden: nicht, daß etwa die Moralgebote für den Christen irrelevant wären—daß sie das nach Thomas ausdrücklich nicht sind, wird unten sofort deutlich werden—, aber das Wesentliche besteht jetzt nicht mehr in der durch die Gnade ermöglichten Erfüllung der von Christus äußerlich gegebenen Gebote, sondern das Wesentliche besteht in der inneren freien Bewegung zu Gott hin, die vor allen Geboten und im Grunde letztlich unabhängig von allen Geboten als Geschenk Gottes, als Heiliger Geist den Menschen treibt. Damit bestätigt und vollendet sich eine Beobachtung, die wir bereits bei Betrachtung des SK im Verhältnis zu Bonaventura und dann wieder bei der Betrachtung der ScG machen konnten: Das ethische Ideal des Thomas besteht letztlich darin, daß der Mensch sich selbst Gesetz ist, nicht darin, daß er dem von außen an ihn ergehenden Anspruch Gottes gehorsam ist, wie es bei Bonaventura der Fall war. Und dieses "Sich-selbst-Gesetz-Sein" Geboten in der liebenden Hingabe an Gott ist der eigentliche Kern dessen, was Thomas in der Sth unter dem "neuen Gesetz" versteht.

31. Ibid., 195.

Gospel is not found until the *Summa theologiae*. It is primarily for this reason that the next chapter will limit itself to looking at this latest work with regard to the New Law. While I will still, to an extent, rely on the added language of "indwelling," which is found more often in the biblical commentaries than in the *Summa*, I limit my treatment of the New Law to the *Summa*, as it is Thomas' most full and robust treatment of this concept.

The evolution and development of Thomas' ideas about the Gifts of the Holy Spirit change along very closely related lines. From his very earliest treatment of the Gifts in his commentary on Isaiah (perhaps as early as 1252),[32] to his final treatment of the Gifts in the unfinished *Summa*, he begins with the authority of Gregory's *Moralia on Job*[33] to frame the discussion of the seven Gifts of the Holy Spirit with the seven virtues. As is nicely explained by Ulrich Horst in his 2001 *Die Gaben des Heiligen Geistes nach Thomas von Aquin*, Thomas' earliest attempts name the seven Gifts as habits that were in support of the virtues. Just as the virtues were the perfection of human action, so the Gifts of the Spirit were the cause of this perfection. Thomas, like Albert the Great, found that one conceptual shortfall in becoming virtuous was that human beings lacked the proper habit. The content of faith asks of us things that are beyond our natural abilities (both in terms of the cognition of the content of faith, and in terms of actions). The Gifts of the Holy Spirit lift up human agency beyond its natural capacity to the perfections of virtue.[34] Most especially in the *Commentary on the Sentences* Thomas

---

32. Horst, *Die Gaben des Heiligen Geistes nach Thomas von Aquin*, 41.

33. Aquinas, *Summa theologiae* I-II.68.1.*sed contra*.

34. Horst, *Die Gaben des Heiligen Geistes nach Thomas von Aquin*, 41. Thomas bedient sich einleitend eines oft zitierten Wortes aus Gregors Moralia, wonach die Gaben zur Unterstützung der Tugenden geschenkt werden, um die Seelenpotenzen zu vervollkommnen, die die normale Handlungsweise des Menschen (modus humanus) lenken. Wie man sich das zu denken hat, illustriert die Tugend des Glaubens, der seinen Gegenstand "im Spiegel und Rätsel" sehen läßt. Das Beispiel—wir haben es bereits bei Albert kennengelernt—verweist auf eine zweifache Unvollkommenheit der Tugend. Eine ist per accidens, sie resultiert aus der jeweiligen Indisposition dessen, der sie hat. Dieser Mangel verschwindet in dem Maß, wie die Tugend wächst. Daneben gibt es es jedoch einen Defekt, der dem Habitus selbst eignet. In bezug auf unseren Fall heißt das: Der Glaube ist seinem Wesen gemäß eine unvollkommene, weil "rätselhafte" Erkenntnis, deren Defizienz durch einen "höheren" Habitus überwunden werden muß. Das geschieht mittels einer von Gott gewährten Gabe, die bewirkt, daß die menschliche Handlungsweise mit ihren naturgemäß begrenzten Fähigkeiten überschritten wird. So vermögen wir, durch das donum intellectus bestärkt, die Glaubensdinge "rein und klar" anzuschauen.

makes clear that the Gifts of the Spirit are necessary because of the very strict distinction he makes between the mode of human action and a *modus supra humanus*—the difference being that while, according to the human mode of action, we can refrain from certain things, we need the Gifts in order to be raised to a higher mode of virtuous action.[35]

According to Horst, Thomas changed his ideas about the Gifts rather suddenly. Sometime between the composition of the *De Caritate* (1269) and his treatment of the Gifts in the *Summa* (written between 1265 and 1272), his approach changed dramatically—a change that Horst believes is due to Thomas' encounter with Eudemus' *Liber de bona fortuna* (which Thomas thought was composed by Aristotle).[36] One might argue with Horst that (as Henri Bouillard points out in his *Conversion et Grâce chez S. Thomas d'Aquin*) in the *Summa contra Gentiles,* completed in 1260, Aquinas cites the *Liber de bona fortuna* eight different times, though never with regard to the Gifts.[37] In any case, in the *Summa*, Thomas explicitly shifts his language significantly from "gift" to "spirit." Thomas writes, "in order to differentiate the gifts from the virtues, we must be guided by the way in which Scripture expresses itself, for we find there that the term employed is 'spirit' rather than 'gift,'"[38] citing Isaiah 11:2–3. Why the change? According to Horst, Aquinas realized that there was a problem with his previous conception. If the dualism overcome by the Gifts was between a natural and a supernatural mode of action, then one still had to account for the transition between wanting to simply refrain from some acts (which were within our natural capacity) and wishing

---

35. Ibid., 78. Dort war die Unterscheidung von modus humanus und modus supra humanus der springende Punkt für die Begründung der Notwendigkeit spezieller Gaben gewesen. Hier ist es—unter einstweiliger Absehung von einzelnen in ein höheres Sein zu erhebenden Tugenden—die menschliche Person, die durch die Gaben befähigt wird, die ihr von Natur eigene "Schwerkraft" zu überwinden, um sich leicht und schnell in Bewegung versetzen zu lassen.

36. Ibid., 71. Da die zeitliche Differenz zwischen den genannten Schriften und der Prima Secundae gering sein dürfte, hat man wohl mit einem ziemlich plötzlichen Wechsel zu rechnen. Das gilt insbesondere für De caritate. Thomas muß, sollte das zutreffen, innerhalb kurzer Zeit Gründe gefunden haben, die ihn veranlaßten, seine einstige Position endgültig aufzugeben. Geht man fehl in der Annahme, daß es die Erkenntnis war, die Lehre vom instinctus Spiritus Sancti und die Anregungen aus dem Liber De bonafortuna seien ihm als besonders geeignet erschienen, die neue Konzeption der Gaben des Hl. Geistes zu entwickeln?

37. Bouillard, *Conversion et Grâce chez S. Thomas d'Aquin*, 125.

38. Aquinas, *Summa theologiae* I-II.68.1.

for an entirely different set of actions that were outside of human capacity. How can one start wanting to do something that was beyond one's capacity? "From the *Liber de bona fortuna*, Thomas obtained one crucial thought: God is the principle for the movement of the soul, which in turn sets will and intellect into action, and is therefore antecedent to every human activity."[39] In order to begin to want to do these virtuous acts, we must be induced to want it from something external to us,[40] and thus a new distinction emerges in Thomas' treatment of the Gifts: the two principles for human action: an interior, the reason, and an exterior, God.[41] Thus he uses the term "Divine inspiration" to denote "motion from without."[42] The agency of the Holy Spirit working by means of "inspiration," illumination, or instinct is certainly not new to Aquinas' theology, but his use of the concept here is a significant departure from his earlier treatments of the Gifts.[43] As indicated above, Horst concludes that this significant change from his earlier approach can be attributed to an attention to Scripture with regard to the Gifts, in which "gift" and "spirit" were associated, and the need for an outside "force" to move the will towards these higher actions, which he realized from his reading of *Liber de bona fortuna*.[44] We are in no less need of "higher perfections," for "human virtues perfect man according as it is natural for him

---

39. Horst, *Die Gaben des Heiligen Geistes nach Thomas von Aquin*, 76. Der Liber de bona fortuna hat Thomas einen entscheidenden Gedanken vermittelt: Gott ist das in der Seele bewegende Prinzip, das Wollen und Denken allererst in Gang setzt und deshalb jeder menschlichen Aktivität vorausliegt.

40. Kühn, *Via Caritatis*, 73. Was zuweilen in actu und zuweilen in Potenz ist, muß von einem anderen Bewegenden bewegt werden. Wenn der Wille etwas zu wollen beginnt, was er vorher nicht wollte, so muß er zum Wollen von jemand bewegt werden.

41. Aquinas, *Summa theologiae* I-II.68.1.

42. Kühn, *Via Caritatis*, 73. See also Aquinas, *Summa theologiae* I-II.68.1.

43. Kühn, *Via Caritatis*, 168. Eine bemerkenswerte Rolle hat schon früh der Gedanke gespielt, der Hl. Geist wirke in der Heilsgeschichte mittels eines instinctus, einer Erleuchtung, einer Eingebung, eines zur Entscheidung drängenden inneren Rufes. Thomas war sich also der theologischen Implikationen des Instinktbegriffs bewußt, als er den Liber de bona fortuna für sich entdeckte und in der Prima Secundae zur philosophischen Erhellung der Lehre von den Gaben verwandte.

44. Ibid. Der Aquinate hat den hier gegenüber dem Sentenzenkommentar zu konstatierenden Wechsel in der spekulativen Begründung des Wesens und der Funktion der Geistesgaben auf zwei Überlegungen zurückgeführt. Zum einen gibt die hl. Schrift Gabe mit Geist wieder, um das Element des Bewegens auszudrücken; zum anderen ist festzuhalten, daß der Wille eines äußeren "Antriebs" bedarf, um in seine erste Bewegung überzugehen, wofür er sich auf den Liber de bonafortuna beruft.

to be moved by his reason in his interior and exterior actions,"[45] but these "higher perfections" are no longer articulated in terms of a *modus supra humanus*. Rather, we need the gifts "to be disposed to be moved by God."[46] Instead of a framework in which the natural and the supernatural modes are firmly separated, Horst says, they now complement each other, and God provides a means for the perfection of our action both by God's causality through the natural light of reason on the one hand, and through the effectiveness of the three theological virtues on the other.[47]

The implications of these ideas for Christian ethics will be explored in the next chapter. I trace the development here to demonstrate why the current inquiry will limit itself to Thomas' treatment of the Gifts of the Holy Spirit in the *Summa theologiae*. Whether or not Ulrich Horst is correct about the impact of the *Liber de bona fortuna* on Thomas' thoughts about the Gifts, it is hard to deny his demonstration that Thomas' approach in the *Summa* is a dramatic departure from his other works, even those that preceded the *Summa* by only a short time. Trying to draw from a variety of Thomas' writings on the Gifts would ignore these crucial changes and would yield a picture of the Gifts that would conflict with itself. Therefore, as with the treatise of the New Law, my examination of Aquinas with regard to the Gifts in the next chapter will look only to the *Summa theologiae*.

Once more, with regard to Thomas' treatment of the conceptual distinctions of grace, his thought undergoes dramatic shifts. Interestingly, at least two modern commentators, Bouillard and Lonergan, also credit the impact of the *Liber de bona fortuna* with leading Thomas to the "concept of the divine initiative as a necessarily interior motion to the will,"[48]

---

45. Aquinas, *Summa theologiae* I-II.68.1.

46. Ibid.

47. Horst, *Die Gaben des Heiligen Geistes nach Thomas von Aquin*, 80. Beide Aspekte—der natürliche und der übernatürliche—liegen nun nicht beziehungslos nebeneinander, sie ergänzen sich vielmehr im Sinne des vorhin gewürdigten duplex principium, das der doppelten Verfaßtheit der menschlichen Vernunft entspricht. Gott sorgt nämlich auf zweifache Weise für deren Vervollkommnung, die unsere konkrete Situation berücksichtigt: Zum einen unter dem Blickpunkt des natürlichen Lichtes der Vernunft, zum anderen, indem er Existenz und Wirksamkeit der drei göttlichen Tugenden in Erkennen und Handeln einbezieht.

48. Bouillard, *Conversion et Grâce chez S. Thomas d'Aquin*, 132. "La decouverture du *Liber de Bona Fortuna* l'a amené à concevoir cette initiative comme une motion nécessairement intérieure à la volunté."

a "premotion"[49] that seems to be behind so much of the development one sees in this concept. In any case, there is a significant change in the ways in which Thomas articulates conceptual divisions of grace across his writings. Bernard Lonergan, in his *Grace and Freedom*, points out that in Thomas' relatively early *Commentary on the Sentences*, grace was articulated as being a habitual gift. Grace was only considered in its habitual effects, probably as a consequence of the writing of his contemporaries. "In referring to habitual grace, Aquinas is hardly innovative. His contemporaries tended to construe grace as principally, even exclusively habitual; and in fact, in his earliest teaching on grace (in the *Scriptum* on the *Sentences* of Peter Lombard), Aquinas himself viewed grace as only habitual."[50] Aquinas draws from Albert's notion that operative grace, by means of formal causality, makes it possible for us to act in such a way that our actions have merit before God.[51] He combines this notion with Bonaventure's idea that grace was a principle of motion as an efficient cause,[52] and affirms that grace is rightly divided into operative grace and cooperative grace.[53] The basic distinction in his early work "is between grace as a formal cause and grace as an efficient cause."[54]

Aquinas divides each of these into operative and cooperative, not without problematic results. As Lonergan explains, formal operative grace is a habit making one acceptable to God. Formal cooperative grace is the combination of grace as the form and free choice as the matter, producing the meritorious action. Effective operative grace referred to grace causing the free will through the virtues, and effective cooperative grace meant the causing of the external action.[55] The third of these four offered a problem: how can the operative grace of God be connected with the free action of the human will? By the time of the *De Veritate*, Aquinas had changed his position somewhat. While the *Commentary* divided both formal and efficient effects of grace into operative and cooperative, in the *De Veritate*, "the formal causality of the habit is said to

49. Lonergan, *Grace and Freedom*, 100.
50. Wawrykow, "Grace," 194.
51. Lonergan, *Grace and Freedom*, 26.
52. Ibid., 28.
53. Aquinas, II *Scriptum super libros sententiarum magistri Petri Lombardi*, 26, q.1, a5.
54. Lonergan, *Grace and Freedom*, 31.
55. Ibid., 31–33.

be *operans* and its efficient causality to be *cooperans*. Essentially this is an improvement to be retained in the *Summa theologiae*, for it eliminates the anomaly of the *Commentary on the Sentences* where an operative grace cooperates with the free will."[56] However, by the time that he wrote the *De Veritate*, he realized that a merely habitual gift was insufficient to move one to meritorious action without an additional help of God's grace; he "affirmed that no matter how perfect the habits one acquires or receives, there always remains the need of divine operation which is a *gratia cooperans*."[57] So, a new division: habitual grace has both an operative and a cooperative effect, but in addition, we need this "help" of God's grace of *auxilium* (a grace that Lonergan calls "actual") cooperating with our free will. As Joseph Wawrykow writes in his 1995 *God's Grace and Human Action*, "the discussion of grace in *De Veritate* marks an intermediary stage between the *Scriptum* and the *Summa*. Thomas continues to view grace, as he did in the *Scriptum*, as primarily habitual but it is in the *De Veritate* that he also introduces the notion of a second grace, a cooperative *auxilium*."[58] Lonergan and Wawrykow both point out that by the time Aquinas wrote *De Malo* (1269–1272), he realized the need to affirm a more internal cause of the movement of human will beyond that of the object provided by the intellect, which certainly didn't necessitate the will's movement.[59] Thus, in the most fully formed and mature of his writings on grace, the *Summa*, "Thomas retains habitual grace but adds a distinctive type of grace, the grace of *auxilium*, and depicts it in much more dynamic terms. In addition, in the *Summa* Thomas divides this *auxilium* into two parts, the operative *auxilium* that inwardly works conversion and grants every good thought as well as perseverance in grace, and the cooperative *auxilium* that confirms the person in the good and strengthens the person in moral activity."[60] For the first time in the *Summa*, Thomas, fully realizing the ways in which grace operates and cooperates in and with human agency, offers four very useful categories for considering God's grace: operative habitual

---

56. Ibid., 37.
57. Ibid., 42.
58. Wawrykow, *God's Grace and Human Action*, 146.
59. Ibid., 49; Lonergan, *Grace and Freedom*, 100. It is at this point that Lonergan affirms the vital importance of Aquinas' encounter with the *Liber de bona fortuna*.
60. Wawrykow, *God's Grace and Human Action*, 146.

grace, cooperative habitual grace, the operative "help" of *auxilium*, and the cooperative *auxilium*.

While the impact of these distinctions for this inquiry will be explored much more fully in the next chapter, here I trace the development of Aquinas' thoughts about grace in order to demonstrate why my inquiry will confine itself to drawing from the *Summa*. Thomas' ideas about grace changed so dramatically throughout his writing career that to draw haphazardly from a variety of sources would ultimately not be very fruitful. Ignoring the evolution of Thomas' thoughts on grace would result in an internally conflicting treatment.

One final reason remains as to why my treatments on Thomas' theology regarding the New Law, the Gifts of the Holy Spirit, and the distinctions of God's grace will all be confined to his *Summa theologiae*: they are profoundly connected. As Albert Patfoort very helpfully points out in his 1983 *Thomas d'Aquin: les clés d'une théologie*, statistically, these three topics fall into an interesting grouping. Patfoort notes that in Thomas' *Prima Secundae*, the Holy Spirit is mentioned in tellingly clustered patterns: 128 times in questions 68–70 (the gifts of the Holy Spirit, the beatitudes, and the Fruits of the Spirit), forty-nine times in questions 106–108 (on the New Law), and twenty-nine times in questions 109–114 (his treatise on grace).[61] This constitutes the bulk of Aquinas' pneumatological treatment in the *Summa*. Such statistics strongly indicate that these are the sections in which Aquinas discusses the impact of the Spirit in the life of the Christian. In this way, they ought to be treated as at least thematically related within this one work. While this alone may not be sufficient reason to neglect Thomas' older texts, it does give some reason why conceptual tools drawn from Aquinas from these three places might interact and support one another in some interesting ways, and should therefore be treated together. Not only do these three subject matters align themselves with the patterns examined in previous chapters in the theologies of Hauerwas and Hütter (and thus, consequently, provide suitable settings for examining the relevance of some of Aquinas' conceptual tools for their systems), they also interconnect in Thomas' own work. They treat, in different ways, the relevance and impact of divine agency on the Christian moral life through God's grace in the Holy Spirit. They likewise complement one another in depicting a picture of the close, integral connection between God's action and our

61. Patfoort, *Thomas d'Aquin*, 83.

own in the Christian moral life. For all of these reasons, then, the following chapter will focus exclusively on Thomas' *Summa theologiae* in seeking to draw out some useful conceptual tools and promptings for the contemporary ethical discourse as represented by Hauerwas and Hütter.[62]

---

62. One brief note about the order in which I have chosen to treat these three topics. In this particular ecumenical attempt I have allowed the contemporary Protestant discourse to set the terms of the conversation, and have allowed them the first word. This has at least one somewhat inconvenient consequence in turning to Aquinas: Do I alter the logical order of the Protestant conversation to fit Thomas' contribution, or do I alter the logical order of Thomas' contribution in order to fit the conversation as it has occurred so far? To be even more specific: the contemporary Protestant discourse that has been treated thus far assumes a particular order in the way Christian ethics works (an order that is most prominently observable in Hauerwas, but has been present in the other two as well): scriptural narrative shapes Christian community. The dynamics internal to this worshipping community, continuing to be shaped by Scripture, shape and, to an extent, redeem and perfect Christian perspective, thinking, judgment, and mindset. Then, with the foundation of this perfection, we act in a way that can be called Christian. This action relies upon God's action as its necessary condition, and thus in the act itself we have a relational bond between God's action and our own agency. As will be shown, the bond between divine and human agency in the Christian moral life is somewhat different for Aquinas, and the relational efficacy between God's agency and our own long precedes the properly "Christian moral act." The perfection of moral willing and moral action is not the beginning of a relational bond between divine and human agency, but the result of it.

Again, the choice is difficult. In treating Thomas' theology of grace, his treatment of the Gifts of the Holy Spirit rests upon the conceptual work accomplished in his treatise on grace. Likewise, in terms of the progression in the moral life, certainly the content articulated in the treatise on grace is chronologically prior to the content articulated in the question on the gifts of the Holy Spirit. The natural order for their treatment is for the Gifts of the Holy Spirit to follow the treatise on grace. However, the importance of Thomas' contribution in this setting is as an ecumenical dialogue partner. Here, I treat his theology as a part of an ongoing conversation. In this discourse, as in any other ecumenical dialogue, conceptual concessions must be made for conversation to continue. In articulating the contemporary discourse in the first chapters, I have allowed Hauerwas and Hütter to set the logical conceptual order. For each of them, God's resituating of our character and agency by gift is a step prior to the relational bond between God's agency and human action. For this reason, I put the heavier burden on Aquinas to respond to this order as it has been thus far presented. Therefore, in the pages that follow, out of consideration for the cohesion of the dialogue, my explanation of the Gifts of the Holy Spirit (as the locus in which Thomas provides those tools best suited for conceiving God's resituating of our character and agency by gift as a part of the bond between divine and human agency) will precede my explanation of the treatise on grace (as the locus in which Thomas provides those tools best suited for conceiving the bond between divine and human agency).

Related Topics

It cannot be denied that Thomas articulates vital pneumatological points in other sections of the *Summa* (especially those concerning the Spirit as "Love" and "Gift"). It cannot be denied that Thomas offers in-depth treatments of the connection between divine and human agency in other sections of the *Summa* (especially those concerning metaphysics). While these sections have been somewhat undertreated in recent literature (and have been left almost entirely aside by contemporary Christian ethical literature), they remain relevant and important. A broad treatment of Thomas' theology of the Holy Spirit would be invaluable to the contemporary Christian ethical discourse, but it is not to be found here. What I have undertaken is the task of fostering a particular conversation surrounding some key patterns and themes in this discourse. I do regret that the boundaries of this project do not allow for a full examination of Thomas' metaphysics or pneumatology as preparatory steps to examining smaller sections of the *Summa*, just as I regret that an examination of Anscomb or Wittgenstein could not pave the way for our assessment of Hauerwas, and that an examination of Karl Barth or Luther could not pave the way for our assessment of Hütter. These preparatory steps would, no doubt, significantly clarify the direction of these theologians, and better help identify some of the roots of the tensions in their respective theologies. Unfortunately, bringing these theologians together in conversation means limiting the extent to which each party can speak. Though it is regrettable, broader treatments of Thomas' metaphysics and pneumatology must wait.

Thomas' theological treatment of grace offers us one more problem: he has very appropriately interconnected his treatise on grace with most other topics of the *Summa*: creation, Christology, virtue, and the sacraments, to name only a few, stand as inextricably intertwined with Thomas' work on grace. Unfortunately, such topics cannot receive the attention due to them here. To those familiar with Thomas' treatise on grace, two further omissions will be even more striking. I plan to leave aside the integral issues of predestination and merit. A part of the definition that Thomas offers for "grace" is that it is gift from God. Grace as gift is nowhere more evident than in Thomas' framing of the questions of predestination and merit. The dynamics of the grace of God in human existence is not a fruitless or occasional relationship, but is purposive. By

God's grace we are directed to a certain end. The showing forth of God's merciful love in grace and God's providential wisdom is the setting for the special love God shows to God's elect in calling them, leading them, and accompanying them (even and especially in terms of agency) to that end. God wills for the elect to attain God's own self, and this willing, the gift of God's love, extends to those actions that, according to Aquinas, have merit before God toward that end. In short, as Wawrykow puts it very nicely, "the human story of responding to grace and working under grace is only correctly told when viewed against the account of God's willing."[63] This is certainly true, and I hope to offer a treatment of God's grace that does take account of God's purposive willing. It is certainly not my intention to articulate an account of Thomas' theology in which God's grace is occasional, or without telos. That being said, keeping this project to a manageable scope requires that I bracket both predestination and merit for the time being. Precisely because these issues are so central do they become difficult to include in an ecumenical conversation. A great deal remains to be said, ecumenically, about the notion that our actions, as a part of the purposive grace of God and the relationship between divine and human agency, are integral to God's will for God's elect to attain a vision of God's self in eternity. A great deal remains to be said, as well, about the notion of God's causation and knowledge by which God's special love extends to some and not to others. Indeed, one cannot speak about Thomas' treatment about the grace of God in a way entirely separated from this larger picture of God's willing. For these important issues, the amount of comparative ecumenical treatment necessary to foster a harmonious ecumenical conversation would constitute a volume all its own. I save treatment of merit and predestination for another venue.

---

63. Wawrykow, "Grace," 204.

4

Thomas Aquinas

ONE OF THE CONSISTENT means that Hauerwas and Hütter employed in speaking about the impact of divine agency on the moral life, and the connection of God's action to Christian moral action, was the Gospel narrative. For both theologians, the effect of the Gospel narrative is closely related to the ways in which God affects human agency in the Christian moral life. Thomas Aquinas is a useful conversation partner in this regard in that he depicts a similar connection in his treatise on the New Law. In the *Prima Secundae* of the *Summa theologiae*, Thomas' treatise on the New Law stands (appropriately) at the end of his treatise on Law (Questions 90–108), and just before his treatise on grace (Questions 109–114). His treatment of the New Law is accomplished in three questions (of the Law considered in itself; of the New Law compared with the Old; and of those things that are contained in the New Law), each containing four articles. Though his treatment of the New Law connects in a number of ways with the treatise on grace that follows it, it still remains firmly a part of his treatise on Law, and thus a preliminary look at the New Law, as law, is important.

The Twofold Sense of the New Law

In considering the New Law, as law, one cannot neglect Thomas' careful explanation of what law actually is. By the time Thomas wrote his *Summa* he had realized the importance of the twofold source of human action: intrinsic and extrinsic. Both law and grace fall under the latter category. In his introduction to his treatise on Law, before he even proceeds to any questions, Thomas writes this: "the extrinsic principle moving to good is God, Who both instructs us by means of his Law, and assists us by His grace, wherefore in the first place we must speak of law, in the second place, of grace."[1] The New Law is just in between these categories of an extrinsic principle by which God instructs us, and an extrinsic principle by which God assists us. More than any other kind of law, the New Law is most closely related to the Old Law, as both are given by God to accomplish what neither the natural law nor human laws could manage. As Aquinas writes in the question regarding natural law, from God as an extrinsic principle in directing human conduct, a Divine Law (being both the "Old" Law of Moses and the "New" Law of the Gospels) is necessary for human beings.[2] This question offers four reasons for necessity of the Divine Law: first, by means of the Divine Law, we are directed "to perform [our] proper acts in view of [our] last end."[3] Aquinas goes on to say that if the end to which we were ordained were none other than that natural end that is proportionate to the kinds of things we can manage as human agents, then we would need no additional law to direct us. But, "since man is ordained to the end of eternal happiness which is disproportionate to man's natural faculty,"[4] God gives us a law directing us to that end. The second reason Aquinas gives for the necessity of the Divine Law is that people tend to differ in opinion on particular matters, and since human judgment tends to vary regarding some of the specifics of how human beings ought to behave, there are differing laws. The Divine Law was given so that "man may know without any doubt what he ought to do and what he ought to avoid."[5] Third, the Divine Law is necessary because, while we may be competent to judge the rightness or the wrongness of an external act, we are not competent to judge "interior movements, that are hidden."[6] For human action to be genuinely virtuous, it must not only be rightly ordered in terms of the way it looks from the outside, but our conduct must be correct in terms of these "interior movements" as well. As Aquinas says, "human law could not sufficiently curb and direct interior acts; and it was necessary for this purpose that

---

1. Aquinas, *Summa theologiae* I-II, introduction to question 90.
2. Aquinas, *Summa theologiae* I-II.91.4.
3. Ibid.
4. Ibid.
5. Ibid.
6. Ibid.

a Divine law should supervene."[7] Fourth, Aquinas argues that just as human law cannot judge the right kinds of internal actions, so human law cannot justly punish evil actions, "since, while aiming at doing away with all evils, it would do away with many good things."[8] So that all sins might rightly be forbidden, the Divine Law was necessary.

This Divine Law, as Aquinas continues in the next article, is divided into the Old Law and the New Law. Thomas briefly comments on the ways in which the New Law surpasses the Old. The Old Law is distinguished from the New, not as two totally different things, but as "imperfect and perfect in the same species, e.g. a boy and a man."[9] The New Law is also said to surpass the Old Law "since it directs our internal acts," while the Old Law only has the capacity to restrain external action.[10] Finally, the Old Law directed human actions by means of the fear of punishment, whereas the New Law directs our actions "by love, which is poured into our hearts by the grace of Christ."[11]

From all of these elements, the New Law is (A) an extrinsic means by which God directs human action that (B) leads to the end of our eternal happiness, so that (C) we may know without doubt what to do, (D) through the governing of our interior acts, and keeping us from sin (E) through love, which is poured into our hearts by the grace of Christ. This definition leaves the reader with the sense that there is quite a lot of work done in the moral life in the New Law, the Law of the Gospel. However, at first glance it would seem that Thomas is falling into the same tensions that present in Hauerwas' theology. One might grant Aquinas that some of the elements of this definition are pretty easily accomplished by the Gospel narrative. Element A seems perfectly fine—the Gospels as revealed narrative can certainly act as an extrinsic means by which God can direct human action. Element B, too, seems plausible—God could certainly reveal things through Scripture that would direct us to an end that is disproportionate to our human capacity (suspending, for the moment, any worry that no matter how well we are directed to it through a narrative, we are no nearer able to accomplish actions toward that end). By the C element, the capability of a narrative is, perhaps, being

7. Ibid.
8. Ibid.
9. Aquinas, *Summa theologiae* I-II.91.5.
10. Ibid.
11. Ibid.

stretched a little bit. After all, the New Law does not offer nearly as comprehensive a picture of prescribed behavior as does the Old Law. How can a narrative like the Gospels hope to leave us without any doubt as to what to do? In the D element, one might ask if Aquinas is demanding of the New Law something that the Gospel narrative could not possibly provide: namely, God's directing of interior movements. We might be willing to allow this if he were only speaking of certain kinds of prescriptions that apply just as much to the condition of the Christian heart and our intentions and motives as they do to the shape of external acts. The final element, E, leaves a lot of unanswered questions. What capacity has a narrative to direct through love? Can a law command love? How can one say that a narrative is connected with the grace of Christ? In short, the issue seems to be that Aquinas, just like Hauerwas and Hütter, holds a very close connection between the effect of the Gospel narrative and the impact of divine agency upon the divine life. He seems to put the Law of the Gospels to tasks that are very connected with how God's grace works in the moral life.

Here emerges the first of the conceptual tools that, I believe, Aquinas has to offer the contemporary ecumenical ethical discourse: the twofold sense of the New Law. Like Hauerwas and Hütter, Thomas seems, initially, to be blending the capacity of the Gospel narrative with God's agency in the moral life. He clears this up, however, in the first article of I-II 106, which asks, "Whether the New Law is a written law?" In the *sed contra* (a section in which Thomas, most often, offers an authoritative citation from Scripture or from the written tradition), Thomas quotes Jeremiah 31, which talks about the promise of a new covenant in which God's law will be written on the heart of the believer. Thomas then concludes, "the New Law is instilled into our hearts."[12] However, this does not constitute a negative answer to his question of whether the New Law is a written Law. Indeed, he begins the *sed contra* thus: "The New Law is the law of the New Testament."[13] He points out in the body of this article that the efficacy of the New Testament is not to be found in the narrative itself but is, rather, "the grace of the Holy Ghost, which is given to those who believe in Christ."[14] That being said, Thomas does not simply dispose of the written New Testament in favor of the "grace of the Holy Ghost" as

12. Aquinas, *Summa theologiae* I-II.106.1.*sed contra*.
13. Ibid.
14. Aquinas, *Summa theologiae* I-II.106.1.

the definition of the New Law. Rather, he writes, "the New Law contains certain things that dispose us to receive the grace of the Holy Ghost, and pertaining to the use of that grace: such things are of secondary importance, so to speak, in the New Law; and the faithful need to be instructed concerning them, both by word and writing, both as to what they should believe and as to what they should do. Consequently we must say that the New Law is in the first place a law that is inscribed on our hearts, but that secondarily it is a written law."[15] The New Law is, then, primarily to be considered that which is inscribed in our hearts—that is, the grace of the Holy Ghost—and secondarily the written law that prepares us for God's grace and instructs us as to its use, which is to say, what we should do. However, one might object that this seems like a very convenient combination. Why can Aquinas simply connect these two things and call them the twofold sense of the New Law? The answer is in a very brief quotation at the beginning of the body of the article from Aristotle's *Nicomachean Ethics* (book 9, chapter 8), which deals with the problem of self-love. In this chapter, part of Aristotle's argument is that the person who is most suitably called a self-lover is the one who grants obedience to the rational soul and does what is virtuous, loving those best, most noble elements in themselves. Just as a city is, above all, the thing within it that has the most authority, within the individual, a person is said to be constituted by the thing that is most in control of that person.[16] From that part of the argument, Aquinas draws out this idea: "each thing appears to be that which preponderates it [*quod in ea est potissimum*]."[17] In other words, any given thing is most correctly said to be that which most dominates it, or that which it is most chiefly or most principally. From this idea, Thomas draws the conclusion, "that which is preponderant [*quod est potissimum*] in the Law of the New Testament, whereon all its efficacy is based, is the grace of the Holy Ghost."[18] In short, it is rather incomplete to talk about the mere written New Law without addressing that which the Law of the New Testament is, principally, which is the grace of the Holy Spirit. Thus, he concludes at the end of the body of I-II 106.1, as was quoted above, that the New Law is primarily the grace of the Holy Ghost, and secondarily a written Law.

15. Ibid.
16. Aristotle, *Nicomachean Ethics*, bk. 9, ch. 8.
17. Aquinas, *Summa theologiae* I-II.106.1.
18. Ibid.

Like Hauerwas and Hütter, Aquinas very closely associates the written Gospels with the grace of God working in the Christian moral life. However, Aquinas points out that this narrative is inseparable from (and, in fact, even secondary to) that on which its efficacy is based: God's agency. This is not to say that we can simply disregard the written text as separate from the grace of the Holy Spirit. Instead, Aquinas argues, "The Gospel writings contain only such things as pertain to the grace of the Holy Ghost, either by disposing us thereto, or by directing us to the use thereof."[19] In harmony with the general instincts of Hauerwas and Hütter, Aquinas closely associates the Gospel narrative with the impact of God's action upon Christian action. However, instead of casing the efficacy of God's agency in terms of the transformative power of the narrative, Aquinas cases the efficacy of the narrative in terms of the transformative power of God. For, as Thomas writes, "the New Law is instilled into man, not only by indicating what he should do, but also by helping him to accomplish it."[20] On both fronts, God's grace is that which constitutes this law principally, or that which preponderates it. This inward bestowing of the Holy Spirit is why, then, Aquinas can affirm that this New Law justifies, without, at the same time, having to affirming that the written letter of the New Law justifies.[21] Thomas argues that "the letter, even of the Gospel would kill, unless there were the inward presence of the healing grace of faith."[22] In this way, he offers a convenient way to separate the transformative grace of God from the transformative power of the Gospels in a way that excludes neither, and rightly indicates God's grace as that which justifies and "helps" us.

After Question 107, in which Aquinas explores the relationship between the Old Law and the New, Aquinas begins to unpack the idea that the New Testament contains content "disposing us to the grace of the Holy Spirit, or directing us to the right use of that grace" in Question 108. In this question, he asks about the sufficiency of the New Law, in its twofold sense, to direct both outward and inward actions, and its ability to provide not only precepts but counsels as well. In the first article, Aquinas asserts that it is fitting for grace to be given to us by external objects (that is, the sacraments) and that it is fitting that external works flow

19. Aquinas, *Summa theologiae* I-II.106.1.RO1.
20. Aquinas, *Summa theologiae* I-II.106.1.RO2.
21. Aquinas, *Summa theologiae* I-II.106.2.
22. Ibid.

from grace.[23] In terms of the second connection Thomas gives between grace and external acts, he writes, "those external acts which ensue from the promptings of grace: and herein we must observe a difference. For there are some which are necessarily in keeping with, or in opposition to inward grace consisting in faith that worketh through love. Such external works are prescribed or forbidden in the New Law."[24] So, one of the ways in which the New Law regulates human action is a means very similar to that of the Old Law—through certain precepts that address things that are in keeping with or are in opposition to inward grace. However, as he indicates above, this is not the only way in which the New Law explicitly addresses external actions, in and of themselves. He continues, "on the other hand, there are works which are not necessarily opposed to, or in keeping with faith that worketh through love. Such works are not prescribed or forbidden by the New Law, but have been left by the Lawgiver, i.e. Christ, to the discretion of each individual."[25] So if this is the case, are such works directed in some way in the New Law? In other words, does the New Law have the capacity to direct our actions beyond simply providing precepts? Here Aquinas seems to be addressing the New Law as written Law (i.e., the Gospels). The answer that he provides is that the written law does not regulate those things that the Lawgiver leaves "at the discretion" of the individual believer. But, that does not mean that this broad range of Christian behavior is simply unaddressed, even in the written sense of the New Law. One might expect Aquinas, here, to use this opportunity to minimize the importance of the New Law in its secondary, written sense, and to speak about the ways in which the Holy Spirit can offer commands and precepts that the written Law cannot. However, Thomas is more careful than that, keeping very firmly to the difference between governing external actions as such, and governing external actions by means of effecting internal actions. Without this distinction, Thomas appears to be simply dismissing the written New Law when he writes in I-II 108.2, "since these determinations are not in

---

23. While it may not be quite fair to Aquinas, if we bracket the first part of connection between grace and external works and treat the second, we can remain focused on the impact of Thomas' account of the twofold sense of the New Law on the contemporary Protestant ethical discourse. While Thomas' notions of the sacraments are rightly and tightly bound up with the bond between grace and external works, I wish to bracket its discussion with regard to relevance to the Protestant discourse.

24. Aquinas, *Summa theologiae* I-II.108.1.

25. Ibid.

themselves necessarily connected with inward grace wherein the Law consists, they do not come under a precept of the New Law, but are left to the decision of man."[26] His conclusion regarding the external regulation of external actions, considered in and of themselves, is that the New Law actually has relatively little to add, and much of what was carefully regulated in the Old Law is now left up to the decision of the individual.

This seeming problem is cleared up in I-II 108.3, in which Thomas addresses the connection between the inward act of the individual and the twofold sense of the New Law. He argues that in the written, secondary sense of the New Law, interior acts are ordered by moments like the Sermon on the Mount, which "contains the whole process of forming the life of a Christian."[27] This process is accomplished by means of the written (Gospel) Law's ability to point to any particular action that has to be done, as well as its ability to direct intention with regard to an end, "teaching that in our good works, we should seek neither human praise, nor worldly riches,"[28] and with regard to how to behave toward our neighbor. He lifts up one more sense in which the written sense of the New Law directs those things that are "left to the decision" of the individual. He writes that in the Sermon, Jesus "teaches us how to fulfill the reaching of the Gospel; viz. by imploring the help of God."[29] Thus, again, Aquinas considers the Gospel narrative as the New Law only in the secondary sense, but at the same time never separate from the grace of God through the Holy Spirit.

In the final article, Thomas again lifts up this secondary, written sense of the New Law as indispensable to the overall conception of New Law, and to addressing the same adaptability (even in the written sense) to individual situations. Thomas affirms that the Gospel narrative directs us not only through precepts, but also by means of counsels: "We must therefore understand the commandments of the New Law to have been given about matters that are necessary to gain the end of eternal bliss, to which end the New Law brings us forthwith: but that the counsels are about matters that render the gaining of this end more assured and expeditious."[30] One of the reasons for the necessity of the Divine Law

26. Aquinas, *Summa theologiae* I-II.108.2.
27. Aquinas, *Summa theologiae* I-II.108.3.
28. Ibid.
29. Ibid.
30. Aquinas, *Summa theologiae* I-II.108.4.

generally, and the New Law specifically, is to direct us to our eternal happiness—a happiness that is beyond our natural capacity. Thus, even in these counsels, the written sense of the New Law points back again to the primary sense of this Law, God's grace, as its most principle element.

The Gifts of the Holy Spirit

The second pattern drawn out from the treatment of Hauerwas and Hütter was their consistent framing of the initial impact of God's agency on the Christian moral life as a fundamental resituating of our character and moral agency by gift, making us more amenable to the shaping power of community and narrative. Both spoke about how perception, vision, and judgment are fundamentally transformed and shaped in the moral life. As seen in turning to Aquinas on the Gifts of the Holy Spirit, his approach shares some common instincts. However, Aquinas has at his disposal some sophisticated conceptual tools that would nicely aid the contemporary ethical discourse in better realizing this important description of the impact of God's agency in the moral life. Like these modern ethicists, Aquinas holds that Christian ethics is rightly conceived of as beginning through God's fundamental resituating of character and moral agency by gift in a way that makes us especially amenable to further formation.

Thomas Aquinas' single question on the Gifts of the Holy Spirit is a part of his larger treatise on habits. Unlike the extrinsic principle of the law, a habit is an intrinsic principle of human action. A habit is a quality, a disposition whereby the subject is disposed, or qualified, with regard to itself or to another.[31] But this qualifying is of the most impactful kind. A habit is the kind of quality that determines the subject and its acts as to the good that is proper to it.[32] A good habit disposes the subject well in its operation with regard to its proper end, while a bad habit disposes the subject to actions poorly in its actions with regard to its proper end. The virtues are good habits, and the Gifts of the Holy Spirit are integrally connected with them. *ST* I-II 68 consists of eight articles, beginning with the question of whether the Gifts of the Holy Spirit differ from the virtues. In this article, Aquinas tries out a number of possible, but incorrect, answers (some of which are similar to his

---

31. Aquinas, *Summa theologiae* I-II.49.1
32. Aquinas, *Summa theologiae* I-II.49.2, 3.

own earlier thoughts), before offering a final answer to the question. Initially, he says that there is no real difference between gift and virtue, "because the word 'virtue' conveys the notion that it perfects man in relation to well-doing, while the word 'gift' refers to the cause from which it proceeds."[33] Again, Thomas employs the same kind of logic he used in speaking about the twofold sense of the New Law. A thing is rightly said to be that which it is most principally. To speak about a thing without speaking about the cause from which it proceeds is incomplete. In this way, at least, the gifts and the virtues are not separate. However, this leads to a conclusion that he dismisses, which is that there is therefore no difference between them, when in fact there are some virtues that are called gifts, and others that are not.[34] He considers and then dismisses a second possibility, that the gifts perfect the faculty of the reason, while the virtues perfect the faculty of the will. However, he says, if this were the case then "all the virtues would have to be in the appetite, and all the gifts in the reason."[35] This is not the case, in fact, as four of the gifts apply to the reason (wisdom, knowledge, understanding, and counsel) and three belong to the will (fortitude, piety, and fear). Next, he considers and dismisses the opinion articulated in Gregory's *Moralia on Job*—an opinion that Thomas himself held in his early writings. According to Thomas' depiction of Gregory, here, the gifts offer the soul "prudence, temperance, justice, and fortitude," and strengthen the soul against any temptation.[36] Thomas rejects this description because the virtues themselves seem to fill this same function in resisting the temptations that threaten them. A final possibility he considers is that since the gifts were in Christ, the virtues are given "that we may do good works, but the gifts, in order to conform us to Christ."[37] This possibility does not work either because, Aquinas argues, Jesus asks us to conform to him (in different places in Scripture) through qualities like humility, meekness, and the virtue of charity.

Dismissing all of these ways as properly depicting the difference between the Gifts and the virtues, Aquinas insists that "we must be guided

---

33. Aquinas, *Summa theologiae* I-II.68.1.
34. Ibid.
35. Ibid.
36. Ibid.
37. Ibid.

by the way in which Scripture expresses itself"[38] in regard to the Gifts. Thomas points out that, in naming the seven Gifts of the Holy Spirit in Isaiah 11:2–3, "the term employed is 'spirit' rather than 'gift.'"[39] This approach yields a very different conception of the Gifts than Thomas' contemporaries and even his own previous writings. The Gifts are given to us through divine inspiration,[40] which shifts the consideration of the Gifts from the framework of different modes of action to different principles from which action proceeds. Thomas notes here, as he does in so many other places, that there is a twofold principle of movement in human beings: the intrinsic (reason) and the extrinsic (God). Suddenly questions arise about Thomas' placement of the Gifts in his treatment on habits. If a habit is an intrinsic principle of action, and if the Gifts are given to us by divine inspiration, then this would seem to make them a part of God's extrinsic causation of our action. Thomas clarifies: "whatever is moved must be proportionate to its mover: and the perfection of the mobile as such, consists in a disposition whereby it is disposed to be well moved by its mover. Hence the more exalted the mover, the more perfect must be the disposition whereby the mobile is made proportionate to its mover."[41] Thomas, thus, sets up a category in which an extrinsic cause is needed to provide a condition or a disposition or a readiness by which the human being can readily be moved by God as an extrinsic principle. There needs to be within the Christian some perfection by which we are "made proportionate" to God's movement of us. No matter how well-polished the cardinal virtues are, Thomas argues, we cannot bridge the gap whereby we are (as free willing agents) well disposed to be moved by God. We can perfect ourselves, by cultivating the virtues, to be well disposed to be moved according to our reason, but "man needs yet higher perfections whereby to be disposed to be moved by God."[42] These perfections, infused by God, are the Gifts.

Aquinas then adds another notion that he draws from the *Liber de bona fortuna*. He writes that "for those who are moved by Divine instinct [*per instinctum divinum*], there is no need to take counsel according to human reason, but only to follow their inner promptings, since they

38. Ibid.
39. Ibid.
40. Ibid.
41. Ibid.
42. Ibid.

are moved by a principle higher than human reason."[43] This seems like a very easy solution to Christian ethics—so easy, in fact, that it seems implausible. If all we have to do is to be moved by divine instinct, then reason and judgment become obsolete; we merely become puppets of God's will, and ethics is no longer an issue. Important to remember, however, is that the "promptings," here, are not God's constraining or moving of the (no longer free) human will. The "promptings" are those things inclining us to actions that our reason could not—actions that lead to our eternal good (a good beyond the reach or even desire of our human capacity). However, whether Aquinas means that this "divine instinct" is an external principle, directing us from without, as the law, or an internal principle distinct from our reason and our other habits, will make an enormous difference to the freedom of our will. Thomas makes this distinction plainer in article 2. He notes that God perfects the reason as to its action in two ways. First, God perfects the reason through the natural light given to it.[44] We are helpfully reminded, here, that our action (that which is our "part" to do) cannot be rightly conceived of without reference to God's action in the overall system of contingent, secondary causes. Aside from this natural perfection of the reason given by God, we are given the supernatural perfection of the theological virtues.[45] However, we cannot, of course, simply make ourselves well disposed to these sorts of actions. Rather the Gifts of the Holy Spirit "are perfections of man, whereby he is disposed so as to be amenable to the promptings of God."[46] These gifts, then, do not result in an extrinsic principle, setting aside the intrinsic principle of reason. Rather, the gifts result in an intrinsic principle by which the intrinsic principle of reason is perfected and disposed to well receive that which would otherwise be beyond its capacity: the promptings of God that constitute the "divine instinct." As Ulrich Horst writes, "the fact that the gifts have an elevating function follows from the movement of the Holy Spirit becoming efficacious in them by which all of the powers of the soul become disposed in such a way that they are subordinated to divine movement. Furthermore, that the Holy Spirit does this is a fact owed to the theological virtues . . . the theological virtues form as it were a

43. Ibid.
44. Thomas Aquinas, *Summa theologiae* I-II.68.2.
45. Ibid.
46. Ibid.

supernatural configuration in humans, which brings about agreement with God and—in a next step, as it were—a unity with the dynamics of the Holy Spirit."[47] This unity with the dynamics of the Holy Spirit is not to be placed in opposition to reason or to any of the powers of the soul, but rather is rightly viewed as elevating and perfecting in which we are well disposed to God's promptings. As Daniel Macguire notes, "the gifts, then—even those which reside in the mind—are essentially linked to love and render us connatural, obedient, and amenable to the movements of the Spirit. The volitional attitude has cognitive impact. There is an affective component in the knowing process."[48] The Gifts are not the promptings themselves, but a kind of habit in which we are made amenable to God's promptings that, for Aquinas, amount to a perfection of the intrinsic principle for human action or, more concisely, a perfection of the reason.[49] For those actions leading to the end proportionate to us, we may be adequately directed there by reason, but for actions leading to the supernatural end of our eternal happiness we must "be moved and led thither by the Holy Ghost. Therefore, in order to accomplish this end, it is necessary for man to have the gift of the Holy Ghost."[50]

Thus, in the overall context of Thomas' moral theology, the Gifts of the Holy Spirit and the primary sense of the New Law point to very similar notions. In the first article on Thomas' treatment of the New Law, he cites John 14:17 in discussing our reception of the Holy Ghost in the New Law.[51] In the *Prima Secundae*, Thomas only cites that passage in one other place: the *sed contra* of I-II 68.3, in which he asserts, "our Lord in speaking of the Holy Ghost said to His disciples, 'He shall abide with

47. Horst, *Die Gaben des Heiligen Geistes nach Thomas von Aquin*, 92. Daß dabei die Gaben eine herausgehobene Funktion haben, ergibt sich aus der in ihnen wirksam werdenden Bewegung des Hl. Geistes, durch die unsere gesamten Seelenkräfte so disponiert werden, daß sie der göttlichen Bewegung unterstellt werden. Ferner: Daß der Hl. Geist dies tut, verdankt sich den theologischen Tugenden, die den Menschen mit dem ihn bewegenden Hl. Geist einen. Glaube, Hoffnung und Liebe stehen also in einer viel tieferen Beziehung zu den Gaben, die zudem durch sie "geregelt" werden, als die natürlichen Tugenden zu den ihnen korrespondierenden Seelenpotenzen. Die göttlichen Tugenden bilden also gleichsam die übernatürliche Grundausstattung des Menschen, sie bewirken die Einigung mit Gott und—gleichsam in einem nächsten Schritt—einen sie ihn auch mit der Dynamik des Hl. Geistes, die ihn "bewegbar" macht.

48. Macguire, "Ratio Practica and the Intellectualistic Fallacy," 28.

49. Porter, "Moral Language and the Language of Grace," 189.

50. Aquinas, *Summa theologiae* I-II.68.2

51. Aquinas, *Summa theologiae* I-II.106.1.RO1.

you, and shall be in you.' Now the Holy Ghost is not in a man without His gifts. Therefore His gifts abide in man. Therefore they are not merely acts or passions, but abiding habits."[52] This is the authority that Aquinas cites in answer to the question of what these Gifts actually are. They are habits. Just as in his questions on the twofold sense of the New Law, while the action of the Holy Spirit is intimately involved in human action, the Holy Spirit is still an extrinsic cause acting on human agency—hence the need for the habit. In the second objection of this article, the objector notes, "insofar as man is moved by the Spirit of God, he is somewhat like an instrument in His regard. Now to be perfected by a habit is befitting not an instrument, but a principle agent."[53] The objector makes a good point here. In a bond between divine agency and human agency, how could we be anything but mere instruments of God? Aquinas answers this way: "This argument holds, in the case of an instrument which has no faculty of action, but only of being acted upon. But man is not an instrument of that kind; for he is so acted upon, by the Holy Ghost, that he also acts himself, in so far as he has a free-will."[54] If we were merely instruments of divine will, then God as an extrinsic cause would simply act upon us and we would respond. However, as creatures with free will, the action of the Holy Ghost upon us operates together with our own action. Thus we are in need of something by which we are well disposed to the promptings of God. Such can only come from outside of us (this he gains from the *Liber de bona fortuna*, as seen in the last chapter), and so there must be within us something that disposes us to God's promptings—in a word, habit.

So, what do the Gifts have to do with God's resituating of character, and how does this treatise aid the contemporary ecumenical ethical discourse? The answer to both questions is in the fourth article, in which Aquinas enumerates the Gifts. This article begins by articulating much of what has been accomplished above, in the citation of the Isaiah 11 passage, and in restating the difference between the Gifts disposing us to follow the promptings of the Holy Spirit, and the moral virtues disposing us to be moved according to reason.[55] As Aquinas goes on to say, however, "just as it is natural for the appetitive powers to be moved by

52. Aquinas, *Summa theologiae* I-II.68.3.*sed contra*.
53. Aquinas, *Summa theologiae* I-II.68.3.Obj.2.
54. Aquinas, *Summa theologiae* I-II.68.3.RO2.
55. Aquinas, *Summa theologiae* I-II.68.4.

the command of reason, so it is natural for all the forces in man to be moved by the instinct of God."[56] Quite a statement. Here Aquinas enjoys the fruits of his careful consideration of free human action in the overall picture of divine causation, as well as his treatment of the Gifts thus far. Just as it is inappropriate to separate that act which is our "part" to do (even those acts which God asks of us) from that which is God's "part" to do, so too it is natural for every one of our movements to proceed from the First Mover. As all of our movement, even and especially movements of our free will, are traceable back to God's causality anyway, it is natural for all of our "powers" to be moved by God. Aquinas continues, "therefore whatever powers in man can be the principles of human actions, can also be the subjects of gifts, even as they are virtues; and such powers are the reason and appetite."[57] So, just as all of our capacity for action is traceable to God anyway, it is fitting and natural that all of our capacities for action be subject to this "habit" by which we are made amenable to God's promptings.

Focusing first on reason, Aquinas divides reason into the speculative and the practical, both of which involve the apprehension of, and judgment concerning, truth.[58] Then he names those Gifts by which our reason is made amenable to God's promptings. Our speculative reason is perfected by the gifts of "understanding" and "wisdom," and our practical intellect is perfected by the gifts of "counsel" and "knowledge."[59] He then goes on to say how our will is perfected in the gifts of "piety," "fortitude," and "fear" (specifically fear of the Lord).[60] In this way, the Gifts of the Holy Spirit, spelled out in this sevenfold way, take the whole person, and render her moveable in all of her abilities.[61] In short, "the Gifts perfect the soul's powers in relation to the Holy Ghost their Mover."[62]

---

56. Ibid.
57. Ibid.
58. Ibid.
59. Ibid.
60. Ibid.
61. Horst, *Die Gaben des Heiligen Geistes nach Thomas von Aquin*, 87. Die Gaben des Hl. Geistes, wiewohl in einer Siebenzahl aufgefächert, nehmen den ganzen Menschen, wofern er dazu bereit ist, in Beschlag, um ihn mit seinen sämtlichen Fähigkeiten "bewegbar" zu machen.
62. Aquinas, *Summa theologiae* I-II.68.8.

It is fairly easy to object to the exact divisions Thomas gives to the function of the intellect, or the location of the "power" of the intellect in the soul, or even his separation between the speculative and the practical reason. It is easy to dismiss the structural connection between reason, God, and action as uselessly antiquated. However, for Hauerwas, Hütter, and others in the contemporary conversation, transitions in the ways we understand, perceive, and judge are spoken of as the roots of the transformation of human action, as well as being very closely connected to how divine action impacts human life. Whatever one makes of Aquinas' conception of reason, intellect, and action, the broad framework of the Gifts of the Holy Spirit fundamentally resituating character and moral agency and making them amenable to God's promptings is an important tool for considering a non-contrastive connection between divine and human agency in the moral life.

Thomas on Grace

Thomas' treatise on grace is considerably larger than the solitary question on the Gifts, and much more detailed in the concepts it provides than the relatively simple twofold New Law.[63] Fortunately, thematic elements in the treatise on grace hold the potential to be very useful to the present inquiry, and as conceptual contributions to the contemporary ethical discourse. For the most part this treatment will concentrate on Aquinas' articulations of (1) what grace is, (2) why it is necessary, and (3) how to conceptually divide it as to its effects. Thomas considers these themes, most closely, in I-II, 109–111.

What Grace Is

In Question 109, Thomas asks, in ten articles, the necessity of grace before going on in question 110 to actually name what grace *is*. Such an approach has the great advantage of inquiring that for which "grace" must provide before looking to see what it is. Thus, question 109 is less

---

63. The present inquiry is not the place for a full exploration of Thomas' treatise on grace, as fully detailing the treatise would take us far from the scope of this chapter and could, at the very best, only duplicate the usefulness of other very adequate studies. Much more thorough examinations are available, especially as found in the sources examined in this and the last chapter, particularly Wawrykow's *God's Grace and Human Action* and Lonergan's *Grace and Freedom*.

about grace and more about human beings, our abilities and our inabilities, as considered from a number of angles, but most especially in terms of intact human nature (before original sin) and fallen human nature (after original sin). However, as the current inquiry will focus on certain distinctions within Thomas' conception of grace, it may be wise to begin with certain indications of what Aquinas means by "grace." While the answer to this question will require very careful examination in the pages that follow, some initial remarks from some of Aquinas' contemporary readers are helpful.

Thomas O'Meara writes in 1997 that "grace is presented as a principle of various activities and potentialities for action. Grace therefore is an intrinsic, fundamental source and not just an extrinsic force."[64] While one might initially object to O'Meara's willingness to stray from Aquinas' clear idea that grace is an extrinsic principle of human action (unlike the intrinsic principle of reason, of which God is still, nevertheless, a part), O'Meara is correct to point out that in Thomas' conception of grace, the action of God as an extrinsic principle becomes much more involved with intrinsic principles for action. This sort of pattern might be expected, based on Thomas' description of the Gifts of the Holy Spirit as habits, and habits as qualities. While a habit, as a quality, can be caused from without, it nevertheless has an enormous impact upon the ways in which the intrinsic principles of our actions operate. As Ægidius Doolan helpfully points out, "quality is the most perfect, the most distinctive and distinguishing of all accidents. It is the accident by which a thing is *qualified*. . . . Quality affects a thing most intimately—it may affect its very nature. The difference between good and bad, health and disease, ugliness and beauty, is a difference of quality."[65] Thus, as Aquinas shows grace to be in some instances a habit or a quality, O'Meara's words indicate that the categories of God's grace as a purely extrinsic principle and our own intrinsic principles become blended. Of course, this is the core reason that Thomas' treatise on grace is so important to prompting an ecumenical ethic of grace in community. Thomas, through his conceptions of grace, is able to deal with the collision between God's causation of our action and our causation of action in a way that blends intrinsic and extrinsic principles of action and does so without compromising either God's sovereignty or the freedom of our action.

64. O'Meara, "Virtues in the Theology of Thomas Aquinas," 260.
65. Doolan, *Sanctifying Grace*, 83.

The domain in which grace has its "effect" with regard to the human being is interesting as well, and will show the synthetic character of Thomas' theology as a whole and his consideration of the interaction between divine and human agency, in particular. Certainly God's grace is connected with human action, and particularly moral action. The reader might call to mind Pinckaers' "two circles" in which the grace of God is illustrated as perfecting every kind of moral action as the lifeblood "in the Christian moral organism as a circulatory system."[66] Jean Porter puts the matter rather more succinctly: "grace is nothing other than a created transformation of the human soul, through which we are enabled to carry out actions that lead to salvation,"[67] the virtues being the vehicle for these actions. As Lonergan has pointed out, however, the idea that grace is an opportunity to speak about God acting upon our agency should cause some worry about violence. When speaking about God co-operating sin-ridden human agency, if God's grace is the lifeblood of the Christian moral organism, can there be room for anything else? Even more worryingly, Wawrykow rightly points out that the "effect" of grace accomplishes this operation within our agency through much more than influencing individual movements alone. Thomas attaches much importance to actions in relation to an end, and this true, eternal end is well beyond the capacity of our human agency. In this way, Thomas looks to "grace" not only to restore a certain kind of action, but to restore the acting person, in order to orient her not just to certain movements, but to a particular end—an end proper to her, but beyond the reach of her nature. "Aquinas in the *ST* speaks of both obstacles to the journey, the ontological and the moral; and therefore grace will have a twofold function, of healing and elevating. Neither seems for Aquinas to take precedence; he views both with equal seriousness."[68] As the realms of ontology and morality are by no means separable for Aquinas, generally, they are by no means separable in terms of the "effect" of grace on our agency.

So, to begin with, these readers have aided in gaining an initial toehold on what grace is, and what grace "does," for Aquinas. Though an extrinsic principle for action, the "effect" of grace operates upon, and co-operates with, intrinsic principles for human action. Part of the "effect"

66. Pinckaers, *Sources of Christian Ethics*, 178.
67. Porter, "Right Reason and the Love of God," 179.
68. Wawrykow, "Grace," 196.

of grace, as a quality, is to qualify us as agents, blending the categories of extrinsic and intrinsic principles. Also, grace has a necessary connection with human action, but not simply in its conception or implementation. Grace addresses our orientation to our final end both through attention to moral action, and attention to our state-of-being from which action proceeds.

Why Grace Is Necessary

Before offering the distinctions between the different effects of grace in I-II 111, Aquinas offers a framework of how we must consider grace with regard to its necessity in different kinds of human action (I-II 109), and what grace actually *is* with regard to its impact on principles of human action (I-II 110). Thus, before even treating the divisions of the effects of grace, Thomas offers a picture of the kinds of human action for which grace is so necessary, and what grace is with regard to the soul. The picture emerging in preparation for offering the distinctions is that there are four kinds of good human action for which grace has relevance in 109: namely (1) those good actions that are natural to us and we can accomplish, (2) those good actions that are natural to us but that we cannot accomplish without some "healing," (3) those good actions that we are asked to do but that are entirely beyond our natural capacity, and (4) those good actions that are an operation of God while they are at the same time our operation. Additionally, the distinctions must account for extrinsic and intrinsic effects of what grace *is* with regard to the soul as found in Question 110.

The first few articles of the treatise on grace frame the matter of God's grace in terms of its necessity. Thomas uses these questions to offer a framework (including some helpful reminders from previous questions) to rightly consider grace. *ST* I-II 109 begins by asking whether, without grace, we can know any truth. Aquinas uses this first article to reiterate a few concepts surrounding cognition and action. After making clear that the act of the intellect still counts as a human action, Aquinas reminds us that all actions rely on the First Mover and one's "form" as principle of human action, also caused by God.[69] No matter how perfect a created nature is supposed to be, one cannot speak about its movement without speaking also about the First Mover, and God's formal causa-

---

69. Aquinas, *Summa theologiae* I-II 109.1.

tion. Aquinas helpfully summarizes, "the act of the intellect . . . depends upon God in two ways: first inasmuch as it is from Him that it has the form whereby it acts; secondly, inasmuch as it is moved by Him to act."[70] With regard to the act of the intellect in particular, through this kind of causation, we can know those things that it is natural and proportionate for our intellect to be able to know through our senses. But there are times in which God instructs us beyond the "natural light" of our intellect. In these times, we need a new light added to supplement our natural abilities, "the light of grace."[71] Thomas here has set the stage of instances in which God grants special help for human action that reaches beyond natural human capacity against the backdrop of a causal setting in which all human intellection is traced back to God anyway. The second article offers tools closely connected to the first. In answering the question, "Whether man can wish or do any good without grace?" Thomas notes that, stained by original sin, we have a twofold shortfall in terms of our doing or wishing good. In the original sin-stained, corrupt state of nature, we are unable to wish or do even those goods that are proportionate to our nature. This does not mean that human nature, in its current, fallen state, is unable to achieve *any* good, "as to build dwellings, plant vineyards and the like,"[72] but that we are unable to do virtuous deeds that should be natural to us. We fall short of the acquired virtues. Thomas equates the current, fallen state of human nature to a "sick man" who can still move, "yet he cannot be perfectly moved with the movements of one in health, unless by the help of medicine he be cured."[73] Without this "healing," we are unable to do good acts that should be natural to us such as loving God above all things (article 3) or being able to fulfill the commandments of the Law of Moses (article 4). Beyond even those good acts natural to us that we can only accomplish after we are healed from our "sickness," Thomas again points to the need of divine agency in accomplishing good acts beyond our natural capacity, "works of supernatural virtue."[74] In article 5, Aquinas adds that such actions that lead to the eternal end of the beatific vision exceed the proportion of human nature, just as the end itself exceeds human nature. A higher force is

70. Ibid.
71. Ibid.
72. Aquinas, *Summa theologiae* I-II 109.2.
73. Ibid.
74. Ibid.

needed for the accomplishment of such acts.[75] Article 6 supplements this picture with the question of whether we can prepare ourselves for grace (elements of which were treated in the last chapter). Grace is necessary here, too, as "we must presuppose a gratuitous gift of God, Who moves the soul inwardly."[76] Being prepared for grace is a free "turning" towards God that we cannot manage without the help of God moving us inwardly.[77] Here, too, divine agency is needed to do that which human agency cannot manage on its own. But, the emphasis in this article is not just that there is the need for some *prior* gift by God that enables us to do that which we could not manage before the gift. Nor is the gift treated as part of God's transforming of the intrinsic principles of our action (in other words, something that stays with us as a part of the causing of a variety of different actions). Instead, here is a moment in which God acts and we act, and one action results. We cannot turn to God unless God turns us, but we cannot turn to God unless we actually turn. This does not mean a preliminary "start" of a turn by God and then our completion of the turn after the gift (or vice versa). Instead we have God's action and our action as one single action. The remaining articles anticipate the divisions of grace, to which I shall turn shortly.

With these opening articles, Thomas offers a very helpful backdrop for the consideration of grace: our action depends on God both in terms of the form by which we act and the movement to act itself. Thomas also offers a difference between those good actions that are natural to us that we can accomplish, those good actions that are natural to us but we cannot accomplish without some healing of our "sickness," and those good actions that are beyond the capacity of our human nature for which we need some additional "help" of God. Finally, Aquinas offers a different kind of good action, our turning to God, in which a new category in the picture of human causation is opened: we act and God acts and a single action results. The setting for the discussion of grace incorporates, then, the potential for a kind of action that is an operation of God at the same time as it is the operation of a free human agent.

With the framework of this picture of human action in terms of divine causation in place, Aquinas turns, in 110, to the question of what grace is. As the first article of 110 makes clear, God's grace, in its primary

---

75. Aquinas, *Summa theologiae* I-II 109.5.
76. Aquinas, *Summa theologiae* I-II 109.6.
77. Ibid.

sense, is "something bestowed on man by God,"[78] or, put another way, an effect of God's will in whoever is said to have God's grace.[79] Aquinas says that the effect of God's "gratuitous" will on human action is twofold: first, those instances in which we are "moved by God to know or will or do something."[80] This is from the second article in which Thomas is asking whether grace is a quality, such as a habit—something that qualifies the soul in a particular way. His answer in this instance is that grace does not have to be. The "effect" of God's will on the one who is said to have God's grace does not have to be in something qualifying the soul, but can simply be a movement. But second, he continues, grace can also be a quality in the soul, "as a habitual gift infused by God into the soul."[81] This is the same sort of thing Aquinas offers in treating the gifts. God bestows upon certain human beings particular intrinsic principles for action, "in order that they may of themselves be inclined to these movements, and thus the movements whereby they are moved by God become natural and easy to creatures."[82] So, God's grace is an effect of God's will on the receiver. Thus far, two possible modes of this effect are apparent—one very simple extrinsic, in which God simply causes action in human beings, and another intrinsic, in which the receiver of God's grace is disposed to a certain kind of action by the habitual shaping of her own inclinations. Such an effect is not an extrinsic movement of the soul to certain actions, but rather, "as a quality, is said to act upon the soul, not after the manner of an efficient cause, but after the manner of a formal cause, as whiteness makes a thing white, and justice, just."[83] With regard to this habitual gift of grace, Thomas addresses an important objection. By grace, Thomas indicates we can do things that are above natural human capacity to an end not in proportionate to our nature. But given the idea of grace as a quality (which is to say, an "accident" that a thing can either gain or lose), how can such a thing be said to produce such effects, when the acting subject is still the human being? Aquinas' reply is very telling: "what is substantially in God, becomes accidental in the soul participating the Divine goodness . . . because the soul participates in the Divine

78. Aquinas, *Summa theologiae* I-II 110.1. Aquinas adds here that "nevertheless the grace of God sometimes signifies God's eternal love."

79. Ibid.

80. Aquinas, *Summa theologiae* I-II 110.2.

81. Ibid.

82. Ibid.

83. Aquinas, *Summa theologiae* I-II.110.2.RO1.

goodness imperfectly, the participation of the Divine goodness, which is grace, has its being in the soul in a less perfect way than the soul subsists in itself. Nevertheless, inasmuch as it is the expression or participation of the Divine goodness, it is nobler than the nature of the soul, though not in its mode of being."[84] Through the gift of grace as a habitual quality, we enjoy an imperfect participation in Divine goodness. While this is still an accident in the soul, our action nonetheless proceeds from the "nobler" nature of God's qualifying of us. The participation in God's goodness (or as Thomas phrases it in articles 3 and 4, "a participation in the Divine Nature"[85]) qualifies the soul in such a way that this qualifying gift of grace enables certain actions. Participation in the Divine Nature enables these actions *not* because it simply overwhelms the soul in its "mode of being." Rather, the Divine Nature qualifies us formally. In short, the result is that just as participation in whiteness makes a thing white, so our imperfect participation in Divine goodness disposes us to actions oriented to God as our eternal end.

The Effects of Grace

Given the content of the last two questions, Aquinas emerges at the beginning of question 111 with a great deal of work to do. In considering how he is to divide up the effects of grace, he must do so with reference to the four kinds of good human action named in I-II 109: (1) those good actions that are natural to us and we can accomplish, (2) those good actions that are natural to us but that we cannot accomplish without some "healing," (3) those good actions that we are asked to do but that are beyond our natural capacity, and (4) those good actions that are an operation of God while they are at the same time our operation. Additionally, Aquinas must account for the two kinds of "effects of God's will" distinguished in I-II 110, namely (A) extrinsic, when we are simply moved by God to certain actions on the one hand, and (B) intrinsic, when we are habitually qualified (through participation in the Divine Nature) to be inclined (in and of ourselves) to act in certain ways toward another person. As Aquinas offers divisions as to the effects of grace, he must, then, not only offer an account of grace that speaks to its necessity in completing the different kinds of human action (1, 2, 3, and 4), but

---

84. Aquinas, *Summa theologiae* I-II.110.2.RO2.
85. Aquinas, *Summa theologiae* I-II 110.3.

also must do so with reference to the two ways in which grace affects the principles for human action (A and B).

Hauerwas and Hütter have consistently indicated the importance of God's action not just in terms of moral premises or norms, but in actual interaction with our own action. Aquinas consistently points to the importance of a very similar notion. But, he employs sufficiently sophisticated conceptual tools to articulate an interactive, noncompetitive connection between divine and human agency in such a way that he does not run into the same problems as even the best of the contemporary discourse encounters. Aquinas shows himself to be a useful conversation partner in his refusal to narrow God's grace to either an extrinsic cause with no effect on the intrinsic principles of our action, or to an extrinsic cause that only has an effect on the intrinsic principles of human action. In short, God's grace is limited neither to something that affects us only from the outside, nor to something that only prompts changes within us. In turning now to I-II 111, Aquinas presents some conceptual tools for considering the grace of God that takes into account the four kinds of human action named above as well as the two ways that God's grace can "affect" the human recipient, named above.

In the first article of Question 111, Aquinas presents the distinction between sanctifying and gratuitous grace. This is an important distinction, especially with regard to the implications of Thomas' theology of grace for the shape of the Christian worshipping community. As later sections focus on this notion, I will suspend treatment of this article, briefly. 111.2 asks about the division of grace into operating and cooperating. Back in I-II 110.2, Aquinas offered a distinction that was treated above, and is nicely summarized at the beginning of the *respondeo* of 111.2. He writes, "grace may be taken in two ways; first, as a Divine help [*divinum auxilium*], whereby God moves us to will and to act; secondly, as a habitual gift divinely bestowed upon us."[86] God, by grace, sometimes simply "moves" us to one sort of action or another. This is the "help" of God's grace of "*auxilium*"—the kind of grace that Lonergan calls "actual." The necessity for setting aside the idea of the additional "Divine help" of grace as opposed to a simply infused habit relies on a metaphysical presupposition in which Aquinas affirms that simply because something is predisposed to act in a certain way through an infused habit, does not necessarily mean that it will spontaneously begin to act in the ways to

---

86. Aquinas, *Summa theologiae* I-II 111.2.

which it was predisposed. In short, "what is in potency to act does not reduce itself to act. . . . In terms of the person who has habitual grace, the mere potency of habitual grace is insufficient to account for graced action. For that action, the potency has to be reduced to act; and that occurs by *auxilium*, by God moving people to actions in accord with habitual grace."[87] Thus, in order to accomplish good action on the part of a human being, the effect of God's grace of *auxilium* must reduce the potency created in us habitually into individual action. However, this is not the only problem for which God's *auxilium* solves. Sin is another barrier between potency and act in this regard (and therefore another corresponding need for Divine *auxilium*), which was presented back in 109.9. Here Aquinas notes that the need for Divine help even after the infusion of habitual grace is not just the problem of moving from potency to act. It is also necessary "for this special reason—the condition of the state of human nature."[88] He goes on to say that while the mind is healed in this infused habit, "it remains corrupted and poisoned in the flesh, whereby it serves 'the law of sin,' (Rom 7:25). In the intellect, too, there seems the darkness of ignorance, whereby, as is written (Rom 8:26): 'We know not what we should pray for as we ought' . . . Hence we must be guided and guarded by God."[89] Aquinas here points out two very important ideas: first, one can see just how interactive these effects are. Because of our sin, participation in the Divine Nature through this habitual gift entails the constant involvement of this additional "help" of God's grace, not only to move us when we are unable to move, but to overcome the remaining corruption of the flesh and to shape our minds where ignorance persists. Thus, while we are formally caused through the infused habit of grace, it is also necessary that we be continually "guarded and guided" by God's consistently present "help." As one might suspect, however, God's "help" is a concept that has application beyond just distinguishing extrinsic from intrinsic. As Wawrykow helpfully points out, indicating this additional movement (as opposed to infused habit) is not the only meaning that Aquinas attaches to the term "*auxilium*." Rather, Thomas also uses this term "in a more general sense, even in the *ST*: simply as God's aid. At times, the word in this undifferentiated sense can even cover what elsewhere is called 'habitual grace' . . . sometimes the word (*auxilium*)

---

87. Wawrykow, "Grace," 194.
88. Aquinas, *Summa theologiae* I-II.109.9.
89. Ibid.

... is used in a more general way, here reflecting the usage of Aquinas' predecessors."[90] While Aquinas uses the term here as a distinction from the habitual effect of grace, and that effect whereby potency is reduced to action, the term also enjoys much more broad usage. Perhaps it is not surprising, then, that Lonergan speaks of this as "actual" grace.

God, by grace, sometimes gives us a gift whereby we are disposed, qualified, "that we might be inclined" to certain actions ourselves. This is habitual grace—the gift of a habit. Alternatively, by Divine "help," an effect of God's grace at other times is in simply moving us to an act. God's grace, as extrinsic cause, can act upon us, simply moving us, or can shape the intrinsic principles of our actions. Unlike his earlier writings, here Aquinas divides both the grace of *auxilium* and habitual grace into operative and cooperative. By the distinction, Aquinas refers to the different effects of God's grace in terms of human agency. Operative *auxilium* refers to that effect of grace (question 110) in which God simply moves the human agent to an action, and ours is the part of passivity before this effect. The operative effect of *auxilium* is the grace in which our agency is only involved as that which is moved by God to act, "in which God is the sole mover . . . in which our mind is moved and does not move."[91] This recalls the "light of grace" that Thomas addressed in 109.1. Distinct from operative grace in which God is the sole mover, Thomas designates the effect of cooperative *auxilium* in which "our mind both moves and is moved, the operation is not only attributed to God, but also to the soul."[92] As both God's agency and human agency move together as an effect of grace, Thomas calls this cooperative grace. The division between operative and cooperative *auxilium* rests on the difference between interior and exterior acts, and hangs on this conceptual knife edge in the responses to the objections in I-II 109.6. As shown there, one of the reasons that grace is so necessary is because of the effects of sin, resulting in the residual corruption of the flesh and the ignorance of the mind, even after the habitual gift whereby the soul is healed. Conversion itself is an instance of operative *auxilium*. God inclines human beings to God's self in a way that we cannot manage. Thus, God moves us and we are moved. In a good action, like beginning to will something good

---

90. Wawrykow, "Grace," 220 n. 26.
91. Aquinas, *Summa theologiae* I-II.109.9.
92. Ibid.

instead of something wicked, "God moves the human mind to this act,"[93] in the operative effect of God's grace of *auxilium*. Yet, again, human acts are twofold, interior and exterior. In I-II 109.6.RO4, Thomas affirms that it is the part of a human being to prepare her soul, while at the same time affirming that this is only accomplished together with God turning her heart to God's self. In other words, for moments in which it is our "part" to do some good act of which we are incapable, even given the habitual gift of God's grace, God's help is required in cooperation with our agency in the accomplishment of the good act. While conversion is the simplest example of the distinction between operative and cooperative *auxilium*, one can also find the necessity of *auxilium* in the reduction of potency to act, and in the overcoming of the sinfulness of the flesh and the ignorance of the mind. In the good act, then, both the operative *auxilium* in which the interior act is accomplished and we are simply moved, and the cooperative *auxilium* of God's grace in which the external action is accomplished, are necessary. While we must be simply moved to the interior reduction of potency to act and the overcoming of sin, this has a cooperative dimension in the good action as commanded by the will "because God assists us in this act, both by strengthening our will interiorly so as to attain to the act, and by granting outwardly the capability of operating,"[94] Thomas calls this effect of grace cooperative *auxilium*.

However, this "help" of God constituting an extrinsic principle for action is only half of the story. Aquinas distinguishes the same twofold effect of grace when considered in terms of an infused habit. By means of this gift of habit, God qualifies the soul formally so as to be well disposed to act in a particular way. Through this habitual gift we imperfectly participate in the Divine Nature. Thomas here divides this habitual gift of grace into its operative and cooperative effects: "habitual grace, inasmuch as it heals and justifies the soul, or makes it pleasing to God, is called operating grace."[95] Also, as seen above, this habitual gift disposes the soul to actions oriented towards our eternal end. Inasmuch as this habitual gift is the principle of these good actions themselves, "which spring from the free-will,"[96] Thomas names this effect cooperative grace. Thomas elaborates a little more in his response to the third objection.

93. Ibid.
94. Ibid.
95. Ibid.
96. Ibid.

"One thing is said to cooperate with another not merely when it is a secondary agent under a principal agent, but when it helps to the end intended. Now man is helped by God to will the good, through the means of operating grace. And hence, the end being already intended, grace cooperates with us."[97] The notion that cooperative grace merely implies a yielding to divine agency is dismissed here. Our operation is not a competitive concession—a forfeit—to the dominance of divine agency, but an effect in which God acts and we act, and a single good act results. As Lonergan writes, "habitual grace like any other form has two effects, *esse* and *operari*. Accordingly, inasmuch as habitual grace cures or justifies the soul or makes it acceptable to God, it is said to be operative. But inasmuch as it is a principle of meritorious acts, it is cooperative."[98] Habitual grace is this "healing" about which Aquinas spoke in I-II 109. The effect of this habitual healing is both the justification of the soul (an action in which human agency is not involved, and indeed could not be, and is, hence, an "operative" effect of grace) and the predisposing of the soul to acts oriented towards its supernatural end (the implication here is that while these actions are not accomplished without God's habitual gift, the realization of the act closely involves our agency as well, and is, hence, a "cooperative" effect of grace).

In opposition to the order in which he treats this distinction of effects in article 2, he explains in article 3 that God's operative grace (habitual operative, in this case) must precede other effects of grace, as prevenient.[99] This ought not to be a surprise, however, as Thomas had already in I-II 109 explained the shortcomings of human action until we are "healed" by some habit. As described in the last article, the operative habitual effect of grace was just this healing. Thomas then makes this further, though not unanticipated, division between prevenient and subsequent effects of grace. However, simply because Aquinas rightly places the healing effect of grace prior to any elevation of our natural capacity for action does not mean that one can necessarily divide the effects of habitual and *auxilium* along the same lines. On this point, Wawrykow is very helpful to point out that the dynamic of "healing" and "elevating" is not strictly divisible into habitual and *auxilium*. As he writes,

---

97. Thomas Aquinas, *Summa theologiae* I-II.111.2.RO3.
98. Lonergan, *Grace and Freedom*, 38.
99. Thomas Aquinas, *Summa theologiae* I-II.111.3.

> Each of Aquinas's two kinds of grace—habitual and *auxilium*—performs both functions of grace. Habitual grace as given at the term of the process of conversion heals the self (at least in principle) of the effects of sin, restoring right order within the self and before God, and so making the person pleasing to God. Habitual grace also elevates the person to the supernatural level, orienting the person and the person's acts to God as end. *Auxilium* too both heals and elevates. In the treatise on grace, Aquinas is clear that an *auxilium* in fact inaugurates the process of conversion. God moves the person who lacks grace into the state of grace, that is, to the reception of habitual grace.[100]

It becomes plain why the distinction between prevenient and subsequent comes only after the explanation of the divisions of operative and cooperative habitual, and operative and cooperative *auxilia*. The effects of grace are divisible based on the differences in how they impact the receiver in terms of the principles of their own action, rather than based on how one kind follows another. The final two articles of question 111 concern "gratuitous" grace whereby one person may help lead another to God. Again, as this concerns the "hints" that Aquinas gives about the necessity of a Christian worshipping community in the dynamics of grace, I shall postpone examinations of these articles until the next section.

The helpfulness of these conceptual tools distinguishing the effects of God's grace cannot be overestimated in describing the Christian moral life. Aquinas helpfully points out through these distinctions that we need God's grace not only to heal our fallen nature, but to move us to righteous action; and not only to point us to righteous action, but to habituate and dispose us to such action; and not only to form us to righteous action, but to turn this potency into act; and not only that, but to then operate with us in a resulting Christian moral action in which our agency and God's agency act cooperatively. Through these distinctions, one can separate the operative help of God's grace on the soul (whereby we are moved internally towards a Christian act to which we could not otherwise be inclined and through the overcoming of our sinfulness in every good act), from the cooperative help (by which such actions are realized in conjunction with our free will), from the operative habit (by which our souls are healed and inclined to God and to our true end),

---

100. Wawrykow, "Grace," 196–97.

and the cooperative habitual effect (in which God grants the principle of operation by which, in conjunction with our free will, the good act is accomplished). In short, Aquinas offers the tools to consider the effect of God's grace on our internal and external acts, both accomplishing in us what we could not, and by cooperating with us.

While certainly the contemporary ethical discourse would not deny the importance of the effect of grace in healing the soul, this discourse needs tools for speaking of the further need for (and the effect of) God's grace in the moral life and in concrete moral actions. Hauerwas and Hütter have so consistently shown the need for a noncompetitive and interactive connection between divine and human agency, that they would likely agree with Aquinas' assertion that "the gift of habitual grace is not therefore given to us that we may no longer need the Divine help; for every creature needs to be preserved in the good received from Him."[101] But just how to articulate the specifics of that preservation while avoiding the ever-present threat of determinism is a difficult task. Hauerwas and Hütter seem to affirm the need for moral theology to grapple with the problem of how God's agency impacts the moral life, not just in terms of an *a priori* healing of the human condition, but in much more interactive terms. They seem to seek a way of speaking about God's action in the moral life in which "the operation of the Holy Ghost, which moves and protects, is not circumscribed by the effect of habitual grace which it causes in us; but beyond this effect He, together with the Father and the Son, moves and protects us."[102] This is the reason that Hauerwas and Hütter stand out as so important in the discourse as a whole, and the reason that presenting more sophisticated tools for their theological instincts is so important as well. They, like Aquinas, seek to articulate a picture in the moral life in which the whole of the Triune God guards, guides, and protects us by grace.

As contemporary ethicists are fully aware, determinism is a constant threat when trying to speak about Christian moral action in its relation to divine agency. External forces (and most especially God) can be depicted as so powerful that they overwhelm the freedom of the human will, and our actions are no longer our own. On the other hand, a reactionary response to the threat of determinism yields a picture of divine agency that is so carefully limited and boxed in, that its impact

---

101. Aquinas, *Summa theologiae* I-II.109.9.RO1.
102. Aquinas, *Summa theologiae* I-II.109.9.RO2.

on the divine life is nominal, at best. Neither position is feasible for Christian ethics, for just as the first compromises the freedom of the will, so the second threatens to make God's grace unnecessary in the moral life, except as a cause of gratitude or guilt. Thomas Aquinas provides a number of useful ways to think about grace that break away from these alternatives. Through the distinction of habitual grace and the grace of *auxilium*, Aquinas offers the tools to think of those actions that can only be accomplished by God, and those effects that are God's shaping of us for certain actions. Through the accompanying distinction of the effects of grace as operative and cooperative, he offers, further, the means to speak about instances in which God alone moves us in ways that we are merely passive, and instances in which our agency and God's intertwine in the production of the good act. Because these divisions are prior to any division of prevenient and subsequent, we cannot simply reduce God's "help" of *auxilium* to moments like conversion, but must instead affirm the constantly intimate involvement of God's agency in the moral life. In offering the category of habitual operative grace, one can speak of grace healing human nature and infusing the inclination in which the Christian moral agent is inclined to actions oriented to her end in God. Another distinct effect Aquinas provides in habitual cooperative grace is that the simple infusion of habit must be accompanied by our own agency in the accomplishment of Christian moral action. These distinctions alone provide much for the contemporary discourse in terms of refusing a separation between God's "part" of healing our human nature and our "part" of the resulting Christian action.

However, the effects of habitual grace are dramatically incomplete without the accompanying concepts of operative and cooperative *auxilia*. While notions of the habitual effects are vital, I believe that the contemporary conversation has the most to gain in giving special attention to operative and cooperative *auxilia*. Because of sin, our habitual participation in divine goodness is imperfect, to the degree that the sinfulness of the flesh and the darkness of the intellect are always a problem. Even before the fall, the grace of Divine "help" was necessary to overcome the reduction of mere potency to actual act. But in the fallen state of human nature, divine *auxilium* is also needed "to provide correct action, to overcome the sin that has disrupted the self in its internal relations, in its relations to others, and in relation, especially, to God."[103] Because we are

---

103. Wawrykow, "Grace," 195.

given the difference between habitual grace and *auxilium* and are told by Aquinas just how closely God's constant "help" is involved in the moral life, one need not simply reduce grace to the creation of a past condition or disposition that has some relevance for us. Even with the habitual gift of God's grace, "it is constantly necessary for God to direct and move the justified person to the good acts which truly fulfill his being—only by God's contribution to human action does the human person in fact do the good."[104] This does not mean that the habitual effects of grace are meaningless, but it does mean that we must rely on the intimate involvement of God's operative and cooperative agency in the accomplishment of the Christian moral act. As Wawrykow beautifully phrases it, "there are as many *auxilia* as there are complete, good human acts of the person who is in the state of habitual grace."[105] Through the distinction between operative and cooperative *auxilia*, Aquinas provides a way of speaking about God's intimate involvement in the moral life that is not competitive with our own agency, but is instead integral to it. God heals human agency and overcomes the remainder of our sinfulness and enables the cooperation by which God and the Christian realize the meritorious act. Human sinfulness is confessed as a problem in the moral life, as is our imperfect reception of the gift of grace. But God's interactive involvement in our own agency is also presented, but not in such a way that the freedom of our human action is compromised. Instead these distinctions allow Thomas to speak in different ways about an intimate bond between human and divine agency in the moral life.

In addition to these benefits, one more important category offered through these distinctions would be of great help to the contemporary ethical discourse: the capacity afforded by God's grace (both habitual and *auxilium*, both operative and cooperative) for the Christian to act above natural human capacity toward the end of union with God. Certainly in terms of the operative and cooperative effects of the infused habit of grace, "does [God] infuse into such as He moves towards the acquisition of supernatural good, certain forms or supernatural qualities, whereby they may be moved by Him sweetly and promptly to acquire eternal good."[106] By means of habit, we are given the capacity to operate beyond the mere capacity of acquired virtue. The Christian ethical

104. Wawrykow, *God's Grace and Human Action*, 172.
105. Wawrykow, "Grace," 199.
106. Aquinas, *Summa theologiae* I-II.110.2.

life, then, becomes more than merely "good" acts, but those acts that are oriented towards the vision of God in eternity. Christian ethical life is the fullest possible realization of the intimate bond between God's agency and our own, elevating us beyond our natural abilities, for those actions oriented to our eternal home. A wonderful passage by Doolan indicates just how important this category is for Christian morality: "A man, without any supernatural gifts, may make a name as a philosopher, scientist, scholar, physician or surgeon; he may distinguish himself as a philanthropist, a soldier, a patriot, and deserve well of his country, or of mankind; he may rightly appear on an honours' list or be given some order of merit; but one thing, without the supernatural grace of God, he cannot do: he cannot live like Jesus Christ; he cannot know and love and serve God as God's own Son knew and loved and served Him."[107] This capacity to "live like Jesus Christ" cannot be accomplished through the shaping power of narrative, or by carefully honing one's perceptions, loyalties, or understanding, but only by the grace of God—in habit and in "help," both operating in us and cooperating with us. Grace is, then, as Chareire elegantly describes it, something grafted onto the natural growth of a tree that allows it to grow well beyond what would be possible without it.[108] The same category of action is indicated in the Gifts of the Holy Spirit, as well, in which we had need of a habitual gift from God by means of which we would become amenable to the promptings of the Holy Spirit, and through which we had the internal principle for action beyond our natural capacity and oriented to our eternal end. Once again, the same category emerges in the twofold sense of the New Law. The primary sense of the New Law was not in the Gospel narrative itself, but the indwelling of the Holy Spirit, which was the extrinsic principle by which we were lead to those acts, beyond our natural capacity, oriented toward our eternal end with God.

The connection between the twofold sense of the New Law, the Gifts of the Holy Spirit, and the distinctions in the effects of God's grace is a pnematological one. Now, additionally, an integral connection between these three sections becomes evident, in that each indicates how

---

107. Doolan, *Sanctifying Grace*, 63.

108. Chareire, *Éthique et grâce*, 162. La grâce est en quelque sorte une greffe entée sur la croissance naturelle de l'arbre qui lui permet de se déployer bien au-delà de ses possibilités; elle fait éclater le désir en l'amplifiant, en le dégageant de sa gangue naturelle trop étroite. La dimension hétéronomique, signifiée par la grâce, nous délivre d'être privé de lien, donc de la mort. Rétablissant le lien, elle est libératrice.

the intimate involvement of God's grace through the Holy Spirit designates a category of properly "Christian" moral action—those actions oriented to an end otherwise out of our reach. Thus the conceptual tools from Thomas' treatments of the New Law, the Gifts, and grace allow one to speak more accurately about the involvement of divine agency in the moral life, and allow one to speak of the source of that action properly called "Christian moral action." Herein, we rely on God's operation, as well as God's invitation into cooperative action, for the accomplishment of that which is beyond our natural capacity, even in spite of our fallen human nature. For the contemporary ethical discourse, the tools Aquinas offers in these sections can lead to the ethic pursued so actively by Hauerwas and Hütter: the interactive connection between our agency and God's grace in the Christian moral life.

5

Toward an Ecumenical Ethic of Grace

Questions for Aquinas on the Context of Christian Community

AQUINAS OFFERS SOME EXTREMELY helpful descriptions of both human agency and God's action that lead to a better description of a noncompetitive connection between the two in the Christian moral life. These concepts are helpful for the contemporary discourse to adapt, if not to adopt, in order to add depth and detail to how Christian ethical life might be described as firmly centered in God's grace. However, such descriptions are not always complete. Part of the benefit of bringing Aquinas into interaction with contemporary Christian ethics is in the ways that theologians like Hütter and Hauerwas can strengthen the tools he offers. More specifically, the great strength of Hütter and Hauerwas is in the way they contextualize Christian ethics in the Christian community and as a part of the worshipping life of that community. These vital promptings in the discourse lead to some hard questions for Aquinas' ethics regarding community and worship.

Divine and Human Agency in the Context of Community

Kathryn Tanner, in her 2001 *Jesus, Humanity and the Trinity*, paints a picture of God's agency and human agency that is (to use her word) non-contrastive. She argues that in the correct conception of Christian action, God's grace operating through us does not entail that our own free agency is any less involved. In Christian moral action, the connection between God's agency and our own is not a contrastive one. "Assumption by Christ in the Spirit therefore should not be identified with moments in our lives when our agency is replaced or interrupted by God's. As was the case with the assumption of Jesus' humanity by the Son of God, to say that is to bind God's workings to the usual contrasts between activity and passivity in our lives, in violation of God's transcendence."[1] The indwelling of the Holy Spirit does not mean having our freedom bound. According to Tanner, if we simply assert that we must be either active in response to grace, or passively yield to grace, then we have failed to take our conviction of God's transcendence with its full gravity. Just as Christ was no less human for being fully divine, and no less divine because he was fully human, our human actions have the capacity for a "non-contrastive" bond between divine and human agency. In point of fact, Tanner argues, this is when Christian action is at its very best, and moral agency most truly our own.[2]

As Tanner's treatment progresses, however, she begins to speak in more detail about the necessity of the context of this Christian action in a Christian worshipping community. Insightfully, she suggests that in conceptualizing the Christian worshipping community, one can rightly employ the same christological and Trinitarian tools used in describing individual human action. If the Trinity subsists in relation, this ought to have some impact on how one considers the connections between people in the worshipping Christian community (though it must be added that she never takes her argument quite that far). She writes, "we gain our perfections as human beings only in our relation to Christ; the members of the Trinity, in whose life together we thereby participate, are only constituted as themselves in virtue of their relations with each other. Doesn't this suggest a general principle for human lives together in their perfection—that the individual is to be him or herself, and for his or her own good, only in relations with others?"[3] She takes the doctrine of the Trinity to heart, to such an extent that she argues for the applications of this doctrine to the dynamics of community, and (more specifically) Christian community. For instance, she asserts that just as God's grace

---

1. Tanner, *Jesus, Humanity and the Trinity*, 72.

2. Ibid., 73. "At our most active—say in loving service to our neighbors—what we are doing should reflect, then, our empowerment to so act by our assumption by Christ in the Spirit. The grace of God can and should be the focal point of our struggle to lead good lives just as it is the whole point of certain acts of ours, say faith and prayer."

3. Ibid., 78.

and God's triune presence come to us in a way that is pure gift, and noncontrastive with our own freedom, so, too, should God's grace be a gift between those of the worshipping community. "All our action is to be like that of the ministers at the Lord's banquet table, distributing outward, to others, the gifts of the Father that have become ours in and through the Son by the power of the Holy Spirit."[4] What happens in the context of the worshipping Church's reception of the Eucharist ought to apply to a consideration of Christian mission and calling in community, as well as the dynamics of God's grace therein. Tanner argues that the dynamics of the Spirit, and our ministry within (and outside of) the Christian community are not even contrastive with our individual identities or our freedom. Instead, "the Holy Spirit respects our differences while uniting us in Christ in the same way that the Holy Spirit respects and maintains the differences between Father and Son even as it attests to and bears the love of the Son back to the Father."[5] She argues that our best human and Christian existence is the noncontrastive combination of our free action and God's action within us. Such a dynamic, however, is not limited only to the conception of the individual Christian, but the dynamics of the worshipping community as well. She writes that "our lives as individuals should be constituted and enhanced in their perfections as we share our lives with others in community, identifying ourselves thereby as persons in community with others and not simply persons for ourselves. We perfect one another in community."[6] The noncontrastive dynamic of God's grace in the heart of the Christian ought to be a paradigm for the life given by God to the Christian community in which our action with each other ought to contribute to the overall project of the reconciliation of humanity to God through Christ.

Aside from utilizing the chance to glance, all too briefly, at another valuable voice in the contemporary Protestant theological discourse, this short examination of Tanner prompts a question: does the interaction of divine and human agency in the Christian moral life happen on a *purely* individual basis? Is the grace of God operative (and cooperative) only in the heart of an isolated individual? Is there simply no need for Church (other than, perhaps, the celebration of the sacraments)? In this dynamic between divine and human agency, is it everyone for him

---

4. Ibid., 80.
5. Ibid., 83.
6. Ibid., 93.

or herself? For a theologian like Tanner, reflection on the dynamics of God's grace and human agency naturally lead to reflection on the context of the Christian community.

Such questions present a much-needed challenge to Thomas' theological ethic of grace. While he may have written for an audience (in thirteenth-century Parisian monastic life) for which he could have safely assumed the presence and dynamic of the background of the Christian worshipping community, that assumption is no longer a safe one for his modern readership. On the surface, the conceptual tools outlining the dynamics between God and the Christian in the moral life treated here seem to have little need for the worshipping community. In fact, the dynamic can seem so elegant and complex that one might even assume that the intrusion of other upon one's ethical journey would constitute a disruption, rather than any kind of aid. While the conceptual tools about God's grace and human agency that Thomas Aquinas provides might quench the thirsty landscape of contemporary theological ethics, the necessity of the context of the Christian worshipping community is in much need of expansion and development. For Aquinas, the Christian worshipping community is often presented as an inert gathering of those who have individual connections to God's grace. The social dynamics of the community are simply not a significant factor in Thomas' explanation of the efficacy of grace in the Christian moral life.

The theology of Thomas Aquinas, examined thus far, has not pointed in any obvious way to the need for a Christian worshipping community. Thomas writes, "The operation of the Holy Ghost, which moves and protects, is not circumscribed by the effect of habitual grace which it causes in us; but beyond this effect He, together with the Father and the Son, moves and protects us."[7] While this may be quite beautiful, the question of whether Christian community and Christian worship are important factors at all in God's gift of grace nevertheless persists. While one might applaud Aquinas, too, for his insight in marking the difference between infused and acquired virtue (for instance), one must nonetheless question whether he has any need for other Christians in properly Christian virtuous action. As seen in his discussion of the Gifts of the Holy Spirit, "the primal union of man with God is by faith, hope and charity: and, consequently, these virtues are presupposed to the gifts, as being their roots. Therefore all the gifts correspond to these

7. Aquinas, *Summa theologiae* I-II 109.9.RO2.

three virtues, as being derived therefrom."[8] If the Gifts of the Holy Spirit find their roots in union with God, and the infused theological virtues are the means by which we are united to God, there seems to be simply no need for any other person in the Christian moral life. When talking about the specific dynamic of Christian moral action and the bond between divine and human agency therein, upon initial examination there seems to be no obvious need for any other Christian.

A closer examination of Aquinas' writings on grace reveals that, rather than an exclusion of the importance of the worshipping Christian community, there is something more akin to neglect. In the following paragraphs, I will indicate some of the ways Aquinas points to the importance of the context of Christian community. However, such indications are usually not central to his arguments about the dynamics of grace, and are often mentioned in passing or as only a part of an answer to an objection. When Aquinas does treat the dynamics of the worshipping community, it is only as a rather passive part of the connection between God's grace and human agency. Though there is no sense that the context of this community is excluded from importance or relevance, it is simply not an important category for Aquinas. While the first few pages of this chapter will indicate some of the ways Aquinas does, in fact, rely on the context of the worshipping community, I bring them forward to demonstrate how such a context is underdeveloped in his treatment.

Sacrament and Worship in Thomas' Theology of Grace

Aquinas points to a twofold connection between grace and external action, "in the first place, as leading in some way to grace. Such are the sacramental acts which are instituted in the New Law, e.g., Baptism, the Eucharist, and the like. In the second place there are those external acts which ensue from the promptings of grace."[9] Thomas goes on from this twofold distinction to speak entirely of the second connection—the external acts that ensue from the promptings of grace. His placing of the communal practice of the sacraments, here, as leading in some way to grace ("*sicut inducentia aliqualiter ad gratiam*") indicates that they are certainly necessary, but perhaps not central. There may be rather good reasons for Thomas' passing so quickly over the necessity of the

---

8. Aquinas, *Summa theologiae* I-II 68.4.RO3.
9. Aquinas, *Summa theologiae* I-II 108.1.

sacramental life of the worshipping body (the most likely being that, for his audience, it was not a point upon which he needed to dwell at great length), but for contemporary readers, the framework of the treatise on grace nonetheless seems to treat the secondary connection between grace and external action in a very thorough way, while passing over its context in the sacramental life of the Christian worshipping community rather quickly. The previous quotation was a part of the answer to the question, "Whether the New Law ought to prescribe or prohibit any external acts?" The next article asks a closely connected question: "Whether the New Law made sufficient ordinations about external acts?" Here, as one might expect, Aquinas gives attention to the twofold connection between grace and external actions. Again, however, indication of the necessity of the worshipping Christian community is only indirect. In treating the reception of grace, Thomas writes, "since we cannot of ourselves obtain grace, but through Christ alone, hence Christ of Himself instituted the sacraments whereby we obtain grace: viz. Baptism, Eucharist, Orders of the ministers of the New Law, by the institution of the apostles and seventy-two disciples, Penance, and indissoluble Matrimony."[10] Again, Thomas does not exclude the worshipping Christian community, but placing the emphasis so thoroughly on Christ, Thomas seems to assume the regular practice and maintaining of these means of receiving God's grace by the Christian community as an integral part of what was instituted under the New Law (and its sufficient provision for external acts) without treating it here. In the context of the questions examined in previous chapters, it is possible to draw the conclusion that since (1) Christian moral action ensues from grace, and (2) grace is received through the practice of Christian sacraments, as instituted by Christ, and (3) the practice of these sacraments occurs in the context of the praying, worshipping Christian community, therefore (4) the continual investment in the worshipping Christian community is central to Thomas' account of a Christian ethic of grace. Thomas' readership might be able to draw such a conclusion on its own, but the fact still remains that these connections are understated implications of Aquinas' readings of the New Law, the Gifts, and grace. While Thomas is clear that the New Law makes sufficient provision for the external acts that sustain the individual Christian life, he does not give a great deal of attention to the necessity of their continual practice or to their setting

10. Aquinas, *Summa theologiae* I-II 108.2.

in the Christian worshipping community as a part of this provision. The inner dynamics of the worshipping community are not a factor on their own. Instead, the community is merely the setting in which individual lives are justified and sanctified. The interactive life of the worshipping community is not a category that carries any importance for the dynamics of grace. Although Thomas argues that we obtain God's grace not on our own, but through the sacraments (and this certainly implies the necessity of the worshipping and sacramental life of the Christian community for Christian moral life), such a context is not given a great deal of emphasis, nor is its full impact upon the Christian ethical life explored at any great length. Given Aquinas' notoriously thorough methodology, this sort of omission is worth noting, especially for his modern readership. But for the contemporary context, in which these moments in the life of the Christian worshipping community *do* have an increasing potential to be practiced without regard to the community interactions in which they are normally situated, the application of Thomas' treatments of grace need some further development in this area. So, even in those places in which Christian community interaction is entailed in Thomas' treatment, I put forward the dynamics of the community itself as an instrument for the efficacy of God's grace.

Further on in the treatise on grace, Aquinas offers another indirect indication of the necessity of the sacramental and worship life of Christian community. In responding to the objection that the sacraments of the New Law *themselves* can be the cause of grace (rather than God alone), Aquinas writes that "in the sacraments of the New Law, which are derived from Christ, grace is instrumentally caused by the sacraments, and principally by the power of the Holy Ghost working in the sacraments."[11] Certainly when speaking of the efficacy of the sacramental and worshipping life of the Church in terms of Christian moral action, the emphasis is very rightly placed on God's agency through the Holy Spirit rather than on the efficacy of the practice of sacrament and worship on its own. Still, as one of the few loci in which the sacraments come up in the treatises on New Law and on grace, the value of the worshipping and sacramental life of the Christian community functions here only to point back to the dynamics of grace that Aquinas has already explained. Aquinas rightly points back to the interaction between the Holy Spirit and the individual Christian that he has already treated, but

11. Aquinas, *Summa theologiae* I-II 112.1.RO2.

in doing so, indirectly takes the emphasis off of the unique importance that the community context might have in the larger picture of Christian moral action. Again, the community appears merely as the setting in which a much more individually oriented interaction takes place.

Just as Aquinas indicates, in perhaps indirect ways, the necessity of the sacramental life of the worshipping community, while at the same time giving somewhat sparse treatment to its importance (at least by the standards of contemporary theology), he likewise highlights the necessity for intercession and prayer in the Christian community (though still only offering fairly minimal arguments for its importance in the Christian moral life). In *ST* I-II 109.9, Thomas asks, "Whether one who has already obtained grace can, of himself and without further help of grace, do good and avoid sin?" This question stands as the logical connection between the previous article, examining whether one can avoid sin without grace, and the end of the question, asking after the need for grace to persevere. Thomas is very clear that one cannot avoid sin without grace, that we need grace to persevere in doing good and avoiding sin, and prayer is at least a small part of this dynamic. In arguing that we need the help of grace ("*auxilio gratiae*") to be moved by God to act righteously, he states that because of the fallen condition of human nature (entailing corrupted flesh and a darkness of the intellect), "we must be guided and guarded by God, Who knows and can do all things. For which reason also it is becoming in those who have been born again as sons of God, to say: 'Lead us not into temptation,' and 'Thy Will be done on earth as it is in heaven,' and whatever else is contained in the Lord's Prayer pertaining to this."[12] Once more, the worship life of the Christian community is given an indirect reference. Though its value is indicated, there is no clear reason why this prayer cannot be offered on one's own, and in isolation from the wider worshipping body, and there is no hint here that one should pray for the perseverance of another person. Perhaps more poignantly, there is no hint that our own prayers for perseverance ought to already be rightly contextualized in our prayers for God's guarding and guiding of our Christian (and non-Christian, for that matter) neighbors. While Aquinas is very clear about the need for prayer, on this point, and even (one might add) liturgically framed prayer, there is only an indirect indication that the worshipping community might be important. While Aquinas will argue in the next article

12. Aquinas, *Summa theologiae* I-II 109.9.

that after one has been justified by grace, "he still needs to beseech God for the aforesaid gift of perseverance, that he may be kept from evil till the end of his life. For to many grace is given to whom perseverance in grace is not given,"[13] there is nothing to suggest that our prayer ought to have some community context, and certainly no indication that our prayers for God's grace in perseverance ought to be not only for ourselves but also for one another. Just to be clear, once more, my argument is not that Aquinas excludes the possibility (and even in some ways the necessity) of these things. My argument is simply that in the instances in which ethics and pneumatology collide in the *Summa*, the context of the Christian worshipping community is underemphasized.[14]

13. Aquinas, *Summa theologiae* I-II 109.10.

14. The final question of the treatise on grace—Question 114 on merit—will not receive treatment here, as I have mentioned. While merit is integral to the treatise on grace, and intertwined with Thomas' ethic, the explanation of such a concept would muddy the waters in this instance and draw us away from our primary goal of framing an ecumenical conversation surrounding the dynamics of human and divine agency in the Christian moral life. Nevertheless, it should be mentioned that we find a similar indication of the importance of intercession in Aquinas' question on merit, exhibiting the same patterns shown in the above paragraph. The question at hand is some variation of, "Can one person merit 'first' grace for another?" This is a complicated question (the full treatment of which would, I believe, lead us quite a distance away from our central argument), the bulk of which is examined in 114.6. This article asks whether there is some action by one human being that God would regard as meritorious enough for God to give grace to another human being. The first objection seems to bring to light the perfect demonstration as to why we need to ask this question. In the ninth chapter of the Gospel of Matthew, a paralytic man was brought to Jesus so that he might be healed. The text (also quoted by Aquinas in this first objection) reads, "When Jesus saw *their* faith, he said to the paralytic, 'Take heart, son; your sins are forgiven.'" This would seem to suggest that one person could merit grace for another. We might expect that this would be the perfect instance for Thomas to speak about the interdependence of Christians, especially with regard to prayer for God's grace. Nonetheless, his answer is that no one can merit the first grace for another person. Without delving into his treatment on merit (a task that has been done very well in other places), it is worth a further glance at the responses to the first two objections in this article. In the first objection, the objector quotes the book of James: "Pray for one another, that you may be saved." The objector naturally concludes that since only grace can save us, we can merit it from one another. Thomas' answer does not deny the need for this prayer, but does deny that God would reward such a prayer, in justice, with grace to another person. He argues that prayer rests on mercy rather than justice (*Summa theologiae* I-II 114.6.RO2), and therefore God does not answer such prayers as reward for meritorious action, but rather out of mercy. Thomas' answers to both the first and second objections are essentially the same, the faith and prayers of one person have bearing upon another person according to God's mercy on that other person, rather than according to any sort of just exchange. Just as before, Thomas does not exclude the context of the Christian worshipping com-

Although it is not strictly within the stated purview of this treatment, it is worth noting that much of the same pattern is evident when Thomas turns to examining the sacraments in the *Tertia Pars*. Thomas offers ample reasons to draw a connection to the grace of God in the moral life and the sacraments themselves in the ways they are there described. Nonetheless, the context of the worshipping community itself and the dynamics therein remain opaque or inert even in this focused treatment on the Church's sacramental life. Aquinas argues that the sacraments are ordained to signify our sanctification, which they do in three ways: "the very cause of our sanctification, which is Christ's Passion; the form of our sanctification, which is grace and the virtues; and the ultimate end of sanctification, which is eternal life."[15] So, Thomas continues, the sacraments do three things: they remind us of the past action of the passion of Jesus Christ, they are a part of the present effect that this passion has upon us in the impact of God's grace in the moral life, and they present a foretaste of glory.[16] Thomas specifies the extent to which the sacraments are uniquely important for the moral life through their distinctiveness as signifiers of Christ's passion, God's grace, and our final end in God. Thomas gives sensory signifiers not only the value of those instruments by which God's grace is given, but of great value in and of themselves. However, the communal dynamics in practicing these sacraments is only given passing reference.

Interestingly, even the physical, motor practice of participating in the sacraments themselves seems to have some efficacy in shaping the moral life. However, these practices do not seem in any way interactive

---

munity, but is careful to note that our prayers for each other are not a cornerstone of the dynamic of grace and human action. While God answers our prayers for one another according to God's mercy, such prayers are not an irreplaceable part of our end in God, or even of the Christian moral life generally. Once again, while we might make excuses for Aquinas based on the audience to which he was writing, it is nonetheless true that we can see that the context of the Christian worshipping community is passed over quickly, and (when present at all) is significantly underdeveloped as a part of Thomas' treatise on grace. As Thomas goes on to mention in a later article, "we [may] impetrate of God in prayer the grace of perseverance either for ourselves or for others," this does not fall under his treatment on merit in a way that would make it necessary, in a way very similar to what we have seen in other places. Prayer, worship, the sacramental life of the Christian community—these are not central to the Christian moral existence in the treatments Thomas offers.

15. Aquinas, *Summa theologiae* III 60.3.
16. Ibid.

with the Holy Spirit in the Christian community dynamic itself. The language remains focused on the individual. Thomas argues that it is fitting for human beings to be led to spiritual matters through material means, and because God provides for God's creatures according to their natures, "Divine wisdom, therefore, fittingly provides man with the means of salvation, in the shape of corporeal and sensible signs that are called sacraments."[17] According to Aquinas, God extends to us a tremendous accommodation here. While God might certainly lead us to a reminder of the gift of the suffering, death, and resurrection of Jesus Christ, along with the gift of sanctifying grace by which we are made holy, and a foretaste of the coming kingdom without sensible signs, God deems it most fitting that we might be led to God by means of these sensible things. God is certainly not confining God's saving agency to these singular moments. Rather, we human creatures are offered these gifts in a way that is easier for us to receive them—by means of things we can see and smell and taste and touch. As indicated, however, Thomas does note that even the physical exercise of practicing the sacramental life has an impact upon us morally. Thomas writes that "bodily action was offered to [human beings] in the sacraments, by which we might be trained to avoid superstitious practices . . . and all manner of harmful action, consisting in sinful deeds. It follows, therefore, that through the institution of the sacraments man, consistently with his nature, is instructed through sensible things; he is humbled through confessing that he is subject to corporeal things, seeing that he receives assistance through them: and he is preserved from bodily hurt, by the healthy exercise of the sacraments."[18] Thomas offers in the above passage a very interesting perspective (which actually echoes Hauerwas and Hütter in a number of ways) on how the practice of the sacraments is fittingly efficacious in the moral life. He argues here that participation in the sacraments by the individual trains her for future moral action, through the efficacy of the passion of Christ and God's grace. Confessing that the magnitude of the gift of God's grace comes through material and sensible action is a humbling experience, and this trains us. He argues that through the actual, motor practice of participating in the sacraments, God's pedagogy regarding spiritual things extends to us through very material things.

17. Aquinas, *Summa theologiae* III 61.1.
18. Ibid.

Such a sentiment seems very much in harmony with Hauerwas and Hütter: we are trained and humbled and taught by God through the shaping power of the physical practices of the Church. After this point, however, Aquinas parts company with them. Hauerwas and Hütter argue, as has been discussed, that the practices of the Christian worshipping community shape the community itself. The worshipping community is not an inert, opaque body, but the practices therein are part and parcel with God's pedagogy. Just as the practice of the sacraments is a means through which God instructs the individual, Hauerwas and Hütter have shown that God shapes and forms the community, and forms us as individuals through its internal dynamics. While certainly such communal notions are harmonious with Aquinas' account, he does not bring them out here. Thomas' account of the pedagogy of God's shaping of Christian life with regard to the practices of the sacraments is certainly important, but only seems to assume the community context, rather than emphasizing it as an important facet of the way God teaches us.

To be fair to Aquinas in this treatment of the sacraments in the *Tertia Pars*, one must acknowledge that he does continually make reference (even if it is rather brief) to the importance of the community context. He is careful to mention that the "use" of the sacraments is twofold: "namely, the worship of God, and the sanctification of man."[19] The practice of worship itself is given special place and separated even from the effect of the sanctification of the individual. The physical act of worship is a valuable effect of the sacraments, and is a part of the efficacy of the passion of Jesus Christ. But, when Thomas does speak to the transformative effects of this physical act, he does so with reference to the individual rather than, in any overt way, to the community. He writes that "the sacraments of the New Law are ordained for a twofold purpose; namely, for a remedy against sins; and for the perfecting of the soul in things pertaining to the Divine worship according to the rite of the Christian life."[20] Once more, Thomas affords the practice of the "Christian rite" of worship its own importance and value. He continues, "Now whenever anyone is deputed to some definite purpose he is wont to receive some outward sign thereof; thus in olden times soldiers who enlisted in the ranks used to be marked with certain characters on the

---

19. Aquinas, *Summa theologiae* III 60.5.
20. Aquinas, *Summa theologiae* III 63.1.

body, through being deputed to a bodily service. Since, therefore, by the sacraments men are deputed to a spiritual service pertaining to the worship of God, it follows that by their means the faithful receive a certain spiritual character."[21] The community of the "faithful" are said to receive an external mark as the result of being a part of God's service through the exercise of the sacraments. Through the sacraments, Christians are made a part of God's service in the world. Like ancient soldiers, marked with tattoos to communicate their identity to the rest of the world, Christians are granted a certain mark—that of a "spiritual character." This "external" mark identifies the Christian as one who is a part of the "spiritual service pertaining to worship." While this is a rather brief moment, Thomas does seem to have some place for the shaping effects of Christian worship on the community, though it is underdeveloped. The practice itself shapes not only the individual but also leaves a "mark" on the community of the "faithful." Still, God's grace in shaping the "faithful" and God's shaping of the individual by means of the "faithful" are different things. Even in this focused discussion of the sacraments, Aquinas does not treat the dynamics of the Christian community as a category in itself, except in passing ways. It stands, rather, as the setting for individually oriented justification and sanctification.

The Interdependence of Christians in the Dynamics of Grace

Aquinas offers a similarly indirect inclusion of the worship life and interdependence of Christian community. In a fairly cursory way, Thomas holds that Christians are dependent upon one another as a part of the work of the Holy Spirit in Christian moral agency. Particularly, he cites the need for Christians to be taught regarding faithful obedience to God. One such instance is in the context of his treatment of the New Law. As the New Law, in its primary sense, was the work of the Holy Spirit in the heart of the Christian, the letter of the law found its completion and fulfillment in the "law of the spirit of life in Christ Jesus." Thus, the law, in its primary sense, is not inscribed on tablets as a strict list of rules to obey, but is "in the first place a law that is inscribed on our hearts."[22] But, this is the New Law in only the first of its twofold senses. Thomas continues, "Nevertheless the New Law contains certain things that dispose

---

21. Ibid.
22. Aquinas, *Summa theologiae* I-II 106.1.

us to receive the grace of the Holy Ghost, and pertaining to the use of that grace: . . . and the faithful need to be instructed concerning them, both by word and writing, both as to what they should believe and as to what they should do."[23] Hauerwas and Hütter go to great lengths to demonstrate the value of Christian community on this point. Precisely because we need instruction in this law of liberty as to what we must do, the Christian community guided by God is of inestimable value and is in fact a means by which God guides and directs. Thomas, however, is content to say that we must be instructed both by "word" and by "writing." Christian community is, perhaps, somewhere implied in this "word," but community seems to be given very little attention here. While the context of Christian community has value for Aquinas, it is underemphasized. Once more the pattern in which Aquinas assumes the community setting as the locus for individual interaction having to do with grace is evident, while the dynamics of the community itself play no role, and are not even treated as a category.

Some explanation for this may be found in looking back again at Thomas' treatment of the New Law, which puts a great emphasis on the grace of God within us, and holds the written New Law as secondary to this more primary sense. However, Thomas does treat this "written" sense, as well. While he says that the moral and judicial precepts of the Old Law (which direct and instruct us concerning our neighbor) are by no means abolished, the Sermon on the Mount takes this instruction to a deeper level. In this sermon, Jesus "directs man's interior movement in respect of his neighbor, by forbidding us, on the one hand, to judge him rashly, unjustly, or presumptuously; and, on the other, to entrust him too readily with sacred things if he be unworthy. Lastly, He teaches us how to fulfil the teaching of the Gospel; viz. by imploring the help of God; by striving to enter by the narrow door of perfect virtue."[24] Perhaps it is possible that Aquinas sees one's community, even one's worshipping Christian community, as neighbors and therefore recipients of moral action only. Perhaps the neighbor is seen primarily as the instance of moral action, rather than a part of that which shapes it. If this is the place of the neighbor in the New Law, then perhaps Aquinas might see the dynamic of moral development through Christian community to be a somewhat backward idea. Our moral instruction from our neighbor

---

23. Ibid.
24. Aquinas, *Summa theologiae* I-II 108.3.

comes perhaps in the opportunity our neighbor presents for obedience and virtue, rather than for the content of moral expression itself. What we learn from each other is, perhaps, given through the opportunity to express how we have been shaped by the New Law, in both its primary and secondary senses. Perhaps even the worshipping Christian community primarily offers the chance for moral expression, rather than moral formation. Again, while Aquinas in no way excludes the context of the Christian community setting, any way in which its internal dynamics might be an instrument of God's grace is left untreated.

Another point at which one can see a present, but underemphasized, treatment of the need for Christian community is in Thomas' discussion of the difference between "sanctifying" and "gratuitous" grace in I-II, Question 111. In this distinction, Thomas tries to demonstrate the difference between the sort of grace whereby we are, ourselves, sanctified by God, and that grace given to us by God that is directed more toward other people than ourselves. The idea here is an interesting one, that God's operation of the grace of Jesus Christ within us would have an effect not just on our reconciliation with God, but upon others as well. The context of the Christian worshipping community would seem to fit ideally with such a notion. One might expect Aquinas to speak about the interdependence of the Christian life with others on their journey toward their end in eternal life. While such an idea is not quite excluded, Thomas speaks to this distinction between sanctifying and gratuitous grace only in terms of the justification of the sinner (in short, a fairly isolated, rather than ongoing, instance in the life of each member of the Christian community). Thomas explains the difference:

> since grace is ordained to lead men to God, this takes place in a certain order, so that some are led to God by others. And thus there is a twofold grace: one whereby man himself is united to God, and this is called "sanctifying grace"; the other is that whereby one man cooperates with another in leading him to God, and this gift is called "gratuitous grace," since it is bestowed on a man beyond the capability of nature, and beyond the merit of the person. But whereas it is bestowed on a man, not to justify him, but rather that he may cooperate in the justification of another, it is not called sanctifying grace.[25]

---

25. Aquinas, *Summa theologiae* I-II 111.1.

The dynamics of God's grace in the Christian moral life necessitate some degree of interdependence with other Christians, but not in any sustained way. We may cooperate in the justification of another, but there is no interdependence necessary beyond that point. From there we may receive God's grace and pray for perseverance in a way that could be totally isolated from those Christians, in cooperation with whom we were justified. Such limits are frustrating, and while they may be explained away in terms of context and the audience to which Thomas was writing, from the modern perspective, the importance of the Christian worshipping community in the Christian moral life is a somewhat marginal one for Aquinas. Again, the Christian community is not totally absent. For instance, in a response to an objection in I-II 111.1, Aquinas quotes the book of Colossians: "'He hath made us worthy to be made partakers of the lot of the saints in light.'"[26] While the "lot of the saints" is not a robust part of his answer to the objection, the suggestion here is that our interdependence in justification entails a broader Christian communal identity. Once more, however, it is passed over rather quickly, and its importance is as a setting for (or, even more simply, a gathering of) a much more individually oriented set of actions.

As Thomas goes on to explain the distinction between gratuitous and sanctifying grace even further, some themes emerge that we have already encountered in Hauerwas and Hütter:

> Gratuitous grace is ordained to this, viz. that a man may help another to be led to God. Now no man can help in this by moving interiorly (for this belongs to God alone), but only exteriorly by teaching or persuading. Hence gratuitous grace embraces whatever a man needs in order to instruct another in Divine things which are above reason. Now for this three things are required: first, a man must possess the fullness of knowledge of Divine things, so as to be capable of teaching others. Secondly, he must be able to confirm or prove what he says; otherwise his words would have no weight. Thirdly, he must be capable of fittingly presenting to his hearers what he knows.[27]

The importance of "teaching" and even "apprenticeship" is hard to miss here. But rather than making this a dynamic within the Christian community that is a part of the Christian life as a whole, Aquinas seems

26. Aquinas, *Summa theologiae* I-II 111.1.RO1.
27. Aquinas, *Summa theologiae* I-II 111.4.

to limit instruction of another through grace to the process leading up to conversion. However, this interdependence through instruction and learning is not always, overtly, limited in this way. In the same question, the fourth article, Thomas explains the same interaction between Christians in terms of the content of faith. "Faith is enumerated here under the gratuitous graces, not as a virtue justifying man in himself, but as implying a super-eminent certitude of faith, whereby a man is fitted for instructing others concerning such things as belong to the faith."[28] Faith is an infused virtue, and therefore a habit—an ongoing disposition necessary in the Christian life. But this particular passage addresses an objection that confuses faith as an infused virtue with faith as the certitude of things unseen. In this particular instance, Thomas does not place the limit of this dynamic of instruction and learning to an end in justification. One might take him here to be addressing not only the instruction given in the process leading to conversion, but the ongoing "improvisation" (to adapt Hauerwas' term) or "narrative casuistry" (to adapt Hütter's) of Christian ethics that happens through instruction and learning. That being said, while Thomas may be speaking to the ongoing task of teaching in the faithful community, Thomas does not go out of his way to show this broader application.

Still, as Thomas explains in a later article of the same question, gratuitous grace is given for the well-being of the Church as a whole. In an article inquiring which of these two graces—gratuitous or sanctifying—is nobler, he writes, "gratuitous grace is ordained to the common good of the Church, which is ecclesiastical order, whereas sanctifying grace is ordained to the separate common good, which is God. Hence sanctifying grace is the nobler."[29] Though Thomas' primary intent was, probably, to address the merits of the saints and the treasury of the Church, one might trace at least some indication that the dynamics of God's grace is ordered not just to the individual, but to the worshipping Christian community as a whole. It is ordained for the well-being of the Church, indicating that the interdependence of the Christian worshipping community is very relevant to the relationship between divine and human agency in the hearts of the individual within that community. Nevertheless, its importance is passed over rather quickly, and (in a sys-

---

28. Aquinas, *Summa theologiae* I-II 111.4.RO2.
29. Aquinas, *Summa theologiae* I-II 111.5.RO1.

tem in which a great number of seemingly small details are explored very thoroughly) the Christian community is significantly underemphasized.

His comparative argument aside, Aquinas names the ways in which gratuitous grace works as a part of the dynamics of the worshipping community to sanctify as firmly secondary. Sanctifying grace unites the individual to God, and is rightly seen as nobler, perhaps, but the picture offered here is that God's grace comes to those who happen to be in a community, rather than in and through the dynamics of that community. The community structures, its internal dynamics are, here, only the collection of relatively isolated Christians in an individual interaction with God. The worshipping context is a setting for this individually oriented life, but Aquinas does not offer much reason to see the community interaction as anything but inert.

In addressing the worshipping context of Christian community, and the importance of the interdependence between Christians in the dynamic between the Holy Spirit and human agency, Thomas Aquinas offers a treatment that is somewhat underdeveloped. In precisely those instances in which Hauerwas and Hütter have relied so heavily on the necessity of God's direction through the worshipping Christian community, Thomas seems to leave it almost entirely aside. The worshipping community seems to be little more than a collection of individuals who are transformed by God's grace. The community setting is certainly implied, but it is rendered neutral. Nowhere is this demonstrated more clearly than when Aquinas speaks to the "counsels" of the New Law, as found in the New Testament. At the end of question 108, Aquinas asks, "Whether certain definite counsels are fittingly proposed in the New Law?" The answer is, yes, there are counsels proposed in the New Law. The difference between a counsel and a commandment is explained at the very beginning of the *respondeo*:

> a commandment implies obligation, whereas a counsel is left to the option of the one to whom it is given. Consequently in the New Law, which is the law of liberty, counsels are added to the commandments, and not in the Old Law, which is the law of bondage. We must therefore understand the commandments of the New Law to have been given about matters that are necessary to gain the end of eternal bliss, to which end the New Law brings us forthwith: but that the counsels are about matters that render the gaining of this end more assured and expeditious.[30]

30. Aquinas, *Summa theologiae* I-II 108.4.

In order to gain our eternal end more assuredly, Thomas argues, there are counsels offered in the New Testament, as supplements to the "commandments" given. But, as he also says, we are not put under any obligation by these counsels. Rather, they are there to aid us to the end in unity with God to which God calls us. He goes on to explain the need for such counsels:

> Now man is placed between the things of this world, and spiritual goods wherein eternal happiness consists: so that the more he cleaves to the one, the more he withdraws from the other, and conversely. Wherefore he that cleaves wholly to the things of this world, so as to make them his end, and to look upon them as the reason and rule of all he does, falls away altogether from spiritual goods. Hence this disorder is removed by the commandments. Nevertheless, for man to gain the end aforesaid, he does not need to renounce the things of the world altogether: since he can, while using the things of this world, attain to eternal happiness, provided he does not place his end in them: but he will attain more speedily thereto by giving up the goods of this world entirely: wherefore the evangelical counsels are given for this purpose.[31]

Thomas argues that in order that we might find our true happiness in God, we must not place our happiness in the "things of this world." The commandments steer us away from this very thing. Aquinas does not infer, though, that the "things of this world" (riches, for example) are evil or in some other way totally forbidden. Instead, we are tempted to make the attainment of temporal goods our hope, our happiness, and our end. Thus, Thomas reasons, the surest path to our true end is simply to avoid sex (and therefore the sin of lust and the potential to hold the end of sexual pleasure more dearly than our end in God); to avoid riches (and therefore the sin of avarice and the potential to hold the end of earthly wealth more dearly than our end in God); and to avoid honors (and therefore the sin of pride and the potential to hold our own love of praise more dearly than our end in God). Again, however, that does not mean that sex, riches, and honors are evil—they are just very significant temptations. We may, Aquinas argues, still gain eternal life without renouncing sex, riches, and honors as long as we do not place them as our true end and happiness, nor love them more dearly than our end and happiness in God. Nonetheless, the counsels of poverty, chastity, and the

31. Ibid.

bond of obedience[32] are offered because they are the surest ways to avoid sinfulness and gain our final end of an eternal bond with God.

Aquinas does not argue here that only those who vow and practice chastity, poverty, and the bond of obedience gain eternal life. What he does say is that these practices are counseled in the New Law as helping us obtain that end by steering us away from clinging to temporal goods too tightly. In a striking way, Aquinas is conscious of the great diversity in Christian vocation and life and does not denigrate those who have chosen a life that includes temporal goods such as sex, riches, and honor. He merely explains that the commands prohibit making such things into ends in and of themselves, and the counsels are issued as the best guides for this goal. For those Christians who have not taken vows of poverty, chastity, and obedience, the question is, how are we to apply such counsels? How are we to know when to be chaste or poor or obedient? How much money is too much money? How much sex is too much sex? When do honors become a distraction? Aquinas realizes that in this short human life, each of us is "placed between the things of this world, and spiritual goods wherein eternal happiness consists." How do we know when and in what way to apply these counsels? In short, to whom or to what do we turn in trying to figure out how to apply the counsels of the New Law to each of our lives? Perhaps even more to the point, to whom do we turn in the task of applying the guidance of the content of Scripture, such as the "counsels" to the individual Christian life? As Thomas Aquinas addresses the application of those deeds neither in keeping with, nor opposed to, the New Law, he says that such works "have been left by the Lawgiver, i.e. Christ, to the discretion of each individual. And so to each one it is free to decide what he should do or avoid; and to each superior, to direct his subjects in such matters as regards what they must do or avoid. Wherefore also in this respect the Gospel is called the 'law of liberty': since the Old Law decided many points and left few to man to decide as he chose."[33] As compared to the Old Law, the New Law leaves a great deal to the discretion of the individual, like the application of the counsels to shaping one's marriage, one's profession, and one's life. Here, too, there is some mention of the great benefit that Christian community can be in this life-long process—that is, each "superior" may direct those under her care about what they should do and

32. Ibid.
33. Aquinas, *Summa theologiae* I-II 108.1.

what they should avoid. Once more, Aquinas does not actually exclude the possibility that the dynamics of the Christian worshipping community could be really important for the moral life. Still, in exactly the place where it might seem most natural to speak to the great value of fellow Christians, Church praxis, and the formation of Christian narrative in the worshipping community, Aquinas uses language like "each one" and "discretion of the individual."

Thomas' treatment of grace, the Holy Spirit, and human agency neglects the importance of the context of the Christian worshipping community in three closely connected ways. In these three ways he undertreats and underemphasizes the importance of the worshipping community—developing his treatments using consistently more individually oriented language. Thomas neglects (but by no means excludes) the importance of the sacramental life of the Christian worshipping community in the dynamics of grace and the Christian moral life. Thomas neglects (but by no means excludes) the importance of the interdependence of members of the Christian community in discussing the effects of grace and the Holy Spirit in the Christian moral life. Thomas neglects (but by no means excludes) the importance and value of the Christian worshipping community in applying the counseling content of Scripture to the Christian moral life. In these three ways, very little of Thomas' arguments on how the Holy Spirit impacts Christian moral existence relies on the dynamics of Christian community. Neither, however, does he exclude the potential importance of this context. Instead, Christian community in itself does not seem to be a category for him.

Contemporary Promptings toward an Ecumenical Ethic of Grace

One purpose of the previous chapters was to show how greatly the contemporary theological ethical discourse could benefit from the kind of sophisticated tools that Aquinas has to offer. However, applying the theology of Thomas Aquinas to a contemporary context is not without its problems, and in his moral theology there are some significantly underdeveloped themes that could benefit greatly from the tools of a community- and narrative-centered ethic, such as the ones found in Hauerwas and Hütter. I hope, here, to show the great value of a conceptual interchange between Hauerwas, Hütter, and Thomas Aquinas for an ecumenical ethic of grace in community, and more specifically, how treatments of the sacramental life of the worshipping Christian community, the interdependence of Christians, and the application of scriptural narrative to the moral life, as these ideas are treated by Hauerwas and Hütter, might provide tools for showing the importance of God's grace in Christian community.

The Sacramental and Worshipping Life of the Church

The first way in which I indicated how the importance of the context of the Christian worshipping community was underdeveloped in Aquinas' treatment on grace, the Holy Spirit, and human action was the way in which he passed rather quickly over the context of the sacramental and worshipping life of the Church. The Christian community for Aquinas appears to be a collection of those who are transformed by God's grace in relative isolation from one another. While it is rather doubtful that Hauerwas and Hütter share all of the same convictions about what is actually happening in the Church's sacraments (or even, for that matter, what the sacraments are), an interaction between these sources remains fruitful in that Hauerwas and Hütter both emphasize the importance of the sacraments in a way that is not doctrinally exclusive. In other words, the valuable contribution of these theologians with regard to the sacraments, as found in Aquinas' theology, is appropriate in that they speak to the importance of the sacramental life of the Church without conditions of specific doctrines regarding those sacraments themselves. I believe that an interaction between these three theologians can be fruitful in that it can occur on the importance of the sacramental and worship life of the Christian community, without unnecessarily highlighting their potential disagreements with regard to doctrine about the specifics of that sacramental and worship life.

In Hauerwas' earliest writings, Christian community seemed to have no place in the determination of Christian moral action. Instead, we human beings can initiate any necessary changes in ourselves. As a human moral agent, "I am not any such event, process, or state that is proposed to be the 'real cause' of my act, such as some intention, motive, or state of willing. . . . I am an uncaused power since no other event is necessary to explain my act other than that I as an agent did it. . . . as the cause of my act nothing further is needed to explain the act's existence beyond the fact that I am the agent of it."[34] This solipsistic viewpoint

---

34. Hauerwas, *Character and the Christian Life*, 88.

was not to last, however. Before long, Hauerwas held very closely to the necessity of ecclesial context even for understanding Christian truth. "Christian beliefs about God, Jesus, sin, the nature of human existence, and salvation are intelligible only if they are seen against the background of the church—i.e., a body of people who stand apart from the 'world' because of the peculiar task of worshipping a God whom the world knows not."[35] The task of worshipping God as a community is not only identity making, but, according to Hauerwas, a necessity to the intelligibility of the Christian moral life. The practice of worship has an impact not only on our understanding of ourselves as a group, but our understanding of revelation, and of its application to each of us individually. In fact, argues Hauerwas, Christian virtue itself is inseparable from this context of sacramental Christian worship. "The sign and substance of this infusion of the Christian virtues is always participation in the body of Christ. This involves our reception of the sacraments of baptism and eucharist, but also includes (and entails) immersion in the daily practices of the Christian church."[36] Our reception of what God has to offer in the sacramental worship life of the Church is as much in community Christian praxis as it is in the sacraments themselves. Both, he astutely observes, are rightly considered as taking part in the body of Christ. To participate in the body of Christ is sacramental, both in moments like baptism and the Eucharist, as well as in the praxis of Christian Church as the body of Christ itself. The sacramental life of the worshipping body, according to Hauerwas, is not an activity that can be rightly conceived of without the context of Christian community and its practices. Like Hütter, Hauerwas speaks of narrative casuistry (though less extensively) as a way of addressing the impact on the Christian moral life of the writing of the New Testament and the community it forms. But, he says, even this activity does not make sense apart from the context of the sacramental and worshipping life of the Church. He writes that "casuistry makes no sense for Christians unless it presupposes the practice of baptism. Only in view of baptism are questions about serving in the military, cooperation with pagans, observance of vows, or behavior during persecution questions at all."[37] Somewhat differently from Aquinas, Hauerwas places the context of community and its worshipping practice

---

35. Hauerwas, "On Keeping Theological Ethics Theological," 34.
36. Hauerwas, *Christians Among the Virtues*, 69.
37. Hauerwas, *In Good Company*, 179.

as the necessary condition for the formation of the individual moral act. Such logic extends to the worship life of the Christian community as a whole. "Worship is what we do for God, but in that doing, we believe our lives are made part of God's care for creation. To be made holy is to have our lives rendered unintelligible if the God who has claimed us in Jesus Christ is not the true God. To be made holy is to have our lives 'exposed' to one another in the hope that we will become what we have been made."[38] The formative power of Christian community is dependent upon its context in Christian worship. Once more, Hauerwas argues for the need of the community, especially in terms of its practice of Christian worship.

Aquinas would say, with Hauerwas, that without the sacramental life of the worshipping Christian community, the idea of a Christian moral theology centered on grace is incoherent. On this point, one must look to Aquinas' treatise on the sacraments, and specifically his answer to the question: "Whether sacraments are necessary for man's salvation?" (III 61.1), the answer to which is an unqualified "yes." As he goes on to note in the third article of the same question, "Sacraments are necessary for man's salvation, in so far as they are sensible signs of invisible things whereby man is made holy."[39] On the precise point of holiness, both Hauerwas and Aquinas assert the need for the sacraments, but Hauerwas reemphasizes their importance with regard to the context of the Christian community in the moral life. When Aquinas addresses the Christian moral existence in terms of the sacraments, there is very little treatment about the impact upon, or the context within, the worshipping Christian community. For Hauerwas, the Holy Spirit at work within the dynamics of community is everything. In outlining an ecumenical ethic of grace, both theologians help by placing the action of the Holy Spirit through the praxis of the church at the foundation of our ethical transformation toward our final end.

Few emphasize the relevance of the sacramental and worshipping life of the Christian community for the moral life like Reinhard Hütter. In fact, Christian worship is so central to his conception of Christian morality (and the action of God therein) that he calls his ethic a "kirchliche Ethik." Hütter's "ecclesial ethics" is meant to emphasize the centrality of God's action in the Christian moral life. In this way, the intention behind

38. Hauerwas, *Better Hope*, 160.
39. Aquinas, *Summa theologiae* III 61.3.

his moral theology is similar to Aquinas. However, unlike Aquinas, the activity of the Christian morality is so dependent on Christian worship and sacrament that labeling it an "ecclesial ethic" is appropriate. Hütter argues that "ecclesial ethics has to ask about 'good works,' which can be described as works done 'through the Holy Spirit.' These are works that bear the promise that God in his actions will bind himself to them."[40] His ecclesial ethics, in ways similar to Thomas' theology, is concerned with those Christian actions that are done "through the Holy Spirit"—the major difference being, of course, that the worshipping and sacramental life of the Christian community is absolutely foundational and totally central for Hütter, whereas it is treated less robustly by Aquinas. There are some moments in Hütter's early writing in which it is difficult to separate the activity of Christian worship and sacrament from the Christian moral life. He writes, "by asking about the basis of the church in God's sanctifying action, the vocation of the Church comes in view and by asking about the vocation of the Church, its reason within God's sanctifying action inevitably comes in view. The theological mode of speech in which both are intertwined, is called Paraklete. *Consequently, Paraklete language is the theological designation of the ethical language of the Church.*"[41] Merely the phrase "ethical language of the Church" already indicates that the activity of the Holy Spirit cannot be modalized. God's grace in the action of the Holy Spirit in the Christian moral life, for Hütter, not only includes, but necessarily entails the worship life of the Christian community. Even after this earliest work, Hütter pursues this same unity between ecclesial and moral activity. In *Suffering Divine Things*, he develops "a notion of the church as the soteriological locus of God's actions, as a space constituted by specific core practices and church doctrine. These practices are understood pneumatologically as acts to be interpreted enhypostatically as 'works' of the Spirit. Rather

---

40. Hütter, *Evangelische Ethik*, 281. Kirchliche Ethik hat m.a.W. nach den »guten Werken« zu fragen, die als die gelten dürfen, die »aus dem Heiligen Geist« sind, d.h. denen die Verheißung gilt, daß Gott sich in seinem Handeln an sie bindet.

41. Ibid., 267–68. Das Eine ist genaugenommen von Anderen nicht abzutrennen. Indem sie nach dem Grund der Kirche in Gottes heilschaffendem Handeln fragt, kommt die Berufung der Kirche in den Blick, und indem sie nach der Berufung der Kirche fragt, kommt unweigerlich ihr Grund im heilschaffenden Handeln Gottes in den Blick. Der theologische Redemodus, in dem beides in dieser Weise verschränkt vorliegt, ist die Paraklese. *Parakletische Rede ist demnach die theologische Bestimmung der ethischen Rede von Kirche.*

than being self-grounded, they participate in the being of the Spirit as the latter's work in the Spirit's mission of the triune God's economy of salvation."[42] Such works of the Spirit constitute the basis for Christian theology and Christian ethical action, and (in many instances) are the ethical actions themselves. As seen before, Christian ethical actions are only rightly understood in an ecclesial context, because this context is the primary locus in which one finds the Spirit's action. For Hütter, the Church, and the worshipping Christian community therein, modeled a conjunction between divine and human action that stands as a paradigm for what Christian ethics ought to be. "God's action is entirely different from human action, in so far as it does *not* compete with it. By God working in the human being through the Holy Spirit, the human being stays a human being, also by staying an agent. . . . Man believes, confesses, prays. As God works in all things, i.e. creates all things new and in doing so proves to be God, man acts holistically as well, and thus, may remain a human being in this 'conjunction.'"[43] It must be mentioned that this strain of Hütter's argument was much more prevalent in his early work, but nonetheless finds less potent expression in his later writing as well. Moments like Christian baptism are meant to be the paradigm for Christian moral life, in that at these moments divine action and human action find an interactive bond (at least to some extent). Such a bond is the core of Christian action. When the Christian believes, confesses, prays, she is right to say that these are moments of Christian action in which God acts, but not in such a way that such actions are any less human, or any less her own. Again, the pattern seen from Hütter is one in which the ecclesial context—the sacramental life of the Christian worshipping community—is central to Christian moral existence. Aquinas,

42. Hütter, *Suffering Divine Things*, 27.

43. Hütter, *Evangelische Ethik*, 102. Gottes Handeln ist darin vom menschlichem Handeln grundverschieden, daß es *nicht* zu diesem in Konkurrenz tritt. Indem Gott am Menschen im Geist handelt, bleibt der Mensch Mensch, auch indem er Handelnder bleibt. Gottes neuschaffendes Handeln im Geist ist ein »Herstellen«, das den Menschen nicht ein totes Produkt verwandelt, sondern ihn in seinem Sein als Handlungssubject beläßt. Der Mensch bleibt nicht nur Handelnder in Gottes Handeln, er wird vielmehr als solcher durch Gottes Handeln an ihm neu in Kraft gesetzt, indem er in die Freiheit geführt wird, Gott an sich handeln zu lassen und dieses Handeln selbst handelnd zu bejahen. Indem Gott den Menschen »neuschafft«, handelt der Mensch selbst. Der Mensch glaubt, bekennt, betet. Wie Gott alles wirkt, also im vollen Sinne neuschaffend handelt und sich darin als Gott erweist, handelt auch der Mensch *ganz* und darf in diesem »Beieinander« somit Mensch bleiben.

too, seems to indicate its importance, but especially regarding the worship and sacramental life, he passes over it rather quickly. The great value of Reinhard Hütter in prompting an ecumenical ethic of grace is the way in which he, like Hauerwas, points to the importance of Christian worship for a system of Christian ethics that demonstrates the close involvement of God's agency in the Christian moral life. Hütter, like Hauerwas, emphasizes the dynamics internal to the Christian worshipping body as themselves valuable, rather than simply as the setting for something valuable. The life of the worshipping community and God's grace are so closely related for Hütter because, for him, "the church, as the *work* of the Holy Spirit, is at the same time the *mode of enactment* of the Holy Spirit's economic mission."[44] The work of the Holy Spirit in the Church as an important parallel to the work of the Holy Spirit in the human heart is presented by Hütter to be a natural one, the reflection on which is fruitful for ethics, and the reality of which makes the worship life of the Christian community a central concern of Christian ethics. As Hütter writes in 2004, "in the proclamation of God's word, in baptism, in the Lord's Supper, the gospel addresses and claims us in tangible and specific ways; in ordained office, prayer, doxology, catechesis, and the suffering walk of discipleship, the gospel engages us in a personal, intellectual, and most deeply existential way."[45] Hütter connects the impact of the discourse of the Christian community with its sacramental life, seeing both as means for God's intimacy in the Christian moral life. Though it would be difficult to make a direct connection between the ways in which Hütter treats the sacraments for Christian ethics and the way Thomas treats them, Hütter, like Thomas, points to the importance of an intimate, interactive bond between divine and human agency in the Christian moral life. But, at the same time, he gives a central role to the worshipping Christian community as the site in which this agency, paradigmatically, occurs.

The Interdependence of Christians

The second way in which Aquinas seems to pass quickly over the importance of the context of the Christian worshipping community is the interdependence between Christians in the dynamic between God's grace

---

44. Hütter, *Suffering Divine Things*, 126.
45. Hütter, *Bound to Be Free*, 50.

and human action. With Hauerwas in particular (in fact, so much so that it leads him into problems), the dynamics of God's agency in the moral life is very closely intertwined with the interdependence of the Christian community. When Hauerwas treats Christian virtue, for instance, our formation by God's grace for God's work and our dependence on each other in formation are hard to separate. For example, in *A Community of Character*, he writes, "if, as I contend, the church is a truthful polity, the most important social task of Christians is to be nothing less than a community capable of forming people with virtues sufficient to witness to God's truth in the world."[46] The formation of virtue for the action of an individual Christian is quite dependent, for Hauerwas, on the other members of the Christian worshipping community. The community itself is capable of forming people. But (while one might say that he does not make this clear often enough) the context of Christian worship, and our interdependence through that activity, stands behind this formation. "The sign and substance of this infusion of the Christian virtues is always participation in the body of Christ. This involves our reception of the sacraments of baptism and eucharist, but also includes (and entails) immersion in the daily practices of the Christian church."[47] The formation of Christian virtue depends on our interaction and interdependence with a community with very distinctive and very transformative practices.

While I have already noted the problems with some of the directions in which he articulated these practices, Hauerwas' voice is valuable in his emphasis on the interdependence of Christians; by contrast, Thomas treats the interconnection between Christians in the worshipping community in an opaque and neutral fashion in most instances. Indeed, for Hauerwas, our dependence on God and our dependence on Christian community are often treated as if they were one and the same. Hauerwas writes that "our moral convictions depend on the experience and wisdom of a people who have been and continue to be on a journey of discovery charted by the God we have come to know through Israel and the life, death, and resurrection of Christ."[48] While God's grace in the moral life, for Aquinas, seems to be always brought back to a somewhat isolated interaction between the individual Christian and God (despite

---

46. Hauerwas, *Community of Character*, 3.
47. Hauerwas, *Christians Among the Virtues*, 69.
48. Hauerwas, *Peaceable Kingdom*, 133.

the occasional notes to the contrary), Hauerwas argues that God's shaping of the community (and the community's shaping of the Christian) *is, in fact,* God's shaping of the Christian. While such a direction can be taken too far, Hauerwas usefully shows that the dynamics of God's grace through the Holy Spirit need not be seen only as a dependence on God, but rightly entails dependence on other Christians. While Aquinas sees problems like the need for prayers for perseverance and the guardianship and guidance of God, he does not treat such matters as occurring as a part of the dynamics of the worshipping Christian community in any overt way. Rather differently, Hauerwas sees that the "immersion in and acquired facility and practiced dexterity with respect to improvisational skills of Christian faith helps account for the way the church trusts, in times of crisis, its own habituation and formation of character."[49] The habitual formation of the Christian, for Hauerwas, happens through community dynamics.

Two of the ways in which Hauerwas uses interdependence to fill out the context of Christian community in the moral life harmonize nicely with how Aquinas seems to treat interdependence: apprenticeship and Christian friendship. The opening pages of this chapter showed how Thomas argues the need for moral instruction under the New Law (especially in his treatment of that Law in Question 106, and his treatment of gratuitous grace in Question 111). The heavy emphasis Hauerwas gives to the interdependence of the Christian community through apprenticeship and instruction fills out this somewhat thin notion very nicely. For Hauerwas, the Christian is instructed in morality through imitation and mutual teaching that yields moral transformation.[50] While some of Hauerwas' ideas about God's grace are not in harmony with those found in Thomas Aquinas, on this point, Hauerwas seems to be providing a richer sense of Christian instruction under the New Law, which Thomas seems to need. The Church, says Hauerwas, "knows that the life of faithfulness is not easily acquired but involves those skills that can be learned only through apprenticeship to a master. Living morally is not simply holding the right principles, [but] . . . the slow training of our vision through learning to pay attention to the insignificant."[51] This means of Christian instruction seems to complete an idea that Aquinas

---

49. Hauerwas, *Performing the Faith*, 91.
50. Hauerwas, *Community of Character*, 131.
51. Hauerwas, *Christian Existence Today*, 103.

argued to be important (even if only in a passing way). Christian formation and instruction indicates the importance of the interdependence of Christians guided by grace. Hauerwas writes that Christian friendship "seems to have three closely related aspects: (1) to enable and assist each friend in the acquisition and practice of Christian virtues, (2) to build up the Christian community as the body of Christ, and (3) to make possible, under God's gracious favor through the Holy Spirit, friendship with God."[52] In a way strikingly absent in Thomas' theology (though occasionally indicated), Hauerwas sees the formation of the Christian by the worshipping community and the formation of the Christian by the Holy Spirit. Especially concerning the third aspect to which he points, the community is a part of God's own formation of us toward an end of friendship with God. Whereas Aquinas speaks very consistently about the Christian being drawn into such friendship using language focused on the individual, Hauerwas points to the importance of the context of the worshipping community. Hauerwas' use of Christian friendship and his emphasis on the importance of Christian instruction bring a much-needed depth to the scant mentions of the context of the interdependence between Christians found in Thomas Aquinas' theology treating the Holy Spirit and Christian moral action.

Drawing heavily from Hauerwas' work, Reinhard Hütter offers a similar contribution to the importance of the interdependence of Christian community in treating the "conjunction" between divine and human agency in the Christian moral life. For Hütter, the ways in which God's grace sanctifies the individual and the ways God sanctifies the community are intertwined, and both are entailed in the "conjunction" between divine and human agency. He writes that "the correctly understood language of the holiness of the community actually presupposes a theological specification of the connection between God's action *and* the action of human beings."[53] Hütter helpfully points out here that the impact of the conjunction of divine and human agency in the moral life is as relevant to the individual as it is to the community. The shaping of Christian agency through God's grace instrumentally uses the dynamics

52. Hauerwas, *Better Hope*, 180.
53. Hütter, *Evangelische Ethik*, 165. Die recht verstandene Rede von der Heiligkeit der Gemeinde setzt im Grunde also eine theologische Präzisierung des Zusammenhangs von Gottes Handeln *und* dem Handeln des Menschen voraus. Erst eine klare Bestimmung dieses »und« kann die Rede von der Heiligkeit der Gemeinde sowohl vor dem Irrweg der »billigen Gnade« als auch dem des Synergismus bewahren.

of Christian community. We are dependent on one another not only for knowledge about Christian ethics, but the holiness that results from the bond between divine and human action. Closely related to how Hütter argues for the importance of the sacramental and worshipping life of the Christian community, he writes,

> *Thus, "discipleship as imitation" can only be developed in the framework of ethical ecclesiology, in whose center there will be those enactments that coincide with God's action . . . The worship service is the place where the church's "discipleship to Christ" is at its center and from which it must proceed. Only in this place does the society that conforms to God's actions have its origin.* In the enactments of the worship service, God's action is communicated and, at the same time, the enactments conform to his action. . . . However, [discipleship to Christ] is not limited to the worship service alone, but develops specific virtues through specific actions, thus molding the character of the individual Christian as well as the whole community.[54]

The praxis of Christian community itself and the rather Hauerwasian discipleship by instruction can only be developed as a part of an interdependent worshipping community. The origin of ethical action—discipleship to Christ—is God's work amongst the worshipping community. What Hütter adds to these notions in this passage is twofold: first, he says that the Christian ethics of ecclesial community has a community origin. Even our dependence on God's action through the worshipping community has its origin in the way God directs the community. A com-

---

54. Ibid., 200. »*Nachfolge als Nachahmung*« *wird letztlich also nur im Rahmen einer ethischen Ekklesiologie zu entfalten sein, in deren Zentrum diejenigen Vollzüge stehen, in denen Gottes Handeln entsprochen wird. Es ist die* »*Geschichte Jesu*«, *die sowohl definiert, wie Gott herrscht, als auch, wie eine derartige Herrschaft eine ihr entsprechende* »*Welt*« *und* »*Gesellschaft*« *schafft. Dabei ist der Gottesdienst der Ort, in dem die kirhliche* »*Nachahmung Christi*« *ihr Zentrum hat und von dem sie ausgehen muß. Denn allein hier hat die dem Handeln Gottes entsprechende Gemeinschaft ihren Ursprungsort.* In den gottesdiestlichen Vollzügen teilt sich Gottes Handeln mit und wird ihn zugleich selbst entsprochen. *Der Gottesdienst selbst ist das Modell dafür, wie das* »*und*« *in Gottes und dem menschlichen Handeln zu verstehen ist. Gottes Handeln bindet sich an bestimmte Vollzüge—ihnen gilt die Verheißung, daß Gott durch sie handelt—, und indem die Mesnchen deise Vollzüge* »*tun*«, *entsprechen sie darin Gottes Handeln und bleiben damit zugleich in ihm.* Ist der Gottesdienst Modell, so hat die kirchliche Nachahmung Christi dort ihren Ursprung und Anfang, bleibt aber nicht auf ihn beschränkt, sondern formt durch bestimmtes Tun bestimmte Tugenden aus und prägt damit sowohl den Charakter der einzelnen Christen wie auch der gesamten Gemeinschaft.

munity of discipleship is not the product of the formation of individuals, but is a product of the functioning of the community itself and God's agency therein. The second important addition comes at the end of the quotation: the interdependence of the worshipping community is in the shaping of actions within that community. We are habituated by the action of the community as a part of the worship life of the Church. We are dependent on one another not only because the origin of community Christian discipleship is in the context of worship, but because the actions that occur therein are a part of Christian habituation. Such notions may be in harmony with Thomas' account of the twofold connection between grace and external action. However, Thomas argues that the connection is both through the sacraments and through Christian moral action as two relatively separate entities. Hütter holds this twofold connection in much tighter tension in a way that seems of extraordinary value for prompting an ecumenical ethic of grace, highlighting the importance of the interdependence of the Christian worshipping community.

Applying Scriptural Counsels to Christian Moral Life

The third and final indication of the need for further conversation regarding the context of the Christian worshipping community as treated by Thomas Aquinas, is in seeking to apply the "counsels" of the New Law that Thomas indicates, and the other specific points of obedience to the New Law which he says are left to the discretion of the individual. Precisely upon this point of applying the "counseling" content of Scripture (and the counsels in the Sermon on the Mount in particular), Hauerwas and Hütter indicate just how imperative the context of the Christian worshipping community can be. By grace, we are freed from sin, and under the New Law—a law described by Thomas (and St. Paul, for that matter) as a law of liberty—many aspects of Christian ethical behavior are left unspecified. Thomas puts this at the feet of the individual Christian, for the most part. Hauerwas and Hütter describe the context of the individual Christian (directed by God's grace) in the worshipping Christian community (directed by God's grace). For them, the point at which the New Law is the least specific is the point at which the content given by Christian community is most valuable. Moral theology as an individual task is only coherent in the context of the shaping of the individual Christian moral life through the worshipping community. As Hauerwas argues, "There can be no normative theory of the moral life that is sufficient to capture the rich texture of the many moral notions we inherit."[55] The application of morality to the life of the individual is the product, for Hauerwas, of story and the formation of the community thereby. In an instance of the Gospels, for instance, the problem is not that they are too bare as moral notions, and therefore a law of liberty. Instead, they are too rich to be bound to a singular theory. So how do we discern well-ordered Christian moral action from such wealth? We do so by means of the community that receives it and is formed by it. Hauerwas argues that "the primary social task of the church is to be itself—that is, a people who have been formed by a story that provides them with the skills for negotiating the danger of this existence, trusting in God's promise of redemption."[56] Whereas Thomas Aquinas admits that a great deal is left to the discretion of the individual in the Christian moral life, he looks primary to the solitary person, and her relationship with God, as the source of moral discernment. Hauerwas indicates the great value of Christian community, and the ways it is formed and directed by God, for moral discernment under the New Law, especially in terms of applying the content of the New Testament. Hauerwas writes that "Scripture is not meant to be a problem solver. . . . The Scripture is not an authority because it sets a standard of orthodoxy . . . but because the traditions of Scripture provide the means for our community to find new life."[57] The great adaptability of the content of Scripture is not just the variety of ways an individual Christian can apply its "counsels" (for example) to her life, but the much larger way in which it forms the community, which in turn forms the individual. When Hauerwas speaks of the formative power of the Gospel narrative, he does so with regard to the community, primarily. Another point at which Hauerwas helps prompt an ecumenical ethic of grace is in showing the value of the context of the worshipping Christian community in the individually and circumstantially specific expressions of Christian morality.

Hütter offers a similar approach to the application of the content of the New Testament in the individual Christian moral life and individual moral circumstance as a function of Christian community. Toward the end of *Evangelische Ethik*, Hütter uses Romans 12:1–2 as a paradigm for his Church ethics. Most especially, he lifts up the "renewal of the mind"

55. Hauerwas, *Truthfulness and Tragedy*, 22.
56. Hauerwas, *Community of Character*, 10.
57. Ibid., 63.

as the product of the formation of Christian community by which we come to know the will of God. But, he cautions, we cannot confuse the knowledge of what is "good, acceptable, and perfect" with the revelation of an ethic on its own. Instead, it points to the place in which the lofty ambition of the individual Christian to know the will of God is best sought, "to the place where judgment is formed and where a renewal of the spirit can be expected: worship in the community."[58] The application of Christian Scripture to Christian morality does leave a great deal to the discretion of the individual. But the "renewal of our minds" of which Hütter speaks does not happen to the solitary individual. In fact, coming to the knowledge of God's will in any one circumstance on one's own is a mistaken enterprise. Instead, he simply points to the context of the Christian worshipping community in which our minds are formed. Christian theology (and, of course, moral theology), for Hütter, is only rightly seen as receptive, passive with respect to the work of the Holy Spirit in the Church. As Hütter writes much later, "theology does not constitute itself 'poietically'; rather, the poiesis of the Holy Spirit constitutes the pathos of theology insofar as theology is shaped by the *poiemata* of the Holy Spirit, namely, by the core practices of the church and by church doctrine.... Theology is undertaken, engaged, performed, 'in' the work of the Holy Spirit, in the temporal and thus ecclesial development of God's *oikonomia*."[59] The activity of speaking beyond where the Bible speaks (the activity of theology) and likewise applying Scripture to the life of the individual Christian life is not in creating something, but rather is a part of the Holy Spirit working in the Church. The application of ideas like the "counsels" to the individual Christian life leaves much to the individual. For Hütter, such application of scriptural ideas to the individual life should be seen as a part of the core practices of the

---

58. Hütter, *Evangelische Ethik*, 273. Kirchliche Ethik als spezifischer kirchlich-theologischer Vollzug innerhalb der kirchlichen Diskurspraxis selbst bleiben immer deshalb schlicht nötig, um auf die Differenz zwischen dem *selbstverständlich Getanen* in der Kirche und dem von Gottes heilschaffenden Handeln her als *selbstverständlich Geltenden* aufmerksam zu machen. Von hier aus wäre dann Paulus' Bezugnahme auf »das Gute, das Wohlgefällige und das Vollkommene« gerade nicht als wie immer geartete Gleichsetzung von Gottes Willen und der »Evidenz des Ethischen« (Ebeling) zu verstehen, sondern als ein grundsätzliches Verwiesensein der Urteilsbildung auf den Ort, an dem die Erneuerung des Geistes zu erwarten ist: den Gottesdienst der Gemeinde.

59. Hütter, *Suffering Divine Things*, 114.

Church, a part of the life to which the context of the community shapes the Christian.

Hauerwas and Hütter offer concrete ways in which the worshipping Christian community is a valuable, and even necessary, asset to Christian moral existence. The dynamics internal to the Christian community are instrumental means for God's grace through the Holy Spirit. Each of these ways is in harmony with Thomas Aquinas' theology of grace and the great tools it provides for demonstrating the connection between divine and human agency in Christian action. Aquinas offers moments in which, as he treats the interaction between the Holy Spirit and human agency, the context of Christian community seems relevant. However, he does not indicate that dynamics internal to the sacramental and worshipping life of this community are at all integral to the connection between God's grace and human action. Thomas also shows how the interdependence of Christians within this community is in the background of Christian moral development. However, the connection between Christians is for the most part an inert context for an individually oriented connection with the Holy Spirit. Finally, he briefly notes how we need to be "taught" under the New Law because of how very many of the specifics of faithful Christian action are left to the discretion of individuals. That being said, he offers no sense in which the internal dynamics of the community are important in and of themselves in the context of the transformation of God's agency itself in the Christian moral life. In all three of these ways in which the context of worshipping Christian community is important, Thomas' treatment is somewhat thin and in need of development. While Thomas by no means excludes the relevance of the worshipping community, he certainly does not dwell on it with his characteristically thorough treatments. Instead, in his treatment of the Holy Spirit and human agency, Christian community seems an assumed context that is simply the gathering of individuals transformed by God's grace, rather than being itself instrumental to that change. Hauerwas and Hütter offer specific ways in which the sacramental life of the Church, the interdependence of Christians, and the function of community in applying the content of Scripture to the individual moral life are an integral and (more importantly) central part of how God's grace impacts the Christian moral life. In past chapters I have focused on the problems of their theologies in order to show the great value of the conceptual tools offered by Aquinas. Here, their great value in this conversation is evident as well. Hauerwas and Hütter need what Thomas has to offer to articulate well the centrality and relevance of God's grace in the Christian moral life for which their theologies advocate. Likewise, Aquinas needs what they have to offer to make clearer and develop more fully how the context of the worshipping Christian community is centrally important to the bond between God's grace and human action in Christian moral life, as directed by the Holy Spirit.

Conclusion

A Community-Centered Ecumenical Ethic of Grace

IN THE CLOSING OF the last chapter, I traced some of the ways in which the very rich articulations of Christian community and its efficacy in the moral life offered by Hauerwas and Hütter might fill out the somewhat thin role that the context of the worshipping community plays for Aquinas' ethics. Yet, filling out a particular facet of Aquinas' theology is only part of the benefit of this ecumenical conversation. While it may be very well to commend Aquinas for his robust theology of grace (and in doing so, point out that these dynamics tend toward a rather isolated picture of human agency), and to commend one strain of the contemporary ethical discourse for their robust theology of Christian community (and in doing so, point out that this setting tends to be a bit thin on articulating the workings of God's grace), very little of this suggests any potential meeting point. After all, what good does it do to tout the importance of Thomas' admittedly individual ethic of grace if there is no ground for applying such dynamics to the context of the worshipping community which Hauerwas and Hütter say is so important? What good does it do to push the importance of the contemporary ethical discourse with regard to this community unless there is some reason to believe that their ideas can mesh with what Aquinas has to say? An ethic of grace in community requires some reason to believe that these two directions do not simply talk past one another. In this concluding section I look at a final framework for an ecumenical ethic of grace by showing the path toward applying the individually oriented dynamics of God's grace in human agency, as seen in Aquinas, to the formative context of the Christian worshipping community, as emphasized in Hauerwas and Hütter.

In different ways, but with the same consistency and emphasis, Hauerwas and Hütter have argued for the importance and centrality of Jesus Christ and of God's grace through Christ for Christian ethics. Thomas clearly concurs with this approach. In the third part of his *Summa theologiae*, Thomas offers a careful consideration of exactly how God's grace through Jesus has an impact on the moral life. Unlike some of the elements of his treatise on grace, the picture offered in the third part is unavoidably oriented toward the Christian worshipping community. Even more, the questions of the third part hold the promise of incorporating Thomas' detailed account of God's grace to the individual into a larger account to God's shaping, moving, and transforming communities of faith. Resonating strongly with the trajectories of Hauerwas and Hütter, Thomas concludes that the efficacy of the grace of Christ is as the Head of the Church. Thomas develops this important move while consistently comparing the work of the Church to a body, with Christ as the Head of that body. The agency of that body is directed, moved, and shaped by the Head, and the Head is involved in every element of the body's actions.

This chapter will trace this explanation and show how, through it, one can apply the intricate explanation Thomas offers on God's grace and human action to the Christian community, the emphasis on which is of inestimable value in the contemporary context. By taking Thomas at his word, that the efficacy of the grace of Christ in the Church is as a Head to a body, one can apply to the shape of this body much of what Thomas has said about grace working through individual bodies. In doing so, the instincts offered by Hauerwas and Hütter to have Jesus at the center of community-centered Christian ethical action are confirmed and enriched. The efficacy of the twofold sense of the New Law, as Thomas describes it, applies well to more contemporary ethical frameworks of the centrality of the Holy Spirit in the Christian community, and the transformative power of the Gospels to its perspective and understanding. The Gifts of the Holy Spirit, described by Thomas as that which makes us amenable to the promptings of God's grace, fills out the importance that Hauerwas and Hütter give to the Holy Spirit and the inner dynamics of community. Thomas' distinctions between the effects of grace upon the individual body apply nicely to the body of the Church as well. The body of the Church, if Hauerwas and Hütter are correct, can be formed habitually and moved by God more immediately in both operative and cooperative ways. In short, if one takes Thomas' proposal about the efficacy of God's grace in the Christian life through the framework of Christ as the Head and the Church as the body, and then augments this proposal with the work of Hütter and Hauerwas to orient these dynamics within a community context, then an ecumenical, community-oriented framework for an ethic of grace emerges.

The Efficacy of God's Grace through the Incarnation

In his *Treatise on the Incarnation* in the third part of the *Summa theologiae*, Thomas uses fifty-nine questions to discuss the fittingness of the incarnation in its specifics. The first eight of these questions deal with the mode of union between the Word and human nature, and the efficacy of the grace of Christ. By the conclusion of question eight, Thomas has carefully led his reader to the notion of the framework of the Church as a body with Christ as its Head. Examining question eight, and some of the progression leading up to it, points toward the application of Thomas' dynamics of God's grace and human action to a concretely ecclesial setting, such as the one insisted upon by Hauerwas and Hütter.

Union of Divine and Human Natures in Jesus Christ

The first four questions of the third part examine the specifics of the incarnation in terms of its necessity, and the mode of the union between divine and human nature in the person of Christ. Reading these opening questions with an eye to the ways in which Thomas will frame the efficacy of God's grace through Christ and its impact on the moral life, it seems at first as if Thomas is carefully leading his reader toward a picture of efficacy based primarily (if not solely) on the union of divine and human natures. In these opening questions Thomas seems to frame the impact of God's grace through Christ in the generic bond forged between God and all those who share human nature. The opening question of the fittingness of the incarnation centers on inquiring as to what is most fitting given the shape of human nature,[1] the necessity of the incarnation due to the fallen shape of human nature,[2] and the timing of the incarnation itself, due to the specific teleology appropriate to human nature.[3] The second question consistently emphasizes the category of nature, as well. This question is most concerned with the mode of the union of human and divine nature in the Person of the Word and the singular hypostasis of Christ,[4] that which can be said to be united or composite in Christ,[5] the difference between the unity of natures and the assumption in the "becoming" of the incarnation,[6] and the fittingness and magnitude of the union of the two natures.[7] Thomas, in this second question, seems to be honing his readers' conception of the union of divine and human nature in Christ, and it would be easy to assume that from here, Thomas will go on to speak of the efficacy of God's grace through Christ only through the union of natures.

This pattern continues in question three, in which Thomas inquires after the fittingness and means by which the person of the Word assumes. Once more, the union of natures emerges as the sole critical and efficacious category. The further development in this question is the added emphasis on the union of natures as the result of the power of God. Articles 5–7 explore some hypotheticals about whether Divine Persons other than the Son could have assumed human nature and whether more than one human nature could be assumed. Thomas' response to each is essentially the same: "since in the mystery of the Incarnation 'the whole reason of the deed is the power of the doer,' as Augustine says (*Ep. ad Volusianum* cxxxvii), we must judge of it in regard to the quality of the Divine Person assuming, and not according to the quality of the human nature assumed."[8] The impact of this approach on the question of the efficacy of God's grace through the incarnation is significant. Saying that the ways in which human and divine nature have been (or could have been) united in Christ being simply the result of divine power means

1. Aquinas, *Summa theologiae* III.1.1. See also III.4.1.
2. Ibid., III.1.2–3.
3. Ibid., III.1.6.
4. Ibid., III.2.1–3.
5. Ibid., III.2.4–7.
6. Ibid., III.2.8.
7. Ibid., III.2.9–12.
8. Ibid., III.3.6.

that the unity of natures emerges as potentially the sole important accomplishment of the incarnation. If Thomas had explained the union of natures as possible only in the way that it actually happened, or had assigned some other reason why the union of natures in the Person of the Word was possible, then the union of natures itself could be seen as some means to an upcoming end. Instead, shaping these questions the way he does, Thomas again seems, initially, to be lifting up the union of natures as the sole efficacious accomplishment of the incarnation, and the result of the sheer power and will of God.

In article 8, this direction seems to be confirmed as Thomas asks after the fittingness of the incarnation as it happened. The restoration of humanity is fittingly accomplished through the union of natures alone—or so it would seem.

> It was fitting that the [human] creature should be restored in order to its eternal and unchangeable perfection; for the craftsman [that is, the Son] by the intelligible form of his art, whereby he fashioned his handiwork, restores it when it has fallen into ruin. Moreover, He has a particular agreement with human nature, since the Word is a concept of the eternal Wisdom, from Whom all man's wisdom is derived. And hence man is perfected in wisdom (which is his proper perfection, as he is rational) by participating the Word of God. . . . And hence for the consummate perfection of man it was fitting that the very Word of God should be personally united to human nature.[9]

Once more the union through nature seems to be the only important category for the efficacy of God's grace through Christ. The shape of human nature is the reason for the fittingness of its assumption by the Son, and the perfection of human beings is fittingly accomplished through the union of natures. No further category is introduced. Even more importantly, the perfection of humanity through the incarnation begins to emerge as happening in a generic way. The efficacy of God's grace through Christ, if it perfects man through the union of natures and if it is fittingly accomplished by reason of the shape of human nature itself, would seem to impact all equally. Humanity seems to be redeemed as a generic collective.

---

9. Ibid., III.3.8.

Redemption as a Generic Collective?

By question four, Thomas begins to turn his readers away from the notion of the impact of God's grace through Christ in terms of the generic collective of humanity alone. After slamming the door firmly closed on adoptionism in article 3, Thomas instructively brings the direction of his discussion of the union of natures to its seemingly inevitable head in the fourth article. There he asks whether the Son of God ought to have assumed human nature abstracted from all individuals. This is an important question for the efficacy of the grace of Christ in Christian life, and for just what is accomplished in the incarnation. If Thomas answers "yes" to this question (and given the trajectory of his inquiries so far in the third part, this seems a real possibility), then his readers can be confident that God's grace through Jesus Christ truly does impact human life on a collective and generic level, even to the point of its accomplishment on the level of nature in the abstract. Before going on to Thomas' answer to this question, the progression of objections that begin the question are quite interesting in terms of the instruction he offers. ST III.4.4.O1 makes the argument that the incarnation was for the salvation of all human beings and so concludes that "the Son of God ought to have assumed human nature as it is abstracted from all individuals."[10] In the second objection, the objector cites the authority of the Platonists, saying that it would have been much more efficacious if the Son had assumed human nature as abstracted from all individuals because the self-existing human nature, abstracted from all individuals, is a much better (and therefore more proper) object for assumption than human nature in an individual. Once more, the objection concludes, "therefore, the Son of God ought to have assumed this."[11] By the final objection, however, the tone shifts slightly, and the argument becomes not "whether the Son ought to have assumed human nature as abstracted from all individuals," but, more accurately, "whether the Son *did* assume human nature as abstracted from all individuals." In objection three, the objector argues that human nature was, in fact, assumed in the abstract because the Son assumed the designation "man," which denotes human nature as it is in every individual, and, therefore, abstracted from all of them. This objection concludes differently than the previous two: "Therefore the

---

10. Ibid., III.4.4.O1.
11. Ibid., III.4.4.O2.

Son of God *assumed* human nature as it is separated from individuals."[12] Suddenly there is much more at stake than a question of the fittingness of a hypothetical incarnation. By the end of the objections, the proposal before Thomas' readership is whether the purpose and the efficacy of the incarnation were in assuming human nature in the abstract. If the answer to this question is "yes," then the impact of God's grace through Christ in the moral life would be set up to occur in all people in the same way. If it was most fitting for the Son to assume human nature in the abstract (being better than human nature in an individual), then the efficacy of God's grace, thereby, would affect human beings in a generic way. Any specific community in which God's grace through Christ was efficacious (the Church, for example) would exist only as a gathering of those generically affected by the assumption of human nature in the incarnation.

Fortunately, Thomas deals very decisively with this notion, barring the way very firmly not only on the idea of the Son's assumption of human nature in the abstract, but on the Platonist underpinnings of the reason for positing such a framework. Thomas answers these objections, first by saying that the assumption of human nature in the abstract by the Son would not actually lead to an incarnation at all, and second by saying that, even if it did, this would not be fitting. Both steps prove important for narrowing down the ways Thomas describes the efficacy of God's grace through Christ. First, Thomas cites the authority of Damascene, stating that the Word's assumption of human nature in the abstract would only yield an incarnation in the abstract, and not a true incarnation at all. Then, in the *respondeo*, Thomas makes a clear choice of Aristotle over Plato in framing the efficacy of the incarnation. He argues that, as Aristotle proves, human nature cannot subsist in itself, "because sensible matter belongs to the specific nature of sensible things, and is placed in its definition, as flesh and bones in the definition of man."[13] In choosing this Aristotelian conception of what is properly human over Plato, Thomas continues to steer his readers away from a generic efficacy in the incarnation. To properly assume human nature is to assume human nature in an individual, rather than in the abstract. A picture emerges of God's grace through Christ impacting us as individuals having human nature, rather than in the abstract. So, Thomas' first answer

12. Ibid., III.4.4.O3. Emphasis mine.
13. Ibid., III.4.4.

to the question is that assumption of human nature in the abstract would not be an incarnation at all. The second answer he offers is that, even if such an incarnation were possible, it would not be most fitting. Thomas writes that "because to a common nature can only be attributed common and universal operations, according to which man neither merits nor demerits, whereas, on the contrary, the assumption took place in order that the Son of God, having assumed our human nature, might merit for us."[14] Again, the progression of Thomas' instruction is worth close attention. In the *respondeo*, Thomas chooses a pattern of efficacy that favors an Aristotelian metaphysics over a Platonist one, and begins to emphasize the importance of the actions of Christ as an individual, rather than in abstraction. The incarnation and the particularity of Jesus was not merely a shadow of a more important union between divine and human nature in the abstract. Instead of a generic importance of Jesus Christ to our salvation, Thomas emphasizes the particulars of his life, death, and resurrection.

This move is completed in the answers to the objections in *ST* III.4.4. The first objection stands out as especially important to the impact of God's grace through Christ in Christian ethics. The objection itself argued that assuming human nature in the abstract would be the best way for God's grace through the Son to be the salvation for all. The objection is answered in this way: "The incarnate Son of God is the common Savior of all, not by a generic or specific community, such as is attributed to the nature separated from the individuals, but by a community of cause, whereby the incarnate Son of God is the universal cause of human salvation."[15] Here Thomas turns his readers from the general trajectory of emphasis on the union of human and divine nature as the sole efficacy of God's grace in Christ to the notion of a *community of cause* bound to Christ, individually. Thomas elegantly accomplishes this move in conjunction with an emphasis on the Son of God as the universal cause of salvation for human beings. God's grace through Christ works via a community of cause, but this does not preclude Christ as the universal cause of human salvation. The response to objection two further dismisses the Platonists by not only reasserting that human nature in the abstract is not a thing that can be said to exist in nature, but also by saying that if such a notion can be said to exist, it is in the divine intellect,

14. Ibid., III.4.4.
15. Ibid., III.4.4.RO1.

and therefore such an assumption would be unnecessary.[16] The answer to the third objection emphasizes the difference between an assumption of human nature in the individual, and the assumption of a human nature in the concrete—which is to say the difference between incarnation and adoption.[17] The third objection argued for the assumption of human nature in the abstract by using adoption, and not assumption of human nature in an individual, as its alternative. Thomas uses this opportunity to highlight the difference between the assumption of human nature in an individual, and the adoption of a human nature in a concrete human being. By the end of this article, Thomas has opened a few new categories for his readers that move them away from the efficacy of God's grace through the incarnation as a generic consequence of the bond between human and divine nature in the incarnation. Instead, the particularity and even visibility of Jesus meet categories like "a community of cause." Thomas begins to bring his readers away from the Platonist aroma of the first three questions, away from a picture of the efficacy of the incarnation as generic in nature, and toward human nature in an individual, without taking away the Son of God as the universal cause of human salvation.

The next article further narrows the efficacy of God's grace through Christ by asking whether the Son ought to have assumed human nature in all individuals. This next step in Thomas' instruction of his readers takes the move towards Aristotle and brings it more pointedly toward the question of the Son of God as the universal cause of human salvation. If, as Thomas said at the closing of the previous article, the Son assumed human nature in an individual, rather than in the abstract (but not in the concrete—by God's adoption of a human being), then would it not have been more effective to assume human nature in all its individuals? Since it would have been possible (as argued in question 3, article 7) for the Son to have assumed more than one human nature, would this not have been more fitting and effective?

Thomas' answers to this proposition even further point towards the eventual picture of "Christ as the Head of the Church" as the framework for mapping out the efficacy of God's grace through the incarnation. Thomas follows a two-step progression similar to the one in the previous article, first noting the impossibility of the proposal, and then add-

16. Ibid., III.4.4.RO2.
17. Ibid., III.4.4.RO3.

ing how, even if it were possible, it would not be most fitting. Thomas begins by noting that if the Word were to assume human nature in all individuals, then concrete individuals would not exist. He writes that "since we must not see any other suppositum in the assumed nature, except the Person assuming . . . if there was no human nature except what was assumed, it would follow that there was but one suppositum of human nature, which is the Person assuming."[18] A suppositum, Thomas reminds his reader in question 3, article 7, is the composition of matter and form—so, an individual human being, having the form of human nature, and the flesh and bones of a human body, constitutes a single suppositum. Since only a singular divine person is assuming (though Thomas concedes that it would be possible for more than one human nature to be assumed), the result would be still a single suppositum—still only the Word of God, Jesus of Nazareth. So, while Thomas seems willing to grant that this is a possibility, any further efficacy would not be possible, and so there would be no additional benefit to be had from the assumption of human nature in all individuals. Even if any such benefits were possible, however, Thomas argues that it would not be most fitting, "because this would have been derogatory to the dignity of the incarnate Son of God, as He is the First-born of many brethren, according to the human nature, even as He is the First-born of all creatures according to the Divine, for then all men would be of equal dignity."[19] Thomas, after many articles in the previous questions that go far toward showing the balanced bond between the human and divine natures in the Son of God, takes a different and telling turn in this statement. The dignity of the Son of God, as the "First-born," means that while there is some equality between his own two natures, there is an important inequality between him and every other human being. Thomas has gone to great lengths, by this point, to show that this difference is not a difference in that which makes the Son of God human, according to his nature. Still, Thomas begins to point his readers toward the category of Jesus as importantly unequal in dignity to other human beings. Once more, Thomas steers his audience slowly toward a description of the efficacy of God's grace through the incarnate Son which does not rest on a kind of corporate or generic foundation, based only on the sharing of our human nature. Already by introducing the importance of Christ as the

18. Ibid., III.4.5.
19. Ibid.

"First-born," important inequalities in dignity begin to have some impact on how he describes God's grace through Jesus.

Christ as the Head of the Church

In questions 5 through 7, Thomas deals with the specifics of the order of the assumption, and the ways in which Christ can be said to have grace. But the careful groundwork that he has laid in the first few questions emerges again in question eight on Christ as the Head of the Church. In this crucial question, Thomas offers a way out of the efficacy of God's grace through the incarnate Son as generic to all who share human nature, completing the trajectory begun by notions such as Christ as the "First-born" influencing a "community of cause." The *respondeo* opens with a bold statement on the nature and shape of the Church, from scriptural authority. Thomas writes that "the whole Church is termed one mystic body from its likeness to the natural body of a man, which in diverse members has diverse acts,"[20] citing the authority of Romans 12 and 1 Corinthians 12. Interestingly, however, Thomas seems to be adapting St. Paul's theology in these passages, to an extent, because, while both chapters do speak of the Church as a body with likeness to a natural body, they speak only of the Church as the body of Christ (see especially Rom 12:5; 1 Cor 12:12, 27), rather than Christ as the Head of the body (as in Eph 1:22; 4:15; 5:23; or Col 1:18). Thomas adds an additional layer to the idea of the Church as a body, which resonates with the notion of the "community of cause" which he indicated in question four. He adds that "Christ is called the Head of the Church from a likeness with the human head, in which we may consider three things, viz. order, perfection, and power."[21] Shifting from a picture of the Church as the body of Christ (in which Christ is not as much any singular member as the whole body), Thomas further narrows this notion of the "community of cause" by naming Christ as the Head of the body that is the Church.

A more complete picture of the efficacy of God's grace through Christ to the Church begins to emerge, which resonates well with the consistent emphasis on the centrality of Christ offered by Hauerwas and Hütter. The Church is a body, with a likeness to a human body, and so subject, in at least a few analogous ways, to the formation of action

20. Ibid., III.8.1.
21. Ibid.

within a human body. Christ is the Head of this community of cause, and Thomas argues that his efficacy in this community is analogous to the influence of a head to a human body, specifying order, perfection, and power as those things that most apply to the analogy of Christ as the Head of the Church. As to the first, Thomas writes, "'Order,' indeed; for the head is the first part of man, beginning from the higher part; and hence it is that every principle is usually called a head."[22] This way of talking about Christ as the Head of the Church harmonizes nicely with St. Paul. If the Church is a body, rightly called the body of Christ, then it follows that the first principle of this body is Christ himself. However, given this category alone, Christ as the Head of a "community of cause" does not seem to apply. Thomas continues, writing that Christ is also the Head of the Church as its "'Perfection,' inasmuch as in the head dwell all the senses, both interior and exterior, whereas in the other members there is only touch."[23] To explain this category further, Thomas cites Isaiah 9:15, which recounts an instance in which the Lord punishes Israel by cutting "off from Israel head and tail,"[24] the head being the elders and the tail being the prophets. The people were being led astray by their head, and so the Lord cut it off. Quite a lot can be made of this comparison, given Thomas' scriptural citation. Christ is placed alongside the tribal elders of Israel, presumably able to direct the body in obedience in ways that the elders of Israel failed to do. The elders—as those members of the community that most perfectly typified the life of that community, and led the community thereby—were the assembly that directed the rest of the body. Here Thomas offers his readers some further details on the efficacy of God's grace through Christ upon this "community of cause." As elders are the "senses" that lead the community of Israel either to obedience of disobedience to God, Christ similarly leads the community of the Church.

Thomas takes this further in the third sense in which Christ is rightly called the "Head," which is "'Power,' because the power and movement of the other members, together with the direction of them in their acts, is from the head, by reason of the sensitive and motive power there ruling."[25] This further step gives the efficacy of God's grace through

22. Ibid.
23. Ibid.
24. Isa 9:14.
25. Aquinas, *Summa theologiae* III.8.1.

Christ an even more prominent place in the Church as a community of cause. More than simply being the principle member, or leading in any indirect way, the head, Thomas argues, directs and moves the actions of the body. Once more, the scriptural citation offered by Thomas is helpful. He quotes 1 Samuel 15:17, in which Samuel, speaking to King Saul, who has just lead the people into disobedience to God's commands, says, "Though you are little in your own eyes, are you not the head of the tribes of Israel?"[26] Saul was commanded by God to utterly destroy the Amalekites, and, through his leadership as the "head," the tribes of Israel had not done so. Here the prophet condemns Saul rather than the people, because Saul is the "head" of those tribes, and so, in some way, the ruler and director of the power and movement of the members of that tribe. At least that is what he is being condemned for in this case. If the Church is that seen and unseen, already begun but not yet complete "body" of members who have Christ as their Head in terms of order, perfection, and power, God's grace through Christ can be said to rule and direct such members in a way similar to the direction and ruling of Saul over the tribes of Israel. Saul bore the responsibility of the actions of the tribes to such an extent that God condemned him for their disobedience. The tribes of Israel, under Saul as their "head," were a fully realized body gathered in one visible location. The Church, on the other hand, is not a fully realized and single visible body. Yet, Thomas deems it appropriate to speak of its connection to Christ as a body to a head.

The Holy Spirit as the Heart of the Church

Thomas' description of the Church, and Christ as its Head, is shown to parallel even further his description of the efficacy of God's grace in an individual as Thomas describes God's grace in the Holy Spirit as a part of this Headship in the responses to the first and third objections. In answering whether Christ, as man, can give "sense and motion to the members"[27] of the body through the gift of grace in the Holy Spirit, Thomas writes, "To give grace or the Holy Ghost belongs to Christ as He is God. . . . And hence by the power of the Godhead His actions were beneficial, i.e. by causing grace in us, both meritoriously and

26. 1 Sam 15:17.
27. Aquinas, *Summa theologiae* III.8.1.O1.

efficiently."[28] Thomas tightens the analogy of the body of the Church, and all that such an analogy would include about what Thomas has said about God's grace in a single body, by saying that grace and the Holy Spirit are given through Christ, rightly making him not simply the "head" of an individual body, but the Head of the "community of cause" that is the Church. Thomas' description of the efficacy of God's grace through the Holy Spirit functions on a strikingly individual level in earlier sections of the *Summa*. So, if Christ is the Head of the Church, and thereby it belongs to him to give the Holy Spirit, *in what way can the Spirit be said to work in the Church as a community of cause?* As a collection of individuals only? When Thomas says that Christ is the Head of the Church because he gives the Holy Spirit, is that gift efficacious only on an individual level, or does the body of the Church have the same capacity to be host to the sort of "indwelling" or "instinct" that operates on an individual level?

The response to the third objection offers a clear answer. The objector argues that in a body, the head is not alone in ruling the body. People also note that there is some kind of bearing that the "heart" has on the formation of action, and even on the head itself. If Christ is the universal principle of the whole Church, then the designation of "Head" would not seem to apply, because a head of an individual human body has some connection with the heart as a principle for its action. The objector raises, helpfully, the problem of just how close the analogy can be between the efficacy of God's grace in an individual human body and the efficacy of God's grace in the body of the Church. Thomas responds, "The head has a manifest pre-eminence over the other exterior members; but the heart has a certain hidden influence. And hence the Holy Ghost is likened to the heart, since He invisibly quickens and unifies the Church."[29] The Church, as a body, has as its heart the Holy Ghost. Not only has Thomas provided language for speaking of both Christ and the Holy Spirit as working in the body of the Church, Thomas has also shown just how deep the analogy of the Church as a body can go. For instance, Thomas spoke of the New Law, in its most primary sense, as "the grace of the Holy Ghost, which is given to those who believe in Christ."[30]

28. Ibid., III.8.1.RO1.
29. Ibid., III.8.1.RO3.
30. Ibid., I–II.106.1.

Thomas also emphasizes that "the New Law is instilled in our hearts."[31] All that Thomas has said about the connection between the action of the Holy Spirit and Christian moral action on an individual level seems to apply to the "community of cause" of the Church, as both the individual human body and the body of the Church have the grace of the Holy Spirit working in the heart and the grace of Christ as their principle.

Thomas describes the Church as a body—a community of cause— with Christ as its Head and the Holy Spirit as its heart. Like the body of a Christian, the rulership of Christ as Head or Holy Spirit as heart is not yet realized fully or in every place. Still, Thomas describes the body of the Church and the body of the Christian with striking similarity in terms of the efficacy of God's grace. Since this is the case, much of what Thomas has said about how the Holy Spirit works in an individual can be applied to the pivotal role that Hauerwas and Hütter rightly place on Christian community.[32]

The Twofold Sense of the New Law in the Body of the Church

One application of the content that Aquinas offers on grace to the framework of community offered by the contemporary ethical discourse is in the impact of the twofold sense of the New Law. In chapter 5, I drew a similarity between the ways in which Hauerwas and Hütter rightly emphasized the formation of Christian ethical action through their emphasis on the Gospel narrative and its impact in Christian community, and Thomas' treatment of the twofold sense of the New Law. If one can take from Thomas the significant similarity between the workings of a human body and the body of the Church, then the formation of that

---

31. Ibid., I–II.106.1.*sed contra*.

32. It must be admitted here that there is a certain mismatch between their conception of Church and that offered by Thomas. For instance, Thomas extends the Headship of Christ to the authority of the pope and of bishops, ruling and governing the physical, visible Church in a way that does not resonate particularly well with Hauerwas and Hütter. Additionally, Thomas seems to describe Christ's rulership of the Church in terms of its mystical body, not fully realized until the coming of the kingdom. Hauerwas and Hütter, on the other hand, seem to have a more immediate, smaller, and more visible community in their sights. Nevertheless, there are enough similarities between the formation of the bodies of which they speak, and God's grace through the body of the Church about which Aquinas speaks, that comparing the two (without necessarily conflating the two) still proves very helpful to an ecumenical ethic of grace that is distinctly community based.

community, not only by the Gospel narrative but also by the Holy Spirit as its heart, reframes Christian moral action as a product of Christian community. The additional depth offered by Aquinas on the centrality of the New Law to individual Christian moral action applies to the inner workings of the "community of cause" of the Church, as well. The twofold sense of the New Law is important not only in the terms of individual transformation traced thus far, but in the context of the worshipping community, too. The indwelling of the Holy Spirit at the heart of Christian life applies to the Christian individual, and to the *poiesis* of Christian community life. At the heart of Christian communities, as well as for Christian individuals, the New Law is the Gospel narrative, offering that reality-making framework so rightly indicated by Hauerwas, and especially Hütter. But, just as Aquinas reminds his readership about the individual, this letter would kill without the New Law of the Holy Spirit "instilled into man, not only . . . indicating what he should do, but also . . . helping him to accomplish it."[33] This New Law is instilled not only into the body of an individual, but into the body of Christian community, as its heart. The adaptation of Christian communities to different ethical circumstances (Hütter's "narrative casuistry," Hauerwas' "moral improvisation") is only secondarily due to the power of narrative. Just as in the life of an individual, the life of Christian community has the Holy Spirit as its heart. The distinctiveness of Church, so cherished by Hauerwas and Hütter, is only secondarily due to the narrative that shapes its language. Rather, "the Law of the New Testament, whereon all its efficacy is based, is the grace of the Holy Ghost."[34] This is true in the body of a Christian, and in the body of the Church.

It must be acknowledged that Christians from different traditions will mean very different things by the "body of the Church." Hauerwas (writing as a Protestant) and Hütter (writing as a Lutheran in most of the documents examined here) seem to think that communities of faith—shaped by the Gospel narrative, with Christ as their center and the work of the Holy Spirit among them—can "count" in some way as Church. Exactly how one distinguishes from communities of that description that do "count" as Church and those that do not is a subject on which both are (quite wisely) reticent. Such a definition probably stands at odds with much of what Aquinas has to say, especially with regard to

33. Aquinas, *Summa theologiae*, I–II.106.1.RO2.
34. Ibid.

Christ's Headship through the office of the pope, and (though he never says as much in the *ST*) the boundaries of the Roman Catholic Church as the one true Church. Here, however, I appeal to the rich tradition articulating the invisible Church as the collection of all of those places in which Christ moves as the Head and the Holy Spirit as the heart. While the mode of that Headship through the office of ecclesial authority will probably remain a point of difference, much ecumenical promise remains for those from different traditions who are willing to define the body of the Church not as a fixed, visible structure, but as those historical and transhistorical moments in which Christ is the Head and the Holy Spirit is the heart of a community of cause. While not asking Thomas to abandon a notion like Roman Catholicism as the true Church, I do appeal to what seems a much more primary definition of the body of the Church: that community of cause over which Christ is principle and in which the Holy Spirit dwells.

The Gifts of the Holy Spirit in the Body of the Church

As with the twofold sense of the New Law, the content that Thomas offers on the Gifts of the Holy Spirit applies not only to the picture of moral agency in the body of an individual Christian (the framework in which Thomas described it), but to the life of the Christian community as a whole, with the work of the Spirit at its heart. In his treatise on the Gifts, Thomas reminds his readers of the distinction between an internal principle (such as reason) and an external principle (God) in the formation of Christian moral action. The Gifts are unique in that they are given by God to be an intrinsic principle by which we are "disposed to be moved by God."[35] They are those perfections that make human agency proportionate to those promptings toward actions that are beyond our natural capacity, and they accomplish, for the Christian individual, that which the cardinal virtues cannot—they form us habitually to be moved not only according to reason, but according to God.

Thomas' explanation of the Gifts offers a picture of the bond between divine and free human agency in an intimately individual way, making connatural to the individual Christian the guidance of the Holy Spirit. He utilizes his description of human agency as secondary instrumental causation, and under the larger umbrella of God as First Mover,

---

35. Ibid., I–II.68.1.

to depict the operation of God's agency within the freedom of our own agency. As Thomas says, "just as it is natural for the appetitive powers to be moved by the command of reason, so it is natural for all the forces in man to be moved by the instinct of God."[36]

Hauerwas and Hütter spill a great deal of ink articulating the depth and magnitude of the impact of community dynamics in Christian ethical life. They also consistently emphasize the degree to which the organic connection between Christians is the natural setting for the formation of Christian action. Thomas shows just how right they are. In taking the body of the Church, with Christ as its Head and the Holy Spirit as its heart, Christian community is structurally, organically well suited to be moved by God to act. If the framework of the Gifts of the Holy Spirit is applied to the dynamics of Christian community so rightly highlighted by Hauerwas and Hütter, then it is possible to apply this same intimate individual bond between divine and human agency to a bond between divine agency and human communal agency. In Christian community, the Gifts of the Holy Spirit make us well disposed to the promptings of divine agency, perfecting the body towards better conformity to God's will—a perfection structured to accomplish with God's aid. Just as with individual human action, God gives Christian community the dispositions necessary to make our judgment, perception, and understanding amenable to the formation and direction of the Holy Spirit. Hauerwas and Hütter have been quite right to lean so heavily upon the Christian worshipping community as the foundation for Christian ethical formation if, as Thomas says is the case, such dynamics are themselves the actions of a body with God's agency at its core. Instead of being a collection of individuals, in whom the Holy Spirit acts in cooperation with their own agency, the Christian worshipping community—and all of the inner dynamics natural to it—is a body gifted by God to be well disposed to the Spirit's promptings toward actions that would otherwise be beyond its reach. Just as in Thomas' description of the operation of the Gifts within an individual, the Gifts are not an imposition upon the free, natural dynamics of Christian community. The ethical action of Christian community has the Holy Spirit as its heart and is thus, in its very being as an entity itself, well disposed to be moved by God.

36. Ibid.

The Effects of Grace in the Body of the Church

Likewise, the distinctions Thomas offers on the effects of grace, when applied to the body of the Church, add considerable emphasis to the laudable trajectory provided by Hauerwas and Hütter. Thomas offers the distinction between the operative effects of grace, the cooperative effects of grace, the effects of grace upon habitual formation, and the effects of grace that are God's immediate *auxilium*, aid, or help, in which those actions poised for accomplishment are realized. Hauerwas and Hütter describe something very closely akin to the ability of the Christian worshipping community to be formed, as a body, habitually. Thomas distinguishes this habitual formation from the grace of *auxilium* in which God pushes this habitual formation into act. Those properly Christian moral acts of the Christian worshipping community, just as for the Christian individual, are the result not only of God's formation of that community, but God's intimate action at the heart of that community. For the Christian community, as well as for the Christian individuals therein, God's habitual formation does not desert human agency in the instance of moral action. Instead, God's gift of grace to the individual and to the Christian community not only forms the shape of moral agency for Christian moral action, but is intimately involved in the accomplishment of an individual action. The body of the Christian community, just like the body of the Christian individual, is created for just such a connection to divine agency. The distinction between the effect of habitual grace and the grace of *auxilium* is another way of showing the centrality of the work of the Holy Spirit to Christian ethics, not only on an individual but within the Christian worshipping community.

The same is true of the distinction Thomas provides between the operative and the cooperative effects of grace. Using Hütter's language, the community of the Church is that group that "suffers" divine action—that is to say, undergoes the formative and transformative work of God as the mark of its identity and the core of its proclamation and action. The Church, as described by Hauerwas and Hütter, is that setting in which God acts. God's operation—God's operative grace—establishes this body, heals it, and moves it to actions well beyond those of which it would be otherwise capable. In the terms of Hütter's "pathos" or Hauerwas' sanctification, God's grace operates upon Christian community. Even more evident in the theology of Hütter and Hauerwas is the deeper desire for a cooperative bond between divine and human agency through the moral action of Christian community. That very tendency in these theologians is what makes them stand out as so promising for a grace-centered Christian community ethic. For both, the noncompetitive bond between divine and human agency in the action of Christian community stands out as a key and defining feature. The distinction between operative and cooperative grace aids a great deal in conceiving of the bond between divine and human agency in individual Christian moral action. This distinction helps frame properly Christian moral action on that narrow knife-edge between freely willed on the one hand, and intimately bound with God's action on the other. Such a distinction goes a long way toward recovering an ecumenical ethic of grace by drawing a clear difference between those effects of God's healing and perfecting grace in which we are purely recipients, and those effects in which we are invited into cooperative action. Combining Thomas' comparison between the body of a Christian and the body of the Church with his work on the distinction between operative and cooperative grace promises to accomplish, in a more thorough way, the kind of community-centered ethic for which Hauerwas and Hütter seem to be reaching. It allows space for the healing and perfecting grace of God in which the Christian community is purely a recipient, while still emphasizing the need for those moments in which God invites the body of the Church into cooperative action, directed by Christ as its Head, and with the lifeblood of the Holy Spirit as its heart.

Applying Thomas' distinctions regarding the effects of grace, like applying his tools of the twofold sense of the New Law and the Gifts of the Holy Spirit, opens the way for a conjunction between Thomas' emphasis on the harmonious mesh between divine and human agency in the Christian moral act and the more contemporary insistence on the importance of Christian community in this cooperative connection. In the end, Thomas, Hauerwas, and Hütter together offer a picture of an organic, natural connection between the shape of human agency (both individual and communal) in which God chooses to be intimately bound in the realization of God's action in the world. God's work is bound up with our redemption and salvation, both as individuals and as Christian community, and depends deeply on the order, perfection, and power of the Head, Jesus Christ, and the breath of life of the heart, the Holy Spirit.

Bibliography

Albrecht, Gloria. *The Character of Our Communities: Toward an Ethic of Liberation for the Church*. Nashville: Abingdon, 1995.
Aquinas, Thomas. *Commentarium super Epistolam ad Romanos*. In *Super Epistolas S. Pauli Lectura*. 8th ed. Turin: Marietti, 1953.
———. *On Evil*. Translated by Richard Regan. Edited by Brian Davies. New York: Oxford University Press, 2003.
———. *On Truth*. Translated by R. W. Mulligan et al. Chicago: H. Regnery, 1952–54.
———. *On the Virtues, in General*. Translated by J. P. Reid. Providence: Providence College Press, 1951.
———. *Scriptum super libros sententiarum magistri Petri Lombardi Episcopi Parisiensis*. 4 vols. Edited by P. Mandonnet and M. F. Moos. Paris: Sumptibus P. Lethielleux, 1933–47.
———. *Summa contra Gentiles*. Translated by Anton Pegis. Notre Dame, IN: University of Notre Dame Press, 1975.
———. *Summa Theologiae*. Blackfriars ed. New York: McGraw-Hill, 1964.
———. *Summa Theologica*. Translated by Fathers of the English Dominican Province. Allen, TX: Christian Classics, 1981.
Aristotle. *Nicomachean Ethics*. Translated and edited by Roger Crisp. New York: Cambridge University Press, 2000.
Basil the Great, Saint. *On the Holy Spirit*. Translated by Stephen Hildebrand. Yonkers, NY: Saint Vladimir's Seminary Press, 2001.
Bouillard, Henri *Conversion et Grâce chez S. Thomas d'Aquin*. Paris: Aubier-Montaigne, 1944.
Chareire, Isabelle. *Éthique et grâce*. Paris: Cerf, 1998.
Christmann, P. Heinrich M. "Einleitung." In volume 14 of *Summa Theologica, Die Deutsche Thomas-Ausgabe: Der neue Bund und die Gnade*. Heidelberg: F. H. Kerle, 1955.
Doolan, Ægidius. *Sanctifying Grace*. Cork: Mercier, 1953.
Hall, Pamela. *Narrative and the Natural Law: An Interpretation of Thomistic Ethics*. Notre Dame, IN: University of Notre Dame Press, 1994.
Hauerwas, Stanley. *A Better Hope: Resources for a Church Confronting Capitalism, Democracy, and Postmodernity*. Grand Rapids: Brazos, 2000.
———. *Character and the Christian Life: A Study in Theological Ethics*. San Antonio: Trinity University Press, 1975.
———. "Characterizing Perfection: Second Thoughts on Character and Sanctification." In *Wesleyan Theology Today: A Bicentennial Theological Consultation*, edited by Theodore Runyon, 251–63. Nashville: Kingswood, 1985.

———. *Christian Existence Today: Essays on Church, World, and Living in Between.* Durham, NC: Labyrinth, 1988.

———. *Christians Among the Virtues: Theological Conversations with Ancient and Modern Ethics.* Notre Dame, IN: University of Notre Dame Press, 1997.

———. "The Church as God's New Language." In *The Hauerwas Reader*, edited by John Berkman and Michael Cartwright, 142–62. Durham, NC: Duke University Press, 2001.

———. *A Community of Character: Toward a Constructive Christian Social Ethic.* Notre Dame, IN: University of Notre Dame Press, 1981.

———. *In Good Company: The Church as Polis.* Notre Dame, IN: University of Notre Dame Press, 1995.

———. *The Peaceable Kingdom: A Primer in Christian Ethics.* Notre Dame, IN: University of Notre Dame Press, 1983.

———. *Performing the Faith: Bonhoeffer and the Practice of Nonviolence.* Grand Rapids: Brazos, 2004.

———. *Sanctify Them in the Truth: Holiness Exemplified.* Nashville: Abingdon, 1998.

———. "Self as Story: Religion and Morality from the Agent's Perspective." *Journal of Religious Ethics* 1 (1973) 73–85.

———. "Toward an Ethics of Character." *Theological Studies* 33 D (1972) 698–715.

———. *Vision and Virtue: Essays in Christian Ethical Reflection.* Notre Dame, IN: University of Notre Dame Press, 1981.

———. *With the Grain of the Universe: The Church's Witness and Natural Theology.* Grand Rapids: Brazos, 2001.

Hauerwas, Stanley, and Richard Bondi. "On Keeping Theological Ethics Theological." In *Revisions: Changing Perspectives in Moral Philosophy*, edited by Stanley Hauerwas and Alasdair MacIntyre, 16–42. Notre Dame, IN: University of Notre Dame Press, 1983.

Hauerwas, Stanley, with Richard Bondi and David B. Burrell. *Truthfulness and Tragedy: Further Investigations in Christian Ethics.* Notre Dame, IN: University of Notre Dame Press, 1977.

Horst, Ulrich. *Die Gaben des Heiligen Geistes nach Thomas von Aquin.* Berlin: Akademie Verlag, 2001.

Hütter, Reinhard. *Bound to Be Free: Evangelical Christian Engagements in Ecclesiology, Ethics, and Ecumenism.* Grand Rapids: Eerdmans, 2004.

———. "The Christian Life." In *The Oxford Handbook on Systematic Theology*, edited by Kathryn Tanner, Ian Torrance, and John Webster, 285–305. Oxford: Oxford University Press, 2007.

———. *Evangelische Ethik als kirchliches Zeugnis.* Neukirchen-Vluyn: Neukirchener, 1993.

———. "St. Thomas on Grace and Free Will in the *Initium Fidei*: The Surpassing Augustinian Synthesis." *Nova et Vetera* 5:3 (2007) 521–54.

———. *Suffering Divine Things: Theology as Church Practice.* Translated by Doug Stott. Grand Rapids: Eerdmans, 2000.

Katongole, Emmanuel. *Beyond Universal Reason: The Relation between Religion and Ethics in the Work of Stanley Hauerwas.* Notre Dame, IN: University of Notre Dame Press, 2000.

Keating, Daniel A. "Justification, Sanctification and Divinization in Thomas Aquinas." In *Aquinas on Doctrine: A Critical Introduction*, edited by Thomas G. Weinandy, Daniel A. Keating, and John P. Yocum, 139–58. London: T. & T. Clark, 2004.

Kelly, Anthony. "The Gifts of the Spirit: Aquinas and the Modern Context." *The Thomist* 38 (April 1974) 193–231.
Kobusch, Theo. "Grace (Ia IIae, qq. 109–114)." In *The Ethics of Aquinas*, edited by Stephen J. Pope, 207–18. Washington, DC: Georgetown University Press, 2002.
Kühn, Ulrich. *Via Caritatis: Theologie des Gesetzes bei Thomas von Aquin*. Göttingen: Vandenhoeck & Ruprecht, 1965.
Lohfink, Gerhard. "Der Not der Exegese mit der Reich-Gottes-Verkündigung Jesu." *Theologische Quartalschrift* 168:1 (1988) 1–15.
Lonergan, Bernard. *Grace and Freedom: Operative Grace in the Thought of St. Thomas Aquinas*. Edited by J. Patout Burns. New York: Herder & Herder, 1971.
Macguire, Daniel C. "Ratio Practica and the Intellectualistic Fallacy." *Journal of Religious Ethics* 10 (1982) 22–39.
McGrath, Alister. "The Influence of Aristotelian Physics upon St. Thomas Aquinas' Discussion of the 'Processus Iustificationis.'" In *Recherches de Théologie Ancienne et Médiévale* 51 (1984) 223–29.
O'Meara, Thomas. "Virtues in the Theology of Thomas Aquinas." *Theological Studies* 58 (1997) 254–85.
Pannenberg, Wolfhart. *Jesus—God and Man*. Translated by Lewis L. Wilkins and Duane A. Priebe. Philadelphia: Westminster, 1977.
Patfoort, Albert. *Thomas d'Aquin: les clés d'une théologie*. Paris: FAC-éditions, 1983.
Pesch, O. H. "Die bleibende Bedeutung der thomanischen Tugendlehre." *Freiburger Zeitschrift für Philisophie und Theologie* 21 (1974) 359–91.
Pinckaers, Servais. *The Sources of Christian Ethics*. Translated by Mary Thomas Noble. Washington, DC: Catholic University of America Press, 1995.
Porter, Jean. "Moral Language and the Language of Grace: The Fundamental Option and the Virtue of Charity." *Philosophy and Theology* 10 (1997) 171–81.
———. "Right Reason and the Love of God: The Parameters of Aquinas' Moral Theology." In *The Theology of Thomas Aquinas*, edited by Rik van Nieuwenhove and Joseph Wawrykow, 167–91. Notre Dame, IN: University of Notre Dame Press, 2005.
Rodgers, Eugene. "Faith and Reason Follow Glory: The Spirit in Aquinas." In *The Theology of Thomas Aquinas*, edited by Rik van Nieuwenhove and Joseph Wawrykow, 442–59. Notre Dame, IN: University of Notre Dame Press, 2005.
Saint Basil the Great. *On the Holy Spirit*. Translated by Stephen Hildebrand. Yonkers, NY: Saint Vladimir's Seminary Press, 2001.
Sokolowski, Robert. *The God of Faith and Reason: Foundations of Christian Theology*. Washington, DC: Catholic University of America Press, 1995.
Stout, Jeffrey. *Democracy and Tradition*. Princeton: Princeton University Press, 2004.
Tanner, Kathryn. *God and Creation in Christian Theology: Tyranny or Empowerment?* Oxford: Blackwell, 1988.
———. *Jesus, Humanity and the Trinity: A Brief Systematic Theology*. Minneapolis: Fortress, 2001.
Velde, Rudi A. te. *Participation and Substantiality in Thomas Aquinas*. Leiden: Brill, 1995.
Wawrykow, Joseph. *God's Grace and Human Action*. Notre Dame, IN: University of Notre Dame Press, 1995.
———. "Grace." In *The Theology of Thomas Aquinas*, edited by Rik van Nieuwenhove and Joseph Wawrykow, 192–221. Notre Dame, IN: University of Notre Dame Press, 2005.

Index

actual grace, 173–74
adopted sons and daughters of God, 25, 27
adoption and adoptionism of human nature, 137, 225, 228
agency, limiting description of, 51–63
Albert the Great, 138, 144
Albrecht, Gloria, 37, 41
Aquinas. *See* Thomas Aquinas
Aristotle, 10, 11, 13, 141, 154, 226–27
assumption vs. adoption of human nature, 228
Augustine, 13, 112, 113, 139, 223
auxilium (help), God's grace of, 124–29, 145–46, 174–75, 178

Baptism, 76, 78–80, 206, 209
Barth, Karl
  Chalcedonian logic, 78–80, 82, 98, 100
  on God's action and human action, 113–14
  on pneumatological connection, 73–74
  post-Chalcedonian Christology, 102
  theological action theory, 78–81
Basil the Great, 1–2
Beieinander, 73, 73n6, 78, 83, 87–88, 98–100, 102–5, 121
  See also conjunction, between divine and human agency

Bonaventure, 144
Bouillard, Henri, 141, 143
Bound to Be Free (Hütter), 69, 105–12

De Caritate (Thomas Aquinas), 141
Chalcedonian logic, 78–80, 82, 98, 100
character
  God's resituating of, 9, 119–21
  and relevance of Protestant church, 92–93
  as the shaping of self, 38–44
Character and the Christian Life (Hauerwas), 37, 40, 43, 44, 53–54, 57, 60
Chareire, Isabelle, 136, 182
Christian act, limiting description of, 59–63
Christian action, 68, 98
Christian community formed by theological narrative, 45–51
Christian ethic, definition of, 3
Christian ethical transformation, 32–33
Christian Existence Today (Hauerwas), 57
Christian life of passivity before God, 97
Christian moral life, 121–22
Christian's, interdependence of, 196–204, 210–15
Christians Among the Virtues (Hauerwas), 57, 58

Index

Christmann, Heinrich, 133–34
Church
  body of, 236–37
  Christ as head of, 230–32
  effects of grace in the body of, 238–39
  Holy Spirit as heart of, 232–34
  linguistic activity of, 95–96, 106
  praxis of, 91–105
Church action, 76–77, 95–96, 107
Church ethic
  Church action and, 76–77
  Hauerwas on, 83–87
  Hütter on, 70, 82, 87–91
Colossians, 199, 230
commandment vs. counsel, 201–3
Commentary on the Sentences (Thomas Aquinas), 140–41, 144–45
community, divine and human agency in context of, 184–88
A Community of Character (Hauerwas), 211
community-centered ecumenical ethic of grace
  Christ as head of the Church, 230–32
  divine and human agency in context of, 184–88
  effects of grace in the body of the Church, 238–39
  efficacy of God's grace through the Incarnation, 222
  gifts of the Holy Spirit and body of the Church, 236–37
  Holy Spirit as heart of the Church, 232–34
  overview, 220–22
  redemption as a generic collective, 225–30
  twofold sense of the New Law in the body of the Church, 234–36
  union of divine and human natures in Jesus Christ, 222–24
  See also ecumenical ethic of grace
confession of sin, 55
conjunction, between divine and human agency
  Barth on, 80, 99
  description of, 77
  Hauerwas on, 83
  in hospitality and truth, 108
  Hütter's on, 68, 73–74, 77, 82, 87–88, 108
  interdependence of Christian community, 213
  in language and understanding, 90
  Lohfink's approach to, 81
  See also Beieinander
contemporary promptings toward ecumenical ethic of grace, 204–19
Conversion et Grâce chez S. Thomas d'Aquin (Bouillard), 141
cooperative *auxilium*, 125, 128–29, 145–46, 175–76
cooperative grace, 144, 175
cooperative relationship (human/Holy Spirit), 26
1 Corinthians, 3, 230
2 Corinthians, 3
counsel vs. commandment, 201–3
creative activity of God, 96
creativity, of theology, 94

Damascene, 226
daughters of God, 25, 27
determinism, 39–42, 65–66, 130, 179
Die Deutsche Thomas Ausgabe (Christmann), 133–34
Die Gaben des Heiligen Geistes nach Thomas von Aquin (Horst), 140

discipleship, 110–11
disclosure of the theological, 6
discursive theological practice, 100
divine agency, centrality of, 33–37
divine and human natures in Jesus Christ, 222–24
Divine causality, 14
Divine instinct, 160–61
Divine Law, 151–52
Divine providence, 20–21
Doolan, Ægidius, 166, 182

ecclesial context of theology practice, 93
ecclesiology and ethics, 70–72
ecumenical ethic of grace
    Christian's interdependence and, 196–204, 210–15
    contemporary promptings toward, 204–19
    Hütter on, 68
    sacrament and worship, 188–96, 205–10
    See also community-centered ecumenical ethic of grace
enhypostasis, 102–3
Ephesians, 230
Erasmus, 112
ethical behavior, 123
The Ethics of Aquinas (Kobusch), 11
Éthique et grâce (Chareire), 136
Eudemus, 13, 141, 142–143, 160, 163
Evangelische Ethik als kirchliches Zeugnis (Hütter), 68–91, 95–96, 98–99, 104–5, 109–10, 114, 118
external mark, 196
external principle, 134, 161, 236
extrinsic principle, 151, 160–61, 166–67, 176, 182

faith, God's work in, 81
Franciscan school, 138

freedom
    of theology, 94, 101
    western notions of, 27
free-will, 18–21, 125

Galatians, 3
gifts of Holy Spirit, 129–32, 140–43, 158–65, 236–37
goals and limits, 52–59
God's action, Holy Spirit and, 75–78
God's gift, 119–20, 122
God's Grace and Human Action (Wawrykow), 22, 145, 165n63
God's grace through the incarnation, 222
God's purposive willing, 149
God's spirit, 18, 26, 27
    See also Holy Spirit
good works, 6, 14, 76, 127, 129, 157, 159, 208
Gospel narratives
    Hauerwas on, 110–11, 117–19
    indispensability of, 9, 66, 117–19
    as shaping Christian community, 147n62
    See also New Law; *specific Bible citations*
grace
    actual, 173–74
    cooperative, 144, 175
    dynamics of, 10, 196–204
    ecumenical ethic of, 68
    effects of, 172–83
    of God, 155
    gratuitous, 173, 178, 198–201
    habitual, 174–75, 177–78, 180–81
    incarnation of God through, 222
    interdependence of Christian's and, 196–204
    as intrinsic principle, 166, 167–68, 173, 175

grace (cont.)
  Kobusch and Thomas' theology of, 10
  and the limiting description of agency, 51–63
  necessity of, 17–20, 168–72
  operative, 144–45, 175–77
  sanctifying, 173, 198–201
  Thomas Aquinas on, 123–29, 143–46, 165–83
  transformative effects of, 6
  what grace is, 165–68
Grace and Freedom (Lonergan), 144, 165n63
gratuitous grace, 173, 178, 198–201
Gregory the Great, 140, 159

habit
  Aristotelian category of, 13–14
  consequences on human agency, 10
  Luther on, 14
  as a quality, 166
  Thomas Aquinas on, 124–27, 158, 160, 162–64
habitual grace, 174–75, 177–78, 180–81
Hauerwas, Stanley
  centrality of divine agency, 33–37
  Christian community formed by theological narrative, 45–51
  Christian Existence Today, 57
  on Christian moral life, 121–22
  Christians Among the Virtues, 57, 58
  on Church ethic, 83–87
  A Community of Character, 211
  comparison with Hütter, 115–17
  on conjunction, between divine and human agency, 83
  contemporary theological ethics, 31–51
  as contemporary voice, 5–8
  goals and limits, 52–59
  God's grace and limiting description of agency, 51–63
  on God's resituating our character, 119–21
  on Gospel narratives, 110–11, 117–19
  on interdependence of Christians, 211–13
  limiting description of the Christian act, 59–63
  morality, application of, 216
  Performing the Faith, 63
  permeability of the self, 63–66
  on pneumatological connection, 73–74
  present treatment of theological ethics, 31–33
  on sacrament and worship, 205–7
  Sanctify Them in the Truth, 54
  self becomes permeable to external determinations, 37–45
  on selfhood of a person, 84
  Truthfulness and Tragedy, 43
  See also Character and the Christian Life
hidden dimension of moral action, 4
Holy Spirit
  action of in the Church, 118
  Aquinas' reflection on, 24–26
  Basil's reflection on, 1–2
  concrete action of, 106, 108, 111
  dynamics of, 162
  ecclesial inquiry and, 72–73
  gifts of, 129–32, 140–43, 158–65, 236–37
  God's action and, 77–78
  as heart of the Church, 232–34
  language of, 90, 95–96, 120
  pneumatological connection, 73–74

Holy Spirit (*cont.*)
  in shaping conviction and perception, 120
  in theological and ethical matters, 92
  work of in the Church, 88, 118
Horst, Ulrich, 140, 141, 142–43, 161
hospitality, practices of, 69–70, 107–10
human and divine natures in Jesus Christ, 222–24
human judgment, 151
human law, 152
Hütter, Reinhard
  Bound to Be Free, 69, 105–12
  "The Christian Life," 113
  on Christian moral life, 121–22
  as contemporary voice, 5–8
  on God's resituating our character, 119–21
  on Gospel narratives, 118–19
  on interdependence of Christians, 211–15
  overview of philosophy, 67–70
  recent literature, 112–14
  on sacrament and worship, 207–10
  Suffering Divine Things, 69, 70, 92, 98–103, 105, 112, 208
  Theologie als kirchliche Praktik, 69, 91–105
  See also Evangelische Ethik als kirchliches Zeugnis

incarnation, 222, 226–27
integrity, 51
intellect, 165, 169, 174
interdependence of Christians, 196–204, 210–15
internal principle, 134, 161, 182, 236
intrinsic principle
  as God's gift, 170–71, 236

grace as, 166, 167–68, 173, 175
habit as, 158
reason as, 160–62
Isaiah, 160, 163, 231

Jeremiah, 31, 153
Jesus, Humanity and the Trinity (Tanner), 184
Jesus Christ, divine and human natures in, 222–24
John, Gospel of, 162
justification, process of, 10, 12–13
"Justification, Sanctification and Divinization in Thomas Aquinas" (Keating), 24

Keating, Daniel A., 24, 27
Kelly, Anthony, 130
Kobusch, Theo, 10, 11, 125
Kühn, Ulrich, 27, 138, 139

language, of Church and Holy Spirit, 90, 95–96, 106, 120
law
  discreation of individuals and, 156–57
  Divine Law, 151–52
  of fear, 138, 152
  human law, 152
  of liberty (*see* New Law)
  of love, 138, 152, 154
  natural law, 138–39, 151
  Old Law, 138, 152, 197, 201
  of sin, 174
  of the Spirit, 28
Liber de bona fortuna (Eudemus), 13, 141, 142–43, 160, 163
Lindbeck, George, 95–96
Lohfink, Gerhard, 74, 81–83
Lombard, Peter, 138
Lonergan, Bernard, 23, 131–32, 143–45, 165n63, 167, 173–74, 177

love relation with God in Christ, 35–36
Luther, Martin, 14, 69, 97, 101, 106, 106n73, 112

De Malo (Thomas Aquinas), 145
mark, external, 196
Matthew, Gospel of, 192n14
McGrath, Alister, 10, 12–13, 125
merit, 148–49, 192–93n14
mind, renewal of, 90, 120, 216
moral life, 47n52
moral progress, 39
Moralia on Job (Gregory the Great), 140, 159
morality, application of, 216

natural causality, 14
natural physics, 10
New Law
  Christian community and, 196–97
  counsels of, 201–3, 215
  law of the Spirit, 28
  moral discernment under, 216
  need for moral instruction, 212
  sacrament and worship, 189–90
  twofold sense of, 150–58, 234–36
  usefulness of, 132–40
Nicomachean Ethics (Aristotle), 154

Old Law, 138, 152, 197, 201
O'Meara, Thomas, 166
On the Spirit and the Letter (Augustine), 139
operative *auxilium*, 125, 128–29, 145–46, 175–76
operative grace, 144–45, 175–77

Pannenberg, Wolfhart, 102, 102n67
Paraklete language, 89–90, 208

Participation and Substantiality in Thomas Aquinas (te Velde), 21
Patfoort, Albert, 146
Paul (apostle and saint), 3, 128, 230, 231
Pelagianism, 11, 35, 82
performing faith, 65
Performing the Faith: Bonhoeffer and the Practice of Nonviolence (Hauerwas), 63
permeability of the self, 63–66
physics, to describe dynamics of grace, 10
Pinckaers, Servais, 3, 133, 135–36, 167
Plato, 226–27
pneumatological connection, 73–74
  See also Holy Spirit
Porter, Jean, 167
prayer, 191–92
predestination, 148–49
premotion, 12, 144
Prima Secundae (Thomas Aquinas), 17, 124, 125, 146, 150, 162
Protestant church, character and relevance of, 92–93
Protestant theologians and Thomas's ethics, 10
providence, 20–21
purposive grace of God, 149

quandary ethics, 37, 39

reason, 13–14, 159
redemption, 55, 57, 225–30
relational bond between divine and human agency, 147n62
Rogers, Eugene, 10, 13–14, 125, 126–27
Romans, 3, 89–90, 120, 128, 174, 230

sacrament and worship, 188–96, 205–10
sanctification, 53–54, 193, 195
Sanctify Them in the Truth (Hauerwas), 54, 63
sanctifying grace, 173, 198–201
Scripture. *See* Gospel narratives
self, as permeable to external determinations, 37–45
self, permeability of, 63–66
selfhood of a person, 84
self-realization, 85
Sermon on the Mount, 157, 197, 215
    See also New Law
sin, 12, 55, 174, 175, 191
Sokolowski, Paul, 4, 6, 125
sons and daughters of God, 25, 27
soul, preparing of, 18
Sources of Christian Ethics (Pinckaers), 3
spirit of God, 18, 26, 27
    See also Holy Spirit
Stout, Jeffery, 35
Suffering Divine Things (Hütter), 69, 70, 92, 98–103, 105, 112, 208
Summa contra gentiles (Thomas Aquinas), 137, 138n26, 141
Summa theologiae (Thomas Aquinas)
    on Christian ethics and pneumatology, 9
    on Gifts of the Holy Spirit, 143
    on grace, 145, 146
    on justification, 13
    on New Law, 138, 139–140
    Prima Secundae (*see Prima Secundae*)
suppositum, 229
synergist model, 81

Tanner, Kathryn, 6, 15, 125, 184–88
te Velde, Rudi, 21
temptation, 202–3

Tertia Pars (Thomas Aquinas), 193, 195
"The Christian Life" (Hütter), 113
theological action theory, 78–81
theological narrative, Christian community formed by, 45–51
Theologie als kirchliche Praktik (Hütter), 69, 91–105
theology
    activity of, 92–93
    of the cross, 107–8
    ecclesial context of practice, 93
    freedom and creativity of, 94
    practice of, 92–95
Third Article of Faith, 72–73
Thomas Aquinas
    anti-Pelagian arguments, 112–13
    De Caritate, 141
    case for, 16–29
    Christian moral life, 122
    Commentary on the Sentences, 140–41, 144–45
    gifts of the Holy Spirit, 129–32, 158–65
    on grace, 123–29, 143–46, 165–83
    Hauerwas and Hütter theology and, 115–16
    De Malo, 145
    on the New Law, 28, 132–40, 150–58
    objections to, 10–16
    overview of philosophy, 122–23
    as a resource, 8–10
    Summa contra Gentiles, 137, 141
    De Veritate, 144–45
    See also Summa theologiae
Thomas d'Aquin: les clés d'une théologie (Patfoort), 146
transcendence, 15, 22–23
transformative effects of God's grace, 6

truth
    ability to perceive, 55
    of the Gospel, 110–11, 119
    honoring, 107–9
    hospitable to, 110, 120
Truthfulness and Tragedy
    (Hauerwas), 43, 60

De Veritate (Thomas Aquinas),
    144–45
Via Caritatis (Kühn), 27
virtues, 34, 159, 169, 206, 211

Wawrykow, Joseph, 22, 134, 145,
    149, 165n63, 167, 174,
    177–78, 181
will, 159
    See also free-will
worship, God's action and, 75–76
worshipping community
    importance of, 49, 73
    sacrament and, 188–96, 205–10

www.ingramcontent.com/pod-product-compliance
Lightning Source LLC
Chambersburg PA
CBHW031726230426
43669CB00007B/255